The Final Co
Tribulation Rising
Volume 2
Modern Technology

FIRST PRINTING

Billy Crone

Copyright © 2019
All Rights Reserved

Cover Design:
CHRIS TAYLOR

To my wife, Brandie.

*Thank you for being so patient
with a man full of dreams.
You truly are my gift from God.
It is an honor to have you as my wife
and I'm still amazed that you willingly chose
to join me in this challenging yet exhilarating
roller coaster ride called the Christian life.
God has truly done exceedingly abundantly above all
that we could have ever asked or even thought of.
Who ever said that living for the Lord was boring?!
One day our ride together will be over here on earth,
yet it will continue on in eternity forever.
I love you.*

Contents

Preface

I've always had a fascination with technology, or should I say a fascination with destroying it. Even as a little kid, I would take apart pens, appliances, you name it, just to see how it worked. Of course, much to my Mother's dismay, the various devices rarely ever went back together again the same. Then in High School, I desperately wanted to major in robotics even though I lived in the middle of nowhere in Kansas with a graduating class of only thirty-nine. So afterwards, I found myself moving to California with my brother to go to Electronics Tech School. Finally, I was able to get the education I so desired and pursue a career in computers, electronics, and "taking things apart" full-time. But God had different plans. Not only did he save me a few years later, of which I am eternally grateful, but I soon hit the education circuit again, this time for Him. I began to get equipped biblically in Bible College and later Seminary, all the while wondering what I was going to do with this technological knowledge. As always, God never lets anything go to waste. It wasn't until my very first Senior Pastorate that it all fell into place. From the start I recorded my sermons on tape and made them available to shut-ins or members who missed a particular service, but about a year later I noticed that hardly anyone would check out a book from my office and only a few would listen to the audio I had. Yet everybody, young and old alike, wanted the videos. That's when I realized that our culture had gone through a shift where everyone now received the bulk of their information via the eyes. Therefore, I realized we needed to start recording the sermons on video. The problem was, nobody knew how to do that. Enter the man with the tech background. I didn't know how to do it either, but I had enough previous electronics experience to give it a try. Lo and behold, this is how Get A Life Ministry began. Now I find myself writing Volume Two of *The Final Countdown: Tribulation Rising*, this time, on of all topics, *Modern Technology*. Go figure. Little did I know that God would use this life-long passion to not only launch a global teaching ministry, but to also get others equipped in our day on the massive amount of ways the Bible says Modern Technology really is a huge sign that we are living in the last days. It's time to get motivated! One last piece of advice; when you are through reading this book will you please READ YOUR BIBLE? I mean that in the nicest possible way. Enjoy, and I'm looking forward to seeing you someday!

Billy Crone
Las Vegas, Nevada
2019

Chapter One

The Increase of Land Travel

"One day this young minister was interviewing for his very first pastorate and the pulpit committee had invited him to come over to their church office for an interview. The committee chairman asked him, 'Son, do you know the Bible pretty good?'

The young minister said, 'Oh absolutely…really good!' Then the chairman asked, 'Alright, which part do you know best?' And he responded saying, 'Oh, I know the New Testament the best.'

The chairman responded, 'Well, which part of the New Testament do you know best?' And the young minister said, 'Oh, several parts.'

The chairman said, 'Okay, well, why don't you tell us the story of the prodigal son.' And the young man said, 'Sure, fine, no problem.'

And he started in, 'There was a man of the Pharisees named Nicodemus, who went down to Jericho by night and he fell upon stony ground and the thorns choked him half to death.

The next morning Solomon and his wife, Gomorrah, came by and carried him down to the ark for Moses to take care of. But, as he was going through the

Eastern Gate into the Ark, he caught his hair on a limb and he hung there forty days and forty nights and afterwards he got hungry and the ravens came and fed him.

The next day, the three wise men came and carried him down to the boat dock and he caught a ship to Nineveh and when he got there he found Delilah sitting on the wall and he said, 'Chuck her down, boys, chuck her down.'

Then they said, 'Well, how many times shall we chuck her down, seven times seven?' And he said, 'Nay, but seventy times seven.' And they chucked her down four hundred and ninety times.

'Then she burst asunder in their midst and they picked up twelve baskets of leftovers and in the resurrection, whose wife shall she be?'

Well, at this the chairman of the committee jumps up and interrupts the young Pastor and says to the rest of the committee, 'Guys, guys, guys…let's hire him! He may be young, but he sure knows his Bible!'"

Wow! Now that joke would be funny, if what? If it weren't so true! How many churches do that? They not only don't know the Bible themselves, but they go off and hire a so-called Shepherd who doesn't know it as well! If you think your church isn't guilty of that, then tell me why your Pastor doesn't teach on nearly one third of the Bible called Bible Prophecy! He might as well be up there saying, "Chuck her down boys! Chuck her down!"

That not only makes for a horrible Shepherd, but it hurts the lost! Why? Because they never hear about the worst time in the history of mankind that's coming to our planet! It's called the 7-year Tribulation and it's not a joke! The Bible says it is an outpouring of God's wrath on this wicked and rebellious planet! Jesus said in **Matthew 24** that it would be a "time of greater horror than anything the world has ever seen or will ever see again." And that "unless God shortened that time frame, the entire human race would be destroyed!" But praise God, God's not only a God of wrath, He's a God of love as well. And because He loves us, He has given us many warning signs to wake us up so that we would know when the 7-year Tribulation is near, and the return of Jesus Christ is rapidly approaching. Therefore, in order to keep you and I from ignoring these biblical warnings from God and risking the danger of being left behind, we're going to continue our series; **The Final Countdown: Tribulation Rising**.

In the first volume, we saw the first sign was **The Jewish People** and **The Antichrist**. We saw sixteen future prophecies concerning the Jewish People, letting us know we're living in the Last days, which was that **Israel would return to the land, Israel would become a nation again, Israel would become a nation again in one day, and Israel would become a united nation, again! Israel would recapture Jerusalem, their currency would return to the Shekel, they would experience a rebirth of the Hebrew language, Israel would blossom as a rose in the desert, Israel would become a light unto the nations, Israel would become a source of world conflict, Israel would have a powerful military, Israel would rebuild the Temple, Israel would become spiritually deceived, Israel would place their hope in the wrong messiah, Israel would place their hope in a deceptive treaty** and that **Israel would face another Holocaust**.

There we saw the horrible news that even after what Hitler did, not that long ago, with the original Holocaust, that another one is coming to the planet upon the Jewish People, very possibly even bigger than the last one! The Bible says two-thirds of the Jewish People are going to be struck down by the antichrist. We saw proof of that anti-Semitic mindset coming again on the international scene and even here in America! We saw that in our own government, leftovers from the previous administration, in politics, especially the new Democratic Freshmen, the media, and even American schools and churches are promoting it through what's called Replacement Theology. No wonder your kids come out of the secular schools and universities hating God and the Jewish People. That's what they're being brainwashed to think! It's crazy, and it's sick, but it's the mindset coming back to the planet just in time for the last days, the 7-year Tribulation! But that's not all.

The **2ⁿᵈ** update on **The Final Countdown: Tribulation Rising** series is none other than **Modern Technology & the AI Invasion**.

Modern Technology is a huge sign that we're living in the last days and most people have no clue how it, or even AI (Artificial Intelligence) fits into that picture! But don't take my word for it. Let's listen to God's.

Daniel 12:1-4 "At that time Michael, the great prince who protects your people, will arise. There will be a time of distress such as has not happened from the beginning of nations until then. But at that time your people – everyone whose name is found written in the book – will be delivered. Multitudes who sleep in the dust of the earth will awake, some to everlasting life, others to shame and everlasting contempt. Those who are wise will shine like the brightness of the heavens, and those who lead many to righteousness, like the stars for ever and ever. But you, Daniel, close up and seal the words of the scroll until the time of the end. Many will go here and there to increase knowledge."

Now, as we saw before with this passage, is that God gives Daniel two signs to be an indicator that we're in the end of times. Notice what it was. Not just the activity of the Archangel Michael, but what? People would be traveling here and there all over the earth like never before, and there would be an explosion of knowledge like never before, right? So, here's the point. Can anybody guess what in the world is happening all around us right now? We are travelling all over the earth like never before and there's an incredible explosion of knowledge, exponentially so! Which means, this very passage is being fulfilled before our very eyes! Which means, we are living in the end times, according to Daniel!

The **1st** way that **Modern Technology** reveals that we're really living in the last days, is by the **Increase of Travel**.

As we saw before, when Daniel wrote down the words of this prophecy, the mode of travel was basically the same for thousands of years. It's only in the last century alone that we see a major change in transportation. In fact, let me show you just how little it's changed throughout history up until modern times.

"In the beginning, the mode of transportation was a canoe or boat, then they started moving around on skis or something to slide on, but around 3,500 BC they developed a way a camel or animal could pull a wheeled cart or wagon. By 1,500 BC they came up with a larger boat that could hold several rowers to transport merchandise or people across the waters.

A horse drawn carriage was used during 600 BC that was used to transport people more conveniently. Then a Junk was developed in AD 200. This could be moved across the waters by the wind blowing in the sails. By AD 230 a wheelbarrow was developed to transport an individual as another was pushing while walking behind it. In the 15th century a Carrack was being used. This was a larger ship with sails that could carry more merchandise and people. In the 16th century a Funicular was invented. This was similar to a train. It consisted of 3 small cars that held one person in each car that was pulled by a cable.

Also, in the 16th century the stagecoach was invented. This could carry more people from city to city and was pulled by horses. Then in 1783 the Hot Air Balloon was invented and in 1785 we had the Steamboat. In 1804 there was the Steam Locomotive and in 1818 the Dandy Horse was being sold on the market. This was the first two-wheeled bicycle. In 1852 there was the Airship, which was similar to the hot air balloon, but it had propellers to move it from place to place. By 1863 we had the subway. This was smaller than a train and would transport people around a localized area.

The Penny Farthing came on the scene in 1870. This was a two-wheeled bicycle that you could peddle. It had one large wheel in front and a small wheel in the back. The Electric Trolley came along in 1882. This was a wagon like vehicle that was controlled by a wire that was attached to a main electrical cord overhead. Then in 1885 the motorcycle was invented. This vehicle looked like a two wheeled bicycle, but this one had an engine and ran on gasoline.

A short time later, in 1886, the first gasoline car came on the scene. The glider came along in 1891, the diesel truck in 1892, and of course the airplane in 1903. The first race car was developed in 1930 and the helicopter in 1939. In 1952 we had our first jetliner and in the 1950's, monster trucks. In 1959 the Hovercraft came along. In 1960 the Bathyscape was invented, something similar to a submarine, and in 1961 the rocket was invented. Also, in 1961, we could enjoy driving the All-Terrain Vehicle.

In 1984 Jet Propulsion suits were introduced. Also, in 1984, people were traveling across country in the Maglev. The Segway was invented in 2001. Now you could ride on the two-wheel motorized vehicle where you stand on it and go anywhere just by holding on to the handlebars. In 2009 the prototype for the self-driving car was introduced."[1]

And that's where we're at today. But as you can see, transportation hardly made any changes for centuries upon centuries, until about the turn of the last century when things started to pick up and that's not by chance. It needed to pick up because that's what Daniel said would happen when you're living in the last days!

The **1st area** of transportation that has seen a major increase in our lifetime is in the area of **Land Travel**.

Now, we left off with self-driving or automated cars on land which we'll get into in a little bit, but you have to understand the prophetic significance of this. You see, when you put the history of land travel on a timeline, you begin to see just how significant the days we are living in really are!

The fastest that mankind could travel for thousands of years was about 30 mph via horseback. From Alexander the Great, to Attila the Hun, to Abraham Lincoln, transportation on land pretty much stayed the same, until now. All in the last century alone, we have gone from the horse to the horseless carriage, to the car. We've gone from a top speed of 30 mph to literally 100's of miles per hour. In fact, the fastest car to date, on record, that we technically could get our hands on, is called the Hennessey Venom GT which was clocked at 270 mph.

But then there's the ultimate dream car on land that can enable you to say goodbye to any long commute forever, it's called the Thrust SSC and goes 1,228 mph!

"This car is being pulled to the desert track by an 18-wheeler. It looks like a black rocket laying flat with large fins on each side of it. It slides across the desert sands like sliding on a lake of ice. It is going straight, so the person inside at the steering wheel is barely turning the wheel. All you see is a little speck of black metal with a long line of sand and smoke behind the incredibly fast-moving car. It is going so fast that it breaks the sound barrier."[2]

That was done here in Nevada in the Black Rock Desert, and to give you an idea of how fast that is, you can hear the sonic boom. The speed of sound is about 761 mph and this thing is almost twice that, at 1,228 mph on land! That's so fast, that you could literally go from San Francisco to New York City in just a little over 2 hours! In a car, on land! It's crazy! But that's not all. It's not just the speed of travel that's increasing, it's the increase of travel options! Many different options have increased on land. For instance, the first car invented was called the Cugnot.

The First Car: Cugnot

It was named after its inventor, Nicolas Cugnot, who apparently "coog not" drive very well because he drove it straight into a stone wall, which then became the first car accident of all time! The Cugnot was steam powered and obviously didn't go very fast, "It went very slow." But then a guy came along after him named Carl Benz and invented the very first gasoline-powered car. It was called the Motorwagen and it could go up to six miles an hour!

First Gas Car: Motorwagen

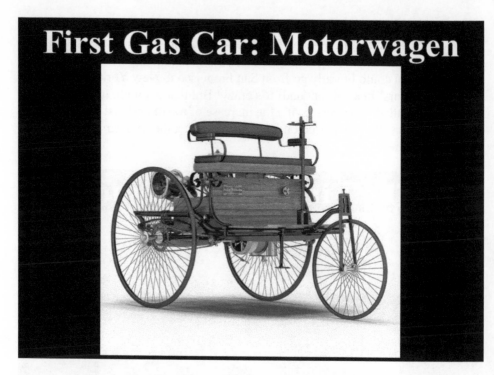

Granted, people could run places faster – but hey, it was a start. Better than steam anyway! Now, what slowed the development of the car initially, was that they were very expensive to make and there was no such thing as auto parts stores back then, let alone gas stations. But then a guy named Henry Ford came along and he not only invented the Model T, which was the most popular of the first mass produced cars, but he also perfected what was to become the modern assembly line and it not only revolutionized the car industry, but the entire manufacturing industry as well.

The Model T Assembly Line

This enabled his cars to come off the assembly line in 15-minute intervals and this was when cars began to take off! It was a total game changer to be able to mass produce them like this which made them much cheaper, and that's when they went from being a rich man's luxury item to an everyday vehicle for the common man. Shortly after that was when you began to see an explosion of many different car manufacturers not only here in the U.S. but around the world, including Toyota, Mitsubishi, Mazda, and others. And now, because of this, in just a few decades from those events, tens of millions of vehicles are made every single year. We now rush here and there on land an average of 16,550 miles per year for males. Ladies, yours is lower than that. My guess is because you ask for directions! Sorry guys! Had to say it! But I will say this, men. Sometimes it might have to do with the helper we have in the car!

Tim Hawkins: *"When you get married, if you're a guy you get a little helper in the car. Ha-ha. I love my little helper in the car. She knows everything about driving. It's very convenient for me. Ha-ha, because sometimes I get confused. I don't know how I get anywhere without my little helper in the car. I'd probably be bouncing off trees and buildings and stuff but she's there to help. She tells me when the light changes colors and everything.*

It's very convenient and helpful. Like, 'It's green.' 'Thank you, I was confused, I didn't know.' I always know how fast I'm going with my little helper. She lets me know. 'You know how fast you are going?' 'Yes, I have a speedometer right here! Thanks for the backup. If that thing ever snaps in half, I've got you.' She gives me statistics when we are in the car. 'You did know that men have the most accidents.' 'Gee, I wonder why that is?'"[3]

Speaking of which, men between the ages of 35-54 drive even more than that! They have an estimated driving of 18,858 miles per year and in some states it's even higher! Now keep in mind it wasn't that long ago that our grandparents could have been born and raised in the same town and lived there their whole lives and had hardly ever gone anywhere on land! But look at us now! Just like Daniel said in the last days we'd be traveling all over the place, and it's increasing massively! There are now 1.2 billion drivers around the world right now and it's estimated that by 2035 there will be 1.7 billion cars on the road, and if you do the math that's almost 1 car for every 4 people on the whole planet! You can't tell me that traveling on land isn't speeding up! It's going nuts! Just like Daniel said! The whole planet has got to drive here and there, whenever we want, wherever we want, as much as we want. We take all this traveling on land for granted, but it's a huge sign we're living in the last days!

There's another land travel technology that has come out just in the last few years that I also believe has to do with End Times Bible Prophecy. Let me explain the technology first, then we'll get into how it's related to Prophecy. It's in the area of Automated Land Travel. A brand-new technology that is just about ready to take over everything on the whole planet!

The **1st automated** land travel technology that's a sign we're living in the last days is **Automated Cars**.

Now I'm not talking about cars that just have automated features like cruise control or even the latest developments with self-parking cars, or even automated braking. I'm talking about full-blown automated cars where you literally do nothing! You don't drive it, it drives you! You just sit back, relax, take a nap if you want and enjoy the ride! And they're already here!

Will Smith driving in his Audi when he says, "Access USR mainframe."

CNN Reports: *"Actor Will Smith in a scene from I Robot in 2004 and it seemed like pure Science Fiction. Now years later self-driving cars have been going way beyond the Hollywood fantasy."*

Bjorn Giesler, Audi: *"You can say I don't want to drive right now, and it will take over. If I want to get back in the driver's seat, I just take hold of the wheel."*

CNN Reports: *"At the consumer show in Las Vegas last week, a demonstration shows that it is possible to catch some zzzz's in this Audi prototype."*

Bjorn Giesler: *"We call it piloted driving, which means there is a driver, but you can concentrate on something else if you don't want to actually drive."*

CNN Reports: *"And it's coming much sooner than you think. The state of California is taking aggressive steps to get driverless cars on the roads as early as this spring. The most well-known autonomous car comes from Google which shows how someday, this car can help the blind."*

Digits WSJ reports: *"In 2015 we completed the world's first driverless ride on public roads. Just a person in a car. No steering wheel, no pedals, navigating traffic."*

Steve Mahan, Former CEO, Santa Clara Valley Blind Center: *"Well, I have never been to Austin, Texas. Now I'm driving in Austin, Texas. It's a profound experience for me to be alone in a car. A very important segment in my life was cut away when my vision failed, and a self-driving car would give me a huge part of my life back."*

Digits WSJ Reports: *"This is just the beginning. So, if auto makers have their way autonomous cars that we communicate with on many levels will be the cars we end up driving in the future."*[4]

That future is here now! It's not coming, it's here now! What you have to understand is that this is not just cool, convenient, and the latest luxury vehicle for traveling on land. I'm telling you, it's about to completely take over all land travel! And it's not just eclectic companies like Google or Tesla, but as of 2016, there are now over 30 companies worldwide utilizing automated AI, artificial intelligence, because that's what's controlling this, and they're all creating driverless cars, automated vehicles, and they're investing not just millions but billions into this! Why? Because they're expecting billions if not more in return! It's big, big business! And again, we're talking all major manufacturers including companies like Apple! Even they are getting in on this. It's like a Wild West boom in Technology! But they're combing it with something else.

The **2nd automated** land travel technology that's a sign we're living in the last days is **Automated Roads**.

You see, apparently, it's not enough to just control and automate the cars we're driving in, as you saw, they also want to control the roads we're on. And this supposedly would give us, once again, a better driving experience. They say it will prevent accidents, reduce travel time, save on fuel costs, and even get rid of ice and snow on the road!

"OK, so actually this time what is it? It's technology that replaces all roadways, parking lots, sidewalks, driveways, tarmacs, bike paths, and outdoor recreation, with solar panels. Not with just lifeless boring solar panels, but it's smart micro processing, interlocking hexagonal solar units. No more useless asphalt and concrete just sitting there baking in the sun needing to be repaved and filling with potholes that ruin your axle alignment. These are intelligent solar panels.

Replace one panel at a time if damaged or malfunctioning. They're covered with a new tempered glass material that's been designed and tested to meet all impact, load and traction requirements and did I mention that they are solar panels? They generate electricity, they generate capital, they pay for themselves, they keep paying more because we're not going to run out of sun for about 15 billion years and that lowers the cost of energy unlike those bills in the mail that keep going up, and it's clean energy. Everyone can theoretically drive an electric car with no pollution and a minimal carbon footprint.

Can you imagine how good our cities would smell; how much heathier we'd all be? 'Excuse me young man, am I being led to believe that this thing is some sort of thing? Yes, it's a thing!' Yes, it's a thing, a real thing, and clean energy is only a primary function. Grab a notepad because this is where it gets interesting. For those in the north the panels use energy they collect to power elements to keep the surface temperature a few degrees above freezing. They're heated. No ice and snow on roads causing traffic delays, accidents and injury.

No more shoveling your driveway and sidewalk, no salt corroding your car or wasting tax money on snow removal, and you can ride your bike or drive your motorcycle all year round. Every panel has a series of LED lights on the circuit board that can be programmed to make landscape designs, warning signs, parking lot configurations, whatever. These roads never have to have lanes repainted.

Just reprogram to whatever we choose or whatever works best. Imagine a highway road lighting up ahead of you, how much safer it would be to drive at night. There would be improved visibility for pilots landing on solar landing strips. Imagine, walking onto a solar recreation court and choosing a sports configuration. Want to play basketball? Cool. Kids want to play hopscotch and foursquare? Awesome. Ball Hockey? Done. With LED lights under your feet it's going to look like Tron out there but real, because this is the real world. The panels are also pressure sensitive so they can detect when large debris like branches or boulders have fallen onto the road or if an animal is crossing. It can warn drivers with LED text to slow down for an obstruction.

Solar roadways use as much recycled material in their production as possible, plus the roadways have two channels that form what's called a cable corridor that runs concurrently with the roadway themselves. One part houses electrical cables meaning power lines, data lines, fiber optics, and high speed internet which replaces the need for telephone poles and hanging wires that can be damaged during storms causing power outages or become extremely dangerous if severed either as fallen live wires or buried cable. The other channel filters storm water and melted snow, moving them to either a treatment facility or treating them on site, greatly decreasing the amount of pollution that enters our soil, lakes, rivers and oceans."[5]

What did he say? This is not coming, it's already happening! Let me give you some examples. The Netherlands is the first country to open a solar road for public use. France is also working on a system that you just place on top of existing roads. And, roads in the U.S. are already starting to be packed with "smart technology." Some states are investing millions of dollars right now to create self-driving highways. They're called "Smart Roads" and the article goes on to say, "President Donald Trump has promised to increase infrastructure spending."

The Guardian reported, *"If all the roads in the U.S. were converted to solar roadways, or Smart Roads, the country would generate three times as much energy as it currently uses and cut greenhouse gases by 75 percent."*

And again, isn't that what the Millennial Generation and the New Green Deal people say we need to do? Sounds like a set up to me! They're the ones who are going to fall for this!

Which brings us to the **3rd automated** land travel technology that's a sign we're living in the last days, and that is **Automated Utopia**.

You see, the pitch they're making to the Millennials with all this new AI controlled Automated Land Travel technology is it will not only "save the planet from blowing up" supposedly, but it will create a Modern-Day Utopia beyond our wildest dreams! We'll have such an amazing self-indulgent convenient travel experience that it will be impossible to say no! Who would say no to this? And again, it's not just cars, but taxis, trucks, subways, trains, buses, pods, you name it! In fact, speaking of Millennials, Chrysler is actually working on an automated car for Millennials that automatically takes selfies! Because we all know how horrible life gets when you get a callous on your thumb from taking all those selfies, this one will do it for you!

CNN reports: *"A minivan for Millennials. The Fiat Chrysler Portal is a concept car designed for Millennials with families. Millennials within the company collaborated with engineers to design the self-driving car. The car's own wi-fi network lets it sync with your mobile devices. Facial recognition will supposedly allow the car to enable custom lighting while driving, and it includes cameras for selfies."*[6]

Obviously is right! But that's the tip of the iceberg! They're also working on autonomous valet parking that would enable drivers to send their car to park itself, and then summon it later using your mobile device…like a trained pet. They're also looking at using automated vehicles for grocery delivery and other purchasing options. The vehicle would be able to take a grocery list and order it from Amazon or from Whole Foods, giving the driver time to handle other errands. It'll do the "buying and selling" for you! We'll get to that in another study. But they also want to, 'Control the whole car experience.' 'Learning the driver's personality, anticipating the cheapest gas station or the closest one when it's time to fill up.' Or, 'Direct a passenger's attention away from their video games or apps to the world around them.' You know…too much screen time! If you're driving past a castle, for example, the passenger would be alerted to pay attention and instantly pull up information about the landmark. I kid you not, pun intended, they will help you, "Calm the kids." If a driver's children are screaming in the backseat, the car would know to switch the programming to trivia or a joke, even point them to an item of interest outside the car turning it into a game keeping them occupied. As one researcher shared, *"How happy we'll all be just to be able to watch Netflix while our cars drive us around."* Oh, wouldn't that be a dream come true. The kids are happy. We're happy. Everyone's happy! It will be one big Land Travel Utopian experience beyond our wildest dreams as this video shows.

Panasonic Pod: *"Future Mobility lifestyle, 20XX, Solar charging, camera monitor systems, autonomous driving mode, mobile teleconferencing, eye-gaze detection, driver monitoring by AI agent. You may be tired, so there is an integrated comfort system. (Lighting – Air conditioning - Premium audio – Massage seat) Cooperative autonomous driving is what is coming. Even driver monitoring and route recommendations. This is moving life forward."*[7]

Yes! Moving life forward! It's going to be amazing! Who can resist? What a Utopia, right? WRONG!

This brings us to the **4th automated** land travel technology that's a sign we're living in the last days and that is **Automated Big Brother**.

Because here's what it's going to lead!

Revelation 13:11-12,14,15-17 "Then I saw another beast, coming out of the earth. He had two horns like a lamb, but he spoke like a dragon. He exercised all the authority of the first beast on his behalf and made the earth and its inhabitants worship the first beast, whose fatal wound had been healed. He deceived the inhabitants of the earth. He ordered them to set up an image in honor of the beast who was wounded by the sword and yet lived. He was given power to give breath to the image of the first beast, so that it could speak and cause all who refused to worship the image to be killed. He also forced everyone, small and great, rich and poor, free and slave, to receive a mark on his right hand or on his forehead, so that no one could buy or sell unless he had the mark, which is the name of the beast or the number of his name."

So here we see how the Bible clearly says that in the 7-year Tribulation the False Prophet is not only going to dupe the whole world into worshiping the Antichrist, but he's what? He's going to make them, he's going to order them, he's going to cause them, he's going to force them to do whatever he says to do, otherwise they will what? They will die, right? And again, focus on the key-words there, "make" "order" "cause" and "force." This implies that we have some serious global enforcement going on here! Because that's the context, it's global. He forces the whole planet to do whatever in the world he wants them to do, or they are going to die! They are, in essence, micro-managing the planet! So, here's the point. In order to pull this off, think about it, you not only need some serious control over the whole planet, but you better have some serious ability to monitor everything and everyone on the whole planet. If they don't do what you say, you have to have the ability to take them out right there on the spot, right? Why? Because you know there's going to be resisters, even in the 7-year Tribulation! The bulk of the planet is going to fall for the antichrist's lies but not everyone does. People are still going to resist. So, what do you do? How do you force, order, make, and cause people to do what you say or kill them on the spot if they don't do what you say? Simple! Stir everything we've seen together so far with this Automated Land Travel technology and I think you have just one of the many ways he's going to do it! Add this to what we've seen so far! Here's what they also want to put in these automated vehicles!

"A Smart car seat senses driver's physical and mental state." This is from L.A. "*A new smart car seat can keep a driver calm by actively monitoring the commuter's physical and mental status, according to the maker.*" And at another L.A. Auto Show they shared how, "*Cars will read your mind in the future.*"

In other words, they will know if you will obey or not obey. Are you a resister? Then add to that how they are already giving this automated smart car information over to authorities to allow them to take control of these automated vehicles if they don't like what you're doing.

"*Automakers could give police control over your self-driving car and they can reroute them or force them to pull over.*"

Why? Because, "*As recent as December 2018 an intoxicated driver fell asleep behind the wheel of a Tesla with the Autopilot engaged.*" "*And this is the kind of problem AV (automated vehicles) manufacturers and law enforcement want to avoid."*

So, they can program the AV's to pull over as soon as they detect flashing police lights behind them, which by the way is already being done by Google's automated car Waymo.

They admit, *"Letting law enforcement control an owner's car seems like murky legal territory and you can see how some people might be opposed to police being able to give instructions to their car — especially if the car is programmed to follow police orders over that of the driver even if the driver isn't doing anything illegal."*

Now, add this to that. This whole system is being controlled by a type of AI Global Cloud system that can be tapped into anywhere around the world. They even admit it in the commercials!

One commercial: *"Did you know that 98% of the cloud runs on Intel? That ride share that you actually rode here, is on the cloud. That driverless car, Intel is driving the future. Traffic lights, streetlamps, business runs on the cloud."[8]*

Including, as you saw, Automated Vehicles. They're already admitting it in the commercials that all these Automated Vehicles are being controlled by an AI Cloud based system which is why articles are starting to say this. *"Some critics have also noted how hackers might be able to exploit this ability for police to control AV's."* In other words, they're concerned that anybody can now get into this cloud system and control your vehicle as well. In fact, it's already being done!

Andy Greenberg. Senior writer at Wired: *"It's not fun having your two-ton SUV's brakes get hacked just as you are parking in front of a ditch. That is what I learned from Chris Valasek and Charlie Miller. They are hackers that have spent the last year developing a piece of software that can wirelessly sabotage this 2014 Jeep Cherokee. It hasn't been altered in any way. There haven't been any devices attached to it. But like many thousands of Jeeps around the world, it can be remotely hacked over the internet through its cellular connection to its entertainment system.*

It would allow someone to take over its steering, transmission and even its brakes. To demonstrate that I am going to take it on the highway here in St Louis while Charlie and Chris hijack its digital system from Charlie's house miles away. They wouldn't tell me what they had planned but they assured me that it wouldn't be life threatening. I have no idea what they might do."

Charlie: *"First we are going to turn the fan on him."*

Chris: *"Yeah, let's turn on the fan and see if he even notices it."*

Andy kind of giggles: *"Something just came on. Like the fan. I didn't do that." "The tricks started small, then a picture of Charlie and Chris showed up on the GPS screen on the dashboard. But as I drove down the interstate things started getting unpleasant and very loud. The radio was blaring, and I couldn't turn it down. Then the window cleaner started spraying and the windshield wipers came on while the radio was still blasting."*

Charlie tells Chris: *"Do it, do it, kill the engine right now!"* And the engine stops.[9]

And you have total control of that car! Now let's put all this together and go back to our text dealing with the 7-year Tribulation. You just made the biggest mistake of your life and you rejected Jesus Christ as your personal Lord and Savior which means you've been left behind at the Rapture, and now you're in the 7-year Tribulation. The False Prophet at some point says to worship the Antichrist or die and you say no, and you try to flee, but because of all this Automatic Travel Technology, you ain't going nowhere! First, you try to flee on land. But maybe they send an automated vehicle to come and take you out! Don't believe me? Listen to this crazy recent patent from Google. The same ones making the automated car!

Fox Business reports: *"Another headline, Google has patented, look at that, a sticky coating on self-driving cars. Let's bring in Laura Seminetti to explain that horrible graphic."*

Laura: *"That is an awful graphic. This is my favorite story or one of my favorite stories this week. Let me explain it to you because we have most of Silicon Valley and most of Detroit working on autonomous vehicles. How do we get them on the road? We are concerned about the safety of the driver and the passengers and we* *are concerned about convenience. How do we make life easier? We don't worry about the other people on the road. So, if you can come up with Google's idea that they are working on, putting a sticker, an adhesive coating on the front of the car so that when you hit a pedestrian or a cyclist, they stick to the car.*[10]

And then you can haul them in or dispose of the body! Crazy stuff! Or maybe you try to get in your automated vehicle to flee from the Antichrist and False Prophet to your so-called bug out shelter you've been working on because you didn't need Jesus, but they control the whole system now! They shut the power off to the automated road and you ain't going nowhere! There's no power! It's all electric now! And remember, they'll know who the resisters are because these cars also know what you're doing, saying, videoing, your pictures, gotta have those selfies, and even what mood you're in! They know it all! Or they let you seemingly flee only to tap into your automated vehicle via the cloud and take control of your car to take you out! Hollywood, believe it or not, is already putting that horrible scenario into our minds. Here's a clip from a recent AI movie called *Upgrade*, which I don't recommend, but watch how they take these people out!

A clip from *Upgrade*: *As the couple is driving down the street the man reaches for the steering wheel and the car tells him, "Do not touch the steering wheel while in motion." He immediately takes his hand off. The lady kind of laughs and then they kiss. But he stops and says, "Where are we?" As he is looking out the window he says, "This is our old neighborhood. We are going in the exact opposite direction of the house. Where is the car taking us?" The lady then says, "Car take us home!" The car says, "I'm sorry there has been an error." The lady then says, "Turn on the freeway and take us home." The car again says, "I'm sorry, there has been an error." The man then says, "Car stop, stop car!" The car doesn't seem to be slowing down, so they try to push the brake pedal. The car just goes faster and faster. He says, "The car is going way too fast." At that point it runs into a barrier and it overturns. Crashing...*[11].

And voila! There goes your resister! I'm sure it was driver error or an accident. Folks, this is the ultimate convenient tool to take somebody out, if you wanted to, for not doing what they were told to do, and nobody would know, all because you got tricked into creating this so-called Automated Travel Utopia! And that's exactly what the Antichrist and False Prophet need to control the whole world in the last days according to the Book of Revelation! That system is being built right now before our very eyes with Modern technology!

And that's precisely why, out of love, God has given us this update on **The Final Countdown: Tribulation Rising** concerning **Modern Technology & the AI Invasion** to show us that the Tribulation is near and the 2nd Coming of Jesus Christ is rapidly approaching. And that's why Jesus Himself said:

Luke 21:28 "When these things begin to take place, stand up and lift up your heads, because your redemption is drawing near."

Like it or not, we are headed for **The Final Countdown**. The signs of the 7-year **Tribulation** are **Rising**! So, the point is this. If you're a Christian and you're not doing anything for the Lord, shame on you! Get busy doing something for Jesus now! Stop wasting your life! We need you! Don't sit on the sidelines! Get on the front lines and help us! Let's get busy working together doing something splendid for Jesus with what time is left and get busy saving souls! Amen?

But if you're reading this today and you're not a Christian, then I beg you, please, heed these signs, heed these warnings, give your life to Jesus now! Because when the Antichrist takes control it won't be a Modern-Day Utopia, don't fall for that lie! It'll be a horrible blood bath! Take the way out now, the only way out, through Jesus Christ, before it's too late! Amen?

Chapter Two

The Increase of Air Travel

The **2ⁿᵈ area** of transportation that has seen a major increase in our lifetime is in the area of **Air Travel**. But again, don't take my word for it. Let's once again look at what Daniel told us.

Daniel 12:1-4 "At that time Michael, the great prince who protects your people, will arise. There will be a time of distress such as has not happened from the beginning of nations until then. But at that time your people – everyone whose name is found written in the book – will be delivered. Multitudes who sleep in the dust of the earth will awake, some to everlasting life, others to shame and everlasting contempt. Those who are wise will shine like the brightness of the heavens, and those who lead many to righteousness, like the stars for ever and ever. But you, Daniel, close up and seal the words of the scroll until the time of the end. Many will go here and there to increase knowledge."

Now again, as we saw before in this passage, God clearly gives Daniel some clear-cut signs that you're living in the end of times. Not only is the activity of the Archangel Michael protecting the Jewish People, but what? There would be an explosion of knowledge like never before. But again, what was the first one? People would be traveling here and there all over the earth like never before. And that's not only happening on land, as we saw in the last chapter, but I'm telling you, it's happening massively when it comes to air travel as well. You see, mankind has always wanted to fly, but nothing ever really changed for centuries and centuries. They had the desire, but they could never pull it off. In fact, at one point, China came out with "Man-carrying kites" that were used for civil or military purposes but sometimes they were used for, I kid you not, "for punishment!" Don't make me put you on that kite! All early attempts at flight were just one big failure after another. In fact, let me show you some examples!

"One attempt at flying was when the pilot put on his heavy-duty suit and stepped into the plane while his assistant turned the handle to make the propeller go around and up and down. It just sat there. So, then they decided maybe it would be better if the pilot had pedals to make the propeller go. But that didn't work. Then they thought maybe if they had more wings, maybe seven wings, that would help the machine to get up off the ground. But no, they were too heavy, and they all caved in on the pilot.

Then they decided that it might work if they had an actual engine. It was small with several wings, but it just went around in circles, mainly scaring the cows in the pasture where they were doing their experimental flight. Well, it was decided that they needed a bigger plane so this one looked like a metal building, but it was too heavy and never made it off the ground. Someone got the great idea to stand on a bridge, jump, and the wind would catch it and away it would go. Fortunately, it was a nice day for a swim.

They started to get a little better this time, one large wing, one small wing, and the pilot just had to hold it up and run as fast as he could so that maybe the wind would catch it and away he would go. Nope, that didn't work. Never got off the ground. So now they go back to the idea of peddling and pulling ropes to make the wings flap like a bird. And to guarantee the flight they even pushed the plane over a hill. The nose went into the ground first and there the pilot was upside down in the dirt.

The next one was a bigger plane. It looked kind of like a bug. The wings started flapping, it started shaking, and it just collapsed there in the field. Just like someone had stepped on a bug. Well, it was time to take things into their own hands and just put wings on a person. He could run and flap his arms and he could fly like a bird. He even put on skates so that he could move faster. Well that didn't work so they made bigger wings and even added a rudder and ran downhill. Nope that didn't work."[1]

As you can see, man has always wanted to fly, the desire's been there for a long, long time with all these crazy inventions. But it was just one big failure after another! Until now! In the last century alone, this is when man began to pull this off! Air flight! Why? Because that's what Daniel said would happen when you're in the last days! It had to happen! Thanks to the invention of the airplane, which also occurred during the last century, the world has become a much smaller place. Now, as we know, the first big breakthrough came through with the Wright brothers.

The Wright Brothers

They actually launched their first glider in 1900 and built a second glider the following year, but it was even worse than the first one. But they didn't give up. After, "hundreds of times," the Wright brothers finally made their first successful attempt at "manned flight" just south of Kitty Hawk, North Carolina on December 17, 1903.

"As one brother gets in, the other helps get him situated and then climbs in beside him. Everyone is holding their breath to see if this thing is going to get off the ground. As they are sitting there, they turn on the engine and it starts to roll

across the ground. Suddenly it lifts off and there is a big sigh of relief and pictures being taken. The airplane stays in the air and flies back over their heads. It is the first flight by the Wright brothers."[2]

Their first flight was made by Orville Wright, it was only 120 feet for 12 seconds, but his brother Wilbur beat him on the same day with another flight of 852 feet in 59 seconds, and this is when manned flight really began to take off...pun intended! Then, a couple of years later, the Wright brother's flight information was published in a French Aviation Magazine called Aerophile, and the next thing you know the French were beginning to experiment with their own planes. This one came out via a Romanian engineer in 1906.

The French Airplane

Then the next year you have the invention of what was called the Voisin Biplane

The Voisin Biplane

But the really big breakthroughs for air travel technology came as a result of the military. As is often the case with military exploits, it often leads to new inventions. And so it was with WWI and airplane technology. There were a

WWI Airplanes

total of 219 different aircraft invented and employed just in WWI for the different militaries around the world. They used them for reconnaissance as well as for dropping bombs.

This is when you had the birth of "The Flying Aces" like the "Red Baron."

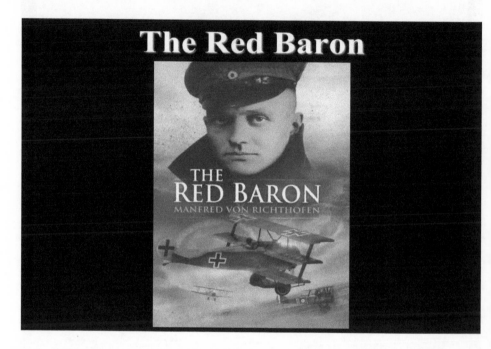

From here, Air Travel Technology really began to explode! Then another war came along and took it even further. With WWII you had the development of the Jet Airplane. The first one was made by a German named Ernst Heinkel called the Heinkel He 178.

Reporter: *On August 27th, 1939 the Heinkel He 178 became the first jet propelled aircraft, producing 1,100 lbs. of thrust. The engine pushed the plane to speeds up to 435 miles per hour but it burned fuel at such a high rate it could only remain airborne for ten minutes.[3]*

Well, that's a gas guzzler! But it was a start and led to the development of a multitude of jet aircraft during WWII, and not just Germany and the United States, but Britain and Russia followed suit.

WWII Jet Airplanes

Post WWII, we see the birth of the commercial jet airplane, with the first commercial jet created by BOAC (British Overseas Airway Corporation) and the De Havilland Comet Jet Airliner. The problem was they lost 3 airliners in 12 months due to structural fatigue which caused them to break up in flight! Not a good advertising campaign!

First Commercial Jet

This paved the way for Boeing to take the lead in aircraft development. They came out with their first commercial jet airliner, the Boeing 707 which became the world's first successful airliner.

The Boeing 707

And this is really when things began to escalate for flying technology. Now you have a multitude of airline manufacturers around the world and soon Boeing came out with its legendary Boeing 747.When you put this into perspective it's amazing! The first flight by the Wright brothers as we saw was only 120 feet. Had they flown from the back of a Boeing 747 they wouldn't have even made it to first class! The first plane had limited seating, but a Boeing 747 can carry more than 400 passengers, fly 8,300 miles without refueling, with 6 million parts, 171 miles of wiring, 5 miles of tubing, and a tail the size of a six-

The Boeing 747

story building. It's from this aircraft that we get the nickname, the "Jumbo Jet." Boeing eventually came out with the Boeing 777 that could seat 550 passengers.

The Airbus A380

This was eclipsed by the current leader, the Airbus A380, a European company, and it can seat 853 passengers making it what they now call a "Super Jumbo." Now stop for a moment. Is it just me or are people in our lifetime traveling to and fro anywhere they want around the planet as much as they want? And it's increasing, or is just me? I mean, where have I heard that before? I'm telling you, we so take for granted this flying technology, but it's a huge sign we're living in the last days!

Air Travel gets even more advanced than that, and again, all in our lifetime! Now we can not only fly a ton of people all over the planet in huge planes, but the speed of which is increasing as well! The Wright brothers flew at a speed of about 30mph, again, about the speed of a horse, not a big deal. But now, oh boy! We not only have aircraft; we have Supersonic Aircraft! The world's first supersonic commercial plane (SST) was made by the Russians

First SST Commercial Jet

and was called the Tu-144 and went about 1,200 mph. But then the British and French came out with the Mach 2 Concorde aircraft and it went about 1,354 mph.

And then of course the military is all about superfast flying aircraft for various reasons and the fastest military jet plane, one record says anyway, was the SR-71 Blackbird that went 2,275 mph.

Mach 2 Concorde

Business Insider: *"The world's fastest manned aircraft is the SR-71 Blackbird. A high-altitude recon aircraft build by Lockheed in the 1960's. It was designed to fly higher and faster than the U-2. It was capable of speeds exceeding Mach 3 (2,200 mph), over three times the speed of sound. The jet could outfly any missile fired at it. At top speed, its titanium skin could reach up to 900 degrees F. Its* *maximum altitude was 85,000 feet forcing crews to wear pressure suits and astronaut-type helmets. Only 32 Blackbirds were made and they were in service from 1964 to 1998. In over 4,000 combat sorties, none were lost to enemy fire. The SR-71 was retired in part because it was costly to operate. A successor, the SR-72 is reportedly in development with aims for the jet to reach Mach 6.* [4]

I wonder how fast that one would go? Well, let's do the math! The SR-71 traveling at 2,275 mph is fast enough to go from Los Angeles to New York City in just a little over an hour! But the SR-72 traveling at 6 times the speed of sound, as they mentioned there, Mach 6, would be 4,603 mph, which means you're going from L.A. to New York in a half an hour! Isn't that crazy! All in

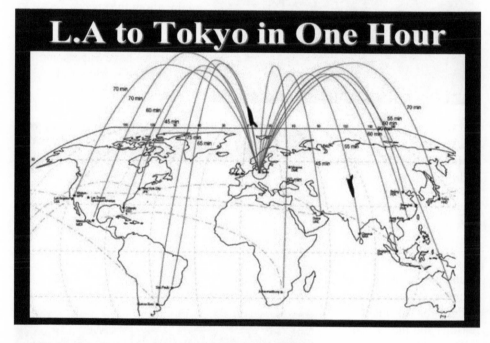

our lifetime! But that's still not all. "Virgin Galactic wants to fly you from L.A. to Tokyo in one hour, through space."

Now it's going commercial, not just military! Richard Branson's company, Virgin Galactic has already built the first commercial spaceport and now he also wants to revolutionize commercial air flights. They want to fly people from L.A. to Tokyo in no more than one hour, through space. And, "It's not clear whether the passengers would be primarily tourists or businesspersons on urgent trips." Yeah, I'd say urgent! But it's being called the world's first commercial spaceline. So, we went from airlines to spacelines! But now you can go anywhere around the whole world in 4 hours!

Buzz 60: *"Let's be honest, air travel can be brutal. Most of us can't afford anything but coach and we spend innumerable hours stuck in that tin can because traveling is awesome. But what if we could tell you that you can go anywhere in the world in about four hours? Well this aircraft can take you anywhere in about four hours. The Sabre Rocket engine was designed by UK-based Reaction Engines, LTD. It combines both jet and rocket engine technologies. The engine quickly cools air drawn from the outside atmosphere and burns it with liquid hydrogen fuel. The company says the technology needed for this heat exchange is extremely lightweight, meaning it could be used in air and space. Once the engine gets above earth's atmosphere, it converts to a regular oxygen-driven rocket. The company says this would enable the aircraft to cruise within the atmosphere at up to 5 times the speed of sound or even fly directly into orbit. Reaction Engines says it plans to do a ground demonstration of the engine by 2020".*[5]

Believe it or not, they're now working on one that will get you from New York to London in just 11 minutes! It's called the Antipode.

TM8 News: *"Canadian engineer designs Mach 24 aircraft Antipode. The Canadians have done it again. They have just released designs for the supersonic aircraft, the Antipode. It is said to carry up to 10 passengers up to 12,430 miles in under an hour reaching speeds up to 16,000 miles per hour. At 16,000 or Mach 24 which is a little over 18,000, Antipode is proposing that it would be possible to go from London to New York in just eleven minutes. A flight that currently takes eight hours."*[6]

Wow! Now we're down to 11 minutes! Now add to the speed the number of passengers traveling to and fro, here and there! Just in the U.S. the FAA provides service to more than 43,000 flights, 2.6 million airline

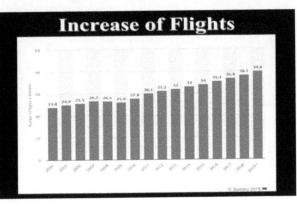

passengers, over 29 million square miles of airspace, and there's about 5,000 aircraft in the air at peak times just in the U.S. But now, around the world there

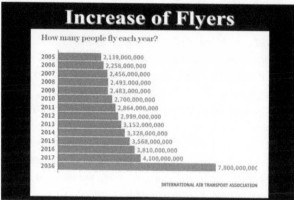

are about 100,000 airline flights per day and that's not counting private aviation, people who have their own planes. There is projected almost 40 million flights this year alone which translates into over 4 billion people traveling each year and by 2036 they estimate there will be 7.8 billion people traveling, in the air around the world, which is just over the whole planet's population!

Don't tell me things aren't speeding up! Air travel has gone ballistic, just like Daniel said it would! In fact, let me show you just how much people are traveling here and there around the world with this screenshot![7]

Wow! What did Daniel say? When you see people traveling all over the world like never before, it's a major sign that you're living in the last days!

But that's still not all. It's not just the increase of the speed of travel and the amount of people traveling that's increasing, it's also the increase of air travel options! There are a ton of different options to travel in the air and many have increased in just the last few years! Including Hoverboards!

A Flyboard Air truck backs up to the water to unload a Flyboard.

Franky Zapata, Zapata Racing: *"Today I'm going to try to break the record of the fastest Hoverboard. I have to fly 218 meters in order to break the record."*

As he flies across the water, several boats follow him to reach his goal.

Franky Zapata: *"I am so happy for my sponsor, for my family, for my city, for my country. I am very happy."*

Sofia Greenacre, Guinness World Records: *"A phenomenal sight to see. A total of 2,252.4 meters, so he beats the record by some margin."*

Franky Zapata: *"No one thought it was possible, not even me, but you see today that we realized our dream and it is just one of the best moments in my life."*

Yeah, clap is right! Marty McFly eat your heart out![8]

Marty's Hoverboard

In fact, speaking of movies, they're now saying, "Star Wars technologies may not be so far, far away." Including the Land Speeder, I guess that's in development as well.

And maybe you're saying well that's not high enough for you to get off the ground. I mean, if you're going to fly here and there whenever you want around the world like Daniel said in the last days, you want to fly on something that can get a little higher than that Hoverboard. Well hey, worry no more! How about your very own Jet Pack! Yeah, they're already here too!

SCI Channel reports: *"Yes this is David Mamen demonstrating his wild side and wowing over 2.5 million people with this fully functional jet pack."*

"I was 10 years old and on the radio was Buck Rogers. He came out of a spaceship, put on his jet pack and I figured I got to have one of those."

"I always wanted to fly myself. Sky divers do that, but I thought that was a little dangerous so let's take up something safe like jet pack flying. The jet pack is science fiction to a lot of people but it's true, it's real, it's sitting right there".

Smithsonian Magazine's Future is Here Festival: *"Is it a bird, is it a plane? No, it's a man flying around the Smithsonian in a jet pack suit."*

"Flying is a really old dream for the human and we are reaching the realization of that dream. I'm not playing with death; I'm playing with life."

And he soars through the air as a jet. Then his partner meets him in the air, and they fly side by side.

Reuters: *"Plunging into the skies of Japan, Ease Rossi, known as Jet Man, streaks through the clouds by Mt. Fuji. It was the latest feat for the 54-year-old swiss pilot who has dedicated 10 years to his passion of flying in the most natural way possible. He says being thrust through the air with only a jet pack on his back is like being in the palm of a giant hand"[9]*

And that same giant hand wrote in the Book of Daniel that all this would be a sign you're living in the last days! And as cool and creepy as that was, maybe you're one of those folks looking for something with a little less of an open concept, you know what I'm saying? I mean, that Jet Pack was cool, but it was a little too much! Maybe they'd make something enclosed like your car, where you feel safer, only it flies! Well worry no more! They have a ton of them now!

WSJ Reports: *"The flying car has long been a feature of pop culture and science fiction. Now a small group of entrepreneurs are turning fiction into reality. Recent advances such as lighter structure and engines finally make their ambitions possible."[10]*

It looks like a small compact car but when you get in it the control panel resembles a plane. You can drive it down the street as a car or you can go to a runway, the wings come out and it turns into a small plane and off you go.

Bye! See you later! Say hi to Jet Man for me! Is this crazy or what? And lest you think this is still going to be a long way off, "10 companies are racing **to** make the flying car a reality." Car makers like Audi, Austin Martin, Rolls Royce and even Aircraft Industry leaders like Boeing and Airbus are getting in on it. And they have a good track record of pulling things off like this! But maybe that still freaks you out because you don't want to have the responsibility of flying. Well hey, worry no more! They are now automating these vehicles like we saw before, only they fly. Just push a button and one of them will come pick you up like a taxi!

"The roads and transport authority in Dubai; adoption of autonomous vehicles technology reflects the Dubai smart autonomous mobility strategy which aims to transform 25% of the city's mass transit system to autonomous driving. To enhance people's well-being and happiness and strengthen Dubai's reputation of technology and the future, RTA has announced the signing of an agreement with the German Volocopter company, a specialist manufacturer of autonomous air vehicles, to launch the world's first autonomous air taxi. The AAT is characterized by its autonomous flight. This enables the movement of people place to place without human intervention or the need of a flight license."[11]

German start-up Volocopter writes aviation history: First ever public demonstration of an autonomous urban air taxi Dubai, 25th September 2017.

Whoa! And that was back in 2017! And what's the point of all this? When you see people rushing here and there, even in the air, in a multitude of ways, you're living in the last days! It's just like the Bible said! And again, keep in mind, your grandparents were born in the same town and lived there their whole lives and basically never ever went anywhere! But look at us now! Just like Daniel said would happen, we're traveling all over the place anywhere in the world, and it's increasing massively in the last days! Don't tell me traveling in the air isn't speeding up! It's going nuts! Just like Daniel said, the whole planet is flying here and there, whenever we want, wherever we want, as much as we want, and it's a sign we're living in the last days!

I also see another aspect of all this air travel technology that also has to do with End Times Prophecy. You see, it also paves the way, I believe, for the global wars the Bible says are coming in the 7-year Tribulation after the Rapture takes place. When the first seal is opened with the rise of the antichrist, he dupes the whole world with his false peace and false utopia. That's the First Seal, and they think he's the best thing since sliced bread, the world's savior, when he's actually Satan's nightmare...God's judgment upon them. But it doesn't take him long to show his true satanic murderous colors because that's what the very next seal does. It unleashes a Global War!

Revelation 6:3-4,8 "When the Lamb opened the second seal, I heard the second living creature say, 'Come!' Then another horse came out, a fiery red one. Its rider was given power to take peace from the earth and to make men slay each other. To him was given a large sword. They were given power over a fourth of the earth to kill by sword, famine and plague, and by the wild beasts of the earth."

So, this global war is so bad that we ultimately see its outcome, one-fourth of the earth, nearly 2 billion people are annihilated. And this is just in the first half of the 7-year Tribulation! In fact, it's the first part of the first half! And so, the question is, "How do you annihilate one-fourth of the planet in such a quick fashion?" Well, simple. I believe, as we saw with all this air travel technology they're using around the world, including the militaries, you now have just one of the means for the first time in the history of mankind to pull it off! Think about it! We can now fly anywhere on the planet in a short amount of time and take out loads of people lickety-split like never before in the history of mankind. All this air travel technology that's ALL emerged in our lifetime, makes it all possible, i.e. this Global War in the 7-year Tribulation! You can fly anywhere in a short amount of time and do your dastardly deed! In fact, maybe it's going to look something like this.

"Revelation 16:15 Behold, I am coming like a thief! Blessed is the one who stays awake.

There is yelling and screaming. People standing in the streets being held back by the police. Bright lights all around. Fear and unbelief run rampant. People are disappearing right and left.

Breaking News: One World Government established! Vacating the Vatican! Pope initiates his move to Jerusalem!

Jerusalem elected capital of the world! Temple complex construction underway!

The course of human history has change today. Peace and Safety! New World leader paving pathway for peace!

The alerts are going off. This is not a test! World currency mandate! All persons to be marked for transactions!

This is an emergency broadcast transmission. Global intelligence agency! New surveillance protocols necessary for peace!

News Broadcasters are saying they are going to stay on the air as long as possible. There is a Global Crisis.

Censored! Religious conservative muzzled for fear mongering!

War is on the horizon! Tensions mount surrounding Israel!

The Pentagon is on alert! Middle East Madness! 10 Kings resign authority to Supreme Caliph Mahdi!

Be Brave!!! Be Brave!!! Golan Heights ... Israeli coast ... World at War! Jerusalem a cup of trembling!

Mediterranean Sea ... What we just witnessed come out of the ocean ... There are massive casualties and losses. Worldwide attacks! Jerusalem conflict incites terror networks! We have lost communication with Tokyo ... France is lost.

High level terror strike! Suitcase nuke detonated in America! Cities are destroyed. U.S. defies world order! Retaliates! Strike forces descend on terror headquarters in Syria!

Syria is decimated!! Damascus a ruinous heap! Nuclear War! Russia and Iran Launch ICBMS, Kings of the East advance on Israel!

People are watching with fear and trembling, crying out for help as they watch the destruction of what used to be their home, city, country, world.

World Government Headquarters ... pushing red buttons, sending missiles, bombs to destroy ... Global directive blocks UK secession! Secret Space weapon impales rebel parliament! Everything is destroyed!

Are You Ready?[12]

This is precisely why, out of love, God has given us this update on **The Final Countdown: Tribulation Rising** concerning the **Modern Technology & the AI Invasion** to show us that the Tribulation is near and the 2nd Coming of Jesus Christ is rapidly approaching. And that's why Jesus Himself said:

Luke 21:28 "When these things begin to take place, stand up and lift up your heads, because your redemption is drawing near."

People of God, like it or not, we are headed for **The Final Countdown**. The signs of the 7-year **Tribulation** are **Rising**! Wake up! If you're a Christian today and you're not doing anything for the Lord, shame on you! Get busy doing something for Jesus now! Stop wasting your life! We need you! Don't sit on the sidelines! Get on the front lines and help us! Let's get busy working together doing something splendid for Jesus with what time is left and get busy saving souls! Amen?

But if you're reading this today and you're not a Christian, then I beg you, please, heed these signs, heed these warnings, give your life to Jesus now! You don't want to be here when the Antichrist takes control! As you saw, it's going to be a total blood bath! Take the way out now, the only way out now, through Jesus Christ, before it's too late! Amen?

Chapter Three

The Increase of
Sea & Space Travel

The **3rd area** of transportation that has seen a major increase in our lifetime is in the area of **Sea Travel**. But again, don't take my word for it. Let's go back one more time to our opening text from the last two chapters.

Daniel 12:1-4 "At that time Michael, the great prince who protects your people, will arise. There will be a time of distress such as has not happened from the beginning of nations until then. But at that time your people – everyone whose name is found written in the book – will be delivered. Multitudes who sleep in the dust of the earth will awake, some to everlasting life, others to shame and everlasting contempt. Those who are wise will shine like the brightness of the heavens, and those who lead many to righteousness, like the stars for ever and ever. But you, Daniel, close up and seal the words of the scroll until the time of the end. Many will go here and there to increase knowledge."

Now again, as we saw before in this passage, God clearly gives Daniel some clear-cut signs that we're living in the end of times. Not only the activity of the Archangel Michael protecting the Jewish People, but what? There would be an explosion of knowledge like never before. But again, what was the first one there? People would be traveling here and there all over the earth like never before.

And that's not only happening on land and air as we saw in the last chapters, but I'm telling you, it's happening massively when it comes to sea travel as well. As we saw before, boats have been around for quite some time, but it wasn't until recently that we saw a major increase of intercontinental boat

The Vikings

travel! Oh, once in a while, throughout history, we hear stories of how the Vikings had made voyages to America, or the Chinese, or Marco Polo, or Magellan in the 1500's sailing around the world, but these were isolated individual experiences. And then we had the age of sailing ships and the pirates and the military campaigns, and even trade routes, but again, these were things the average person did not take part in. In fact, an interesting side note, most people were deathly afraid of the sea because they were convinced that this was where darkness and evil dwelled, and where monsters

roamed and swallowed up ships, including the Jewish People. They never really had much of a maritime presence. I learned this while I was in Jerusalem recently, because they believed the sea was full of evil and this was where the power of God stopped, at the edge of the coast. This is why Jonah not only tried to escape, but of all places he tried to escape from God, was from

Marco Polo

Tarshish, a seaport, to board a ship. Why? Because they believed that the sea was where the power of God stopped and thus he would be safe from God's reach! But he learned the hard way that God's power goes there too, and God sent a whale to get him. And this is also why the Bible says:

Revelation 21:1 "Then I saw a new heaven and a new earth, for the first heaven and the first earth had passed away, and there was no longer any sea."

It's not that there won't be any oceans on the New Earth, it's speaking of the fact that there will no longer be any sea (i.e. any evil or darkness) which is what the Jewish People thought the modern seas were full of!

But be that as it may, sea travel for the average Joe didn't change much for centuries upon centuries, it stayed the same. But not anymore! At the turn of the last century, sea travel has gone ballistic. That's because with the development of the internal combustion engine as we saw before, not only launched the automobile industry, it also revolutionized the shipping industry, Sea Travel! Ocean liners came along and even massive Superliners they were called, like the Titanic. Even though that one sunk, it didn't stop the trend. Now the average Joe was traveling to and fro, by the boatloads, pun intended, in what was now called transatlantic or transpacific voyages! Boats are now going all over the world! In fact, we have around 50 different Cruise Lines to choose from, from around the world. This is not counting private yachts, cargo ships, submarines you name it.

The Titanic

In fact, to give you an idea of how much we are traveling now on the sea, here's a live screen shot from maritimetraffic.com. Go check it out. This is just the amount of ships going from the Atlantic to Europe at any given time.

Cruise Lines

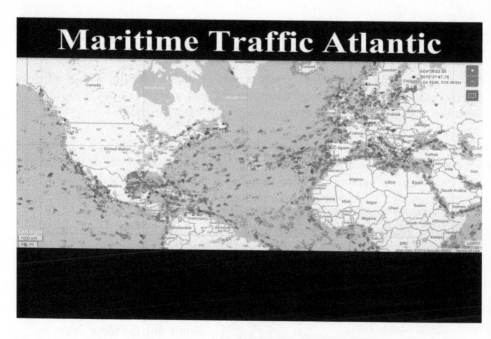

Looks to me like it's increasing like never before in the history of mankind, how about you?

But it's not just the amount of sea travel that's increasing, it's also the speed. The fastest boat on record to date is the Spirit of Australia which can go almost 318 mph.

Now the Chinese are working on a Submarine called a Supersonic Submarine using what's called "Supercavitation Technology" and it will go from Shanghai to San Francisco in 100 minutes, underwater!

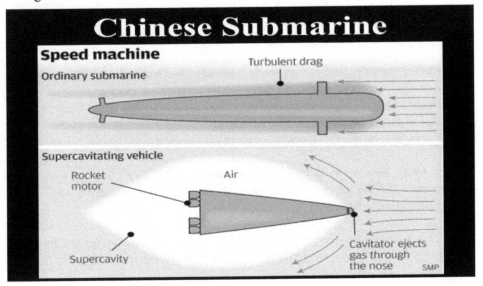

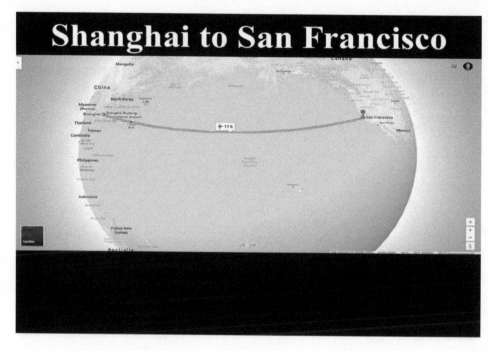

Shanghai to San Francisco

A plane trip takes over 11 hours, but this thing will go halfway across the planet in 100 minutes, underwater!

And it's not just the speed that's increasing, so are the options! How would you like to have this Seaworthy Car that can go on both land and sea! It's called the Panther!

"'WaterCar' into the future, powered by Honda. On the road, as it drives down the street, the WaterCar looks like an ordinary jeep. It even drives through the desert with 4-wheel drive like an ordinary jeep would do. But when it comes to the water it doesn't slow down. The wheels go up and it speeds across the water as if it were still on the land, passing everything in its way."[1]

Okay, how many of you want one of those? But that's still not all! Now they're even making underwater homes and cities to apparently drive your underwater vehicle to one day!

Deep Ocean Technology: "As you sit on the sand at the beach there is a large object that looks like an alien ship that is sitting above the water. It is the Sea

Orbiter. The Sea Orbiter is 190 ft. tall. Over half of the futuristic ship will be submerged and be on the constant lookout for new species, lost cities and creatures. Construction on the ship is scheduled to begin 2014. H2ome says, 'If you are tired of living above sea level, check out this builder.' For about ten million dollars, depending on the amenities and such, they can whip up a sea lovers' home.

The homes are built at surface pressure, so no decompression is needed. Well, this is one way to see the sea level rise. A city that can exist submerged in water, designed as a floating bowl with a massive atrium up to the sky where sunlight will be able to reach all the underwater levels. The buildings themselves are built at varying levels made accessible to one another via stairs. Water Discus is the underwater hotel. It was named for its design which consists of two inhabitable discs. One is located above water while the other sits beneath the surface giving guests the option to enjoy warm breezes or watch vivid sea life swim by as they please.

Atlantica Expeditions: Dennis Chamberlin, the man behind this concept has already built a two-person underwater habitat but his total vision stretches so much further. He wants to build a whole city which he describes as sort of like the Jetson's hometown but on the ocean floor.

Subviosphere Two: If everything goes as planned, designer Phillip Pauley will one day open this underwater community that will accommodate 100 people. Incidentally that is the number of humans it would take to repopulate the earth if something happened that wiped just about everybody out."[2]

Whoa! You really think you're going to escape God's judgment by hiding underwater? I don't think so...Jonah! He'll find you even there, but we'll get to that in a little bit. But here's the point, never before in the history of mankind have we had all these kinds of sea travel until now! All in our lifetime. We have seen a massive explosion of sea travel, just like Daniel said would happen in the end times, it's a sign we are living in the last days that we take for granted, and we better wake up! But that's not all. We have one more mode of travel to deal with.

The **4th area** of transportation that has seen a major increase in our lifetime is in the area of **Space Travel**.

Now this is another desire that man has had for a long time. To travel to

the stars, into outer space, to go where no man has gone before! Starting with early science fiction book writers who informed us that apparently the moon was full of cheese and space Martians, to legendary space travelers like Buck Rogers or Flash Gordon.

Or writers like Jules Verne and his classic "From the Earth to the Moon" and Edgar Rice Boroughs and his "John Carter" series going all the way to Mars. But that's pretty much where it stayed for space travel, all in the books, until now! All in our lifetime, even in the last few decades, Space Travel has gone ballistic!

The History of Space Travel: There is no easy way from the earth to the stars, Seneca the Younger, c. 40 A.D.

March 16, 1926, The first liquid-fueled rocket launch by Robert H. Goddard (USA)

October 20, 1928, "Hoopskirt" rocket launch failure by Robert H. Goddard (USA)

May 7, 1931, First German liquid-fuel rocket launch by Herman Oberth (Germany)

May 19, 1937, Successful liquid-fueled rocket launch by Robert H. Goddard (USA)

1942 to 1945, V-2 development by Wernher von Braun (Germany)

June 20, 1944, First man-made object in space V-2/MW 18014 (Germany)

September 8, 1944, First long-range rockets strike Allied forces V-2 (Germany)

1946 to 1951, White Sands proving grounds, Werhner von Braun (USA)

October 24, 1946, First photographs from space V-2 (USA)

July 22, 1951, First dogs in space R-1 Rocket (USSR)

August 1957. First inter-continental ballistic missiles R-7 Semyorka (USSR)

October 4, 1957, First artificial satellite in orbit, Sputnik 1 (USSR)

December 6, 1957, Failed American satellite launch Vanguard TV-3 (USA)

January 31, 1958, First American satellite in orbit, Explorer 1 (USA)

April 12, 1961, First man in space Yuri Gagarin (USSR)

May 5, 1961, First American in Space, Alan Shepard (USA)

May 25, 1961, Address to Congress on Urgent National needs, John F. Kennedy (USA)

June 16, 1963, First woman in space Valentina Tereshkova (USSR)

March 18, 1965 First spacewalk, Alexei Leonov (USSR)

June 3, 1965 First American spacewalk, Ed White (USA)

July 14, 1965 First photo of Mars from space, Mariner 4 (USA)

December 15, 1965 First American rendezvous, Gemini 6 & 7 (USA)

July 16, 1969, Apollo 11 Launch, Armstrong/Collins/Aldrin (USA)

July 20, 1969 First humans on the Moon, Armstrong/Collins/Aldrin (USA)

1969 to 1972 Last manned mission to the Moon Apollo 12 through 17 (USA)[3]

      Now what you need to understand is that what started out as "One small step for mankind" in 1969, as you just saw, when the first man stepped on the moon, Neil Armstrong, it turned into a global space race! You see most of us think that man going into space kind of took a nosedive or major detour or even a pause after the moon landings in the 60's and 70's, and it kind of did for the most part. I mean, we had the space shuttles and the space station, but nobody was really going back to the moon let alone to Mars and the edges of space. And part of the reason why was a funding issue. I recently visited NASA, as you can see

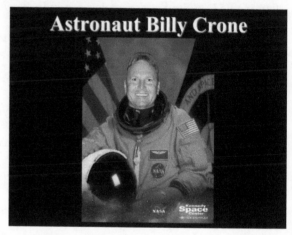

Astronaut Billy Crone

here, and I talked with one of the Astronauts. I asked him that question, "Why was there a pause?" And he said it was a funding issue, especially in the Obama years. But now they're going like gang busters! And not just the U.S. and Russia, like it was before, but a lot of countries all around the world! Like China, Japan, the European Union, India, Germany, the UK, even Israel is getting in on the action! Here's their moon trip!

I24News Reports: *"Continuing on Israel's contribution to the future of space travel our next guest is the director of the Israel Space Agency, Avi Blackburger, here to talk about the exciting new partnership with NASA, Israel's upcoming mission to the moon."*

"In 2019 Israel will become the 4th country to reach the moon. In December 2018, for the first time in its history, Israel will launch a spacecraft to the Moon. The Israeli spacecraft is scheduled to land on the Moon on February 13, 2019

and hoist the Israeli flag on its surface. The spacecraft was manufactured by Spaceil in collaboration with Israel Aerospace Industries.

When it lands on the moon, it will be the smallest spacecraft ever built to land there. Israel will join three countries that have already reached the moon: The United States, Russia, and China. This challenge marks a new peak for Israel's decades-long space program. The Israeli space program was formed in the 1980's: in 1983, the Israeli Space Agency was founded.

In 1988, Israel became the world's 8th country to successfully launch satellites into space. Israeli satellites are world acclaimed. Among them are the Amos, Ofek and EROS satellites. In 2003, Ilan Ramon became the first Israeli astronaut to reach space. Ramon was onboard the space shuttle Columbia which exploded in the air.

Earlier this year, 6 Israeli scientists completed the D-MARS experiment simulating life on Mars in Israel's Negev desert. Many of these projects are carried out in collaboration with space agencies around the world. Israel's space program is reaching new heights, see you on the moon!"[4]

Who would have thought little teeny tiny Israel, 20½ of them could fit in the one state of California, would even be getting in on space travel? It's almost like it's speeding up all over the world. Where have I heard that before? In fact, speaking of foreign countries going to the moon, one of the countries doing this is China. China wants to put a fake moon into orbit to create more light!

SJZ13 Reports: *"China wants to launch a fake moon into the sky by 2020, announced last week at an Innovation Conference. A southwestern Chinese city wants to launch a satellite into orbit that would reflect the sun's rays at night. It will reportedly be 8 times brighter than the real moon and it could replace streetlights saving that city more than $200,000,000 per year. However, astronauts are concerned about the increased light pollution it could cause."[5]*

Okay, that's not only weird but it looks like the Death Star to me! I hope it's not a ruse!

Oh no, it's not a Death Star, it's just a fake moon. We need more light you know. Save on electricity. Go Green!

In fact, it's not just the amount of space travel that's increasing, so is the speed of space travel which is now leading to the possibility of other trips even beyond the moon in the near future. First, they're developing what's called the Em Drive. This is a new technology that could, "Get us to the moon in just 4 hours." Then there's another technology NASA is working

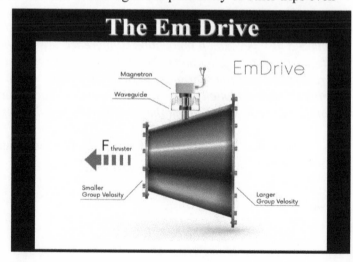

on that could get a craft to Mars in just 3 days called Photonic Propulsion. And even faster than that, there's technology being developed that would enable

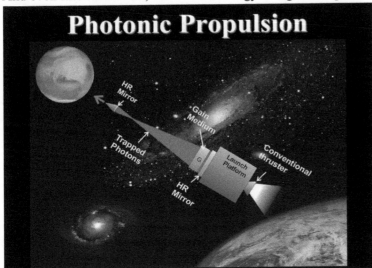

us to travel at the speed of light which means we could get from here to the Moon in just 1.3 seconds, and Mars in 12.5 minutes. And I kid you not there's even talk of developing warp drives just like in Star Trek where now you're going faster than the speed of light and it's all happening in our lifetime! Science fiction is not science fiction anymore! We're in the last days and not only is the amount of space travel and the speed of space travel increasing, but so are the space travel options including that for the average Joe! First of all, they're developing what's called a Space Elevator for those of you that are afraid of rockets. Now you can ride an elevator into space!

Julian Huguet @Jhug00: *"A space elevator is one of those ideas that sounds ultra-crazy at first but when you learn more about it, it still sounds absolutely crazy, but you can see the upside. It's exactly what it sounds like. A giant elevator that you get on down here on earth and you step off in space. You need an anchor on earth that would act as a loading station for the elevator car, a tether stretching into space for the car to travel on and a counterweight way out in space to keep the tether taught.*

Designs vary but it looks like the counterweight could have to be as far as 100,000 km above the earth. More than a quarter of the distance of the moon. Sounds nuts but to some it's not just a pie in the sky idea, it's something that they are actively working towards. The experiment is working in collaboration with the construction firm Obayashi which six years prior released plans to build a space elevator by the year 2050.

They are not the only ones toying with the idea. China intends to build one by 2045. And NASA has commissioned studies to look into how feasible the idea is. But once built, by one estimate, it could cost as little as $200.00 to get one kg into space, meaning that I would need only $13,000.00 to get off this planet as opposed to $175,000. A space elevator would open up so many possibilities. Like building and launching ships in orbit.

Hello, Starfleet. It could make trips to Mars less fuel intensive because a ship could plummet towards earth like an Olympic skydiver using the earth's gravity to boost it on to the Red Planet. Tourists could make trips up regularly. Just get in, listen to the Girl from Ipanema, make small talk for a few thousand kilometers and get a selfie of a lifetime."[6]

And we all know how important that is! In fact, all kinds of countries are getting in on this space elevator action, including the Canadians. Believe it or not they even want to make a Space Tower to save even more costs.

TOMO News Reports: *"A Space Elevator would climb 20 kilometers into the sky. A Canadian space company wants to build a space elevator that would reach 20 kilometers high. You heard that right, 20 kilometers, or more than 12 miles. The idea is to build the tower with reinforced inflatable sections, the middle is hollow. An elevator car would circle the tower until it reaches the top. It is estimated that the cost would be $5,000,000,000 to construct. As a demonstration project they would build a precursor tower measuring one and a half kilometers tall. The main purpose of the tower is to provide a take-off and landing platform for spacecraft. If your spacecraft takes off at a 20-kilometer altitude you can get to space in a single stage without the need for additional fuel stages."[7]*

But wait a minute. Didn't mankind try to build a tower once before in the sky? How did that work out? Not good! But now even the options for space travel are moving to the average Joe! Now we have private firms who are not only going into space, but even to the moon. And there's talk of making it commercially available to us, just like with a commercial airliner, except we're going to the moon! It's crazy, and it's happening right now!

Believe it or not, "Private Firm Reveals its Plans of Taking Tourists to the Moon and Back by 2026." It's called the Moon Express. And it has the backing of a billionaire entrepreneur named Naveen Jain from India who is also

Moon Express

working with Elon Musk of America and they have been, "Granted permission to travel beyond earth's orbit and land on the moon."

In fact, there's so much of this private activity going on now that, "The FAA is Regulating Business on the Moon" and there's talk of building,

"inflatable habitats on the moon." So, I guess you can vacation there now! Even, Bigelow Aerospace here in Nevada is getting in on the action. Now, what's helped to push this drive of the private sector to bring the average Joe into space was a challenge by Google called, "The Google Lunar XPRIZE Contest." The winner got $30 million dollars to successfully land a robot on the surface of the moon, and 29 teams registered from around the world to do so. This is what's helped fuel the surge for the average Joe to get into space. So much so that we even now have people like Elon Musk who leads his own space exploration company called SpaceX.

He has recently gone on record saying, *"We Need a Moon Base,"* and *"We'll create a city on Mars with a million inhabitants."* The billionaire said, *"He hopes to build a 'Mars Colonial Fleet' of more than 1,000 cargo ships that would depart 'en-mass' and could transport 200 passengers at a time, along with materials to build homes, industrial plants and shops."*

And this isn't 100 years down the road, listen to this, Musk is already planning the first manned flight to Mars in 2023 and has said he wants to die on Mars, although he has stipulated 'not on impact.' I guess that's a space joke! But again, he's not the only billionaire doing this. Many others are jumping on the bandwagon to get into space and not only for tourism, but for other business opportunities like mining as well. In fact, the media is even calling it, "The New Space Race."

Bloomberg Reports: *"Sixteen of the world's 500 richest people have made space investments. Who are we talking about here? Who surprises you the most when you are talking about investing?"*

Tom Metcalf, Bloomberg News: *"Well, you expect the technology tycoons to be in there but there are a couple, but one that is surprising is Ricardo Salinas, a Mexican retail billionaire."*

Bloomberg: *"Do any of these aspire to go into space themselves?"*

Tom Metcalf: *"For sure Jeff Bezos and Elon Musk. Elon Musk said he would be on the first ever SpaceX trip to Mars and he's not pulling back on that."*

Bloomberg: *"Is this going to be profitable or is this just a vanity project?"*

Tom Metcalf: *"Things are vastly changing. I think 10 years ago, maybe not a vanity, maybe a passion project. So you have Bezos spending maybe a billion dollars a year but what their presence has done, Bezos and Musk, have done by making space more accessible, perhaps not to you and me, but for a wealthy investor he can see a rather viable business model here. That is what is developing."*

Bloomberg: *"What are the different kinds of startups? I mean we all know about SpaceX, right, but are there different business models at work here?"*

Tom Metcalf: *"Yes, the ones that get all the attention are the SpaceX and the Blue Origin. That's all in the launch business, that's the most expensive. They're also more downstream with services around the idea of people going into space with the classic example being Expedia, so they are buying the whole rocket and then parcel out the payload to various operators."*

Bloomberg: *"What about space mining? I remember a few years ago I think some Google people were talking about that, is that actually some viable thing that could happen at some point?"*

Tom Metcalf: *"The one that was most interested in that was Planetary Resources. And there were some very excitable analysts commenting about maybe one big asteroid that has two trillion worth of platinum, well, maybe not trillion, but billions and billions, enough to wreck the earth bare market."*[8]

Well, that's not good, for us anyway! But as you can see there's big money in that venture if you can pull it off and these guys have a history of doing so. But here's the point. This is just what Daniel said would happen in the end times! We're traveling to and fro, here and there, wherever we want even into space! And again, keep in mind, our grandparents were born in the same town and lived there their whole lives and basically never went anywhere! But look at us now! Just like Daniel said would happen, we're traveling all over the place, anywhere in the world and even outside the world and it's increasing massively in our lifetime! Don't tell me travel in the air, land, sea, or space isn't speeding up! It's going nuts! Just like Daniel said would happen when you're living in the last days! I mean, it appears as if nothing is holding us back from being able to rush here and there wherever and whenever we want, except God. You see, the sad thing is that this explosion of **Modern Travel Technology** has made us arrogant and overconfident like the Edomites of long ago who also tried to escape the boundaries of Almighty God.

Obadiah 3-4 "The arrogance of your heart has deceived you, you who live in the clefts of the rock, in the loftiness of your dwelling place, who say in your heart, 'Who will bring me down to earth?' Though you build high like the eagle, though you set your nest among the stars, from there I will bring you down, declares the LORD."

People, even if we can one day arrogantly boast that we don't need God because we can rush here and there even to the edge of the stars, even like Elon Musk and others are saying, to boldly go where no one has gone before; God will one day, just like the Edomites, bring us down. And speaking of arrogance, I see another historical mistake being repeated here with all this travel technology concerning God's Judgements. Now, did you see the list of all the billionaires that are going into space? Not just Elon Musk but Mark Zuckerberg from Facebook, Jeff Bezos from Amazon, Larry Page and Sergey Brin from Google. Makes you wonder if there's a secondary reason why these billionaires have plans for going into space personally. I mean could it be an "Insurance Policy" in case the world faces some sort of global calamity? And lest you think that's a crazy idea, they're already doing it down here on earth with Luxury Bunkers.

Inside Edition Reports: *"You are in the middle of nowhere, rural Kansas. The site of a nuclear missile silo. Armed security control the entrance to the doomsday bunker that has been preserved for the wealthy elite. And sales are booming!"*

Larry Hall: "*Since the election of Donald Trump we've seen a whole new demographic of people calling, people that didn't even know we existed.*"

Inside Edition: "*Larry Hall is the owner of the Survival Condo Project. These 16,000 lb. doors will lock you inside. We are headed deep below the surface of the earth to an underground bunker like no other.*"

Larry Hall: "*We in a typical 4/4 residential unit and even though we are 100 ft underground right now you can certainly see that it is not a claustrophobic area.*"

Inside Edition: "*Twelve luxurious condos exist here with fireplaces, high end appliances, Jacuzzi's and windows, yes, even windows. High definition TV broadcasts images of the outside world right into your living room. The price tag for this 3-bedroom 2 bath condo is $2.3 million.*"

Larry Hall: "*Well, as the sign says, 'Welcome to the beach.'*"

Inside Edition: "*Look at this! It's a swimming pool with a slide and waterfalls. Other common areas include a movie theatre, rock climbing wall, and shooting range. There is even a farm to grow all the fresh fruits and vegetables you will need.*"

Larry Hall: "*This can grow up to seventy species of plants, lettuce, tomatoes, carrots.*"

Inside Edition: "*The Bunker runs on power sources like wind and diesel generators.*"

Larry Hall: "*We have enough fuel to run these diesels for two and a half years.*"

Inside Edition: "*Plenty of time to ride out world-wide chaos should it ever erupt.*"[9]

Oh, it'll erupt. And it will be a lot longer than two and a half years! But you really think you're going to ride out and escape God's wrath by building that? You sound just like the people who make a big mistake in the 7-year Tribulation!

Revelation 6:15-17 "Then the kings of the earth, the princes, the generals, the rich, the mighty, and every slave and every free man hid in caves and among the rocks of the mountains. They called to the mountains and the rocks, 'Fall on us and hide us from the face of Him who sits on the throne and from the wrath of the Lamb! For the great day of their wrath has come, and who can stand?"

Well, certainly not you! You should have accepted Jesus as your Savior, but no, you had all your money and riches! You don't need Him! You thought you could escape, big mistake! And here's my point. Maybe the billionaires realize that the earth is going to get pummeled and their posh bunkers will not survive. So, is this why they're switching gears and going in the opposite direction into space? Could be! Maybe they think they can get so high that not even God could reach them, like the Edomites?

When are we going to learn? The only way to escape God's wrath is to receive His Son, Jesus Christ, as your personal Lord and Savior. You don't need any money for that! No ocean or bunker or spaceship is going to protect you! And how slick of the enemy to get people to think this! In fact, it reminds me of the Tower of Babel incident. It's like history is being repeated.

Genesis 11:1-4 "Now the whole world had one language and a common speech. As men moved eastward, they found a plain in Shinar and settled there. They said to each other, 'Come, let's make bricks and bake them thoroughly.' They used brick instead of stone, and tar for mortar. Then they said, 'Come, let us build ourselves a city, with a tower that reaches to the heavens, so that we may make a name for ourselves and not be scattered over the face of the whole earth.'"

Now, what's interesting is that for those of you who went through our 42-week study on Creation vs. Evolution, we came across an interesting tidbit of information as to the reason why mankind was building a tower into the sky. Now, there are over 500 different flood accounts around the world outside the Bible which is what you would expect if this were a real historical global event, and it was. But it was the Toltec Legend where we found this:

Discovered in the histories of the Toltec Indians of ancient Mexico is a story of the first world that they say lasted 1,716 years and was destroyed by a great flood that covered even the highest mountains.

Their story tells of a man named Tapi who was a very pious man. The creator told Tapi to build a boat that he would live in and escape the destruction. He was told that he should take his wife and a pair of every animal that was alive into this boat. Naturally everyone thought he was crazy. Then the rain started, and the flood came. The men and animals tried to climb the mountains, but the mountains became flooded too.

Finally, the rain ended and Tapi decided that the water dried up and let loose a dove.

Following the great flood, people began to multiply and built a very high, great tower to provide a safe place in case the world were destroyed again. However, everyone started to speak different languages and the people became confused, so different language groups wandered to other parts of the world.

The Toltecs claim they started as a family of seven friends and their wives who spoke the same language. They crossed great water, lived in caves and wandered 104 years until they came to southern Mexico. The story reports that this was 520 years after the great flood.

People, when are we going to learn? You can try to escape God to the ocean like a Jonah or build a bunker under the earth like the people of Revelation 6, or even try to escape to the heavens like the Edomites of long ago. But there's only one way to escape God's wrath in the coming 7-year Tribulation. It's called get saved NOW through Jesus Christ! That's it! One day the Bible says the "door" of opportunity is going to shut at the Rapture of the Church! Just like it did in Noah's day when God closed the door to the Ark, and people were left outside banging on that boat, it's the same thing! In fact, maybe it looked like this.

"The Ark is completed, and the animals are all in their places. You can hear their sounds coming from their stalls and cages. The final door is closed, and it is dark inside. The ocean waters are calm, and the fish are swimming like any other day when suddenly there is a tremor and the ground starts to split across the ocean floor. The crack gets larger and larger when suddenly water shoots out, straight up like a wall coming up out of the ocean causing a tsunami, bigger than any before or after ever existed and it is rushing towards land.

What makes this tsunami different is that it not only goes towards one coastline, it is so huge it is heading towards all the coastlines of all the continents. The occupants of the Ark are busy doing their daily routines of cooking, cleaning and feeding the animals. They do not see what is coming. A huge wall of water is coming towards the Ark.

But God has given the instructions as to how to build the Ark and they are safe. But the people of the village, are unaware of what is coming. When they do see the wall of water they are stunned. They had made fun of Noah for so long while he was building the Ark, while he was trying to warn them. They had never seen water like this before.

What were they supposed to do now, now that it was too late to get on the Ark? They start running to get away but as they run north, they find the water is also coming from the south. When they run east, they find that the water is also coming from the west. There is no way to get away from the walls of water. They have to make it to the Ark in order to be saved. But it is too late."[10]

God judged this world once, and He's getting ready to do it again. The signs are all around us! The door is about to be closed with the Rapture of the Church!

And that's precisely why, out of love, God has given us this update on **The Final Countdown: Tribulation Rising** concerning **Modern Technology & the AI Invasion** to show us that the Tribulation is near and the 2nd Coming of Jesus Christ is rapidly approaching. And that's why Jesus Himself said:

Luke 21:28 "When these things begin to take place, stand up and lift up your heads, because your redemption is drawing near."

People of God, like it or not, we are headed for **The Final Countdown**. The signs of the 7-year **Tribulation** are **Rising**! Wake up! And so, the point is this. If you're a Christian today and you're not doing anything for the Lord, shame on you! Get busy doing something for Jesus now! Stop wasting your life! We need you! Don't sit on the sidelines! Get on the front line and help us! Let's get busy working together doing something splendid for Jesus with what time is left and get busy saving souls! Amen?

But if you're not a Christian, then I beg you, please, heed these signs, heed these warnings, give your life to Jesus now! Because when the Rapture of the Church happens, which can happen any moment, the door will be shut on you and you will be deluged with God's Judgement and Wrath! Don't make that mistake! Take the way out now, the only way out now, through Jesus Christ, get into the Ark of the Cross before it's too late! Amen?

Chapter Four

The Increase of
Global Communication

The **2ⁿᵈ** way that **Modern Technology** reveals that we're really living in the last days, is by the **Increase of Communication**. And believe it or not, that's exactly what's going to happen in the 7-year Tribulation when the Antichrist and False Prophet micro-manage the whole planet and connect them in order to rule them! They need to communicate to the whole planet. In fact, it's the same thing that was done in another time of rebellion called The Tower of Babel. But don't take my word for it. Let's listen to God's.

Genesis 11:1-9 "Now the whole world had one language and a common speech. As men moved eastward, they found a plain in Shinar and settled there. They said to each other, 'Come, let's make bricks and bake them thoroughly.' They used brick instead of stone, and tar for mortar. Then they said, 'Come, let us build ourselves a city, with a tower that reaches to the heavens, so that we may make a name for ourselves and not be scattered over the face of the whole earth.' But the Lord came down to see the city and the tower that the men were building. The Lord said, 'If as one people speaking the same language, they have begun to do this, then nothing they plan to do will be impossible for them. Come, let us go down and confuse their language so they will not understand each other.' So, the Lord scattered them from there over all the earth, and they stopped building the city. That is why it was called Babel – because there the Lord confused the language of the whole world. From there the Lord scattered them over the face of the whole earth."

Now, according to our text, the Bible clearly tells us the unfortunate news that right after the flood, the last time God judged this planet, that mankind once again was already rebelling against God! It's like a whole giant global flood didn't get your attention! It's crazy but true! And good thing we don't have hard hearts like that today…yeah right! But notice what mankind had in common that apparently helped produce this rebellious global society at that time. They didn't just work together, they what? They had a common speech, i.e. one language. And it was this universal form of communication that not only enabled them to work together effectively in their rebellion against God, but it was so powerful that God had to shut it down and confuse the whole thing! And that's why we have the languages we have today! In fact, there are an estimated 6,500 spoken languages throughout the world! Talk about confusion! And it's this multitude of languages that are keeping us separated, and from totally rebelling against God on a worldwide basis, until now! I'm telling you, all in our lifetime, just in time for the 7-year Tribulation, we are seeing a repeat of the Tower of Babel incident that will unite our world with the Antichrist in his total rebellion against God.

Revelation 13:3-4,7-8 "The whole world was astonished and followed the beast. Men worshiped the dragon because he had given authority to the beast, and they also worshiped the beast and asked, 'Who is like the beast? Who can make war against him?' And he was given authority over every tribe, people, language and nation. All inhabitants of the earth will worship the beast – all whose names have not been written in the book of life belonging to the Lamb that was slain from the creation of the world."

The enemy has been slowly but surely working ever since the turn of the last century, to recreate this last days rebellion against God and unite our planet not only with travel, that's step one, but even with the uniting of our communication back to a common universal language! It's all happening right now!

The **1ˢᵗ way** the enemy is uniting our world for the 7-year Tribulation rebellion is by **Connecting All People with Communication Technology**.

You see, for the longest time, mankind was not only separated by the continents throughout the world, but as we saw in the previous chapters, being reconnected by Modern Travel Technology, we can travel wherever we want now. But we also had a communication gap. We had no clue whatsoever of other people and what they were doing or saying around the world, until now! Just like the travel technology, so it is with communication technology, it's not by chance! At the turn of the last century, the enemy began to put even communication technology into high gear, and increase it to slowly but surely, unite the planet! Don't believe me? Let me show you!

Newspapers

First, we had the birth of newspapers which was a big deal because prior to this, mankind wrote on forms of communication like cuneiform tablets, pressing shapes into clay, or parchment, or animal skins, or even discarded pieces of pottery. But that's about it! And it stayed that way for the longest time! But then along came another invention called the Gutenberg Press which occurred in the mid-1400's, invented by a guy named Johannes Gutenberg, that allowed for the mass production of printed material.

Gutenberg Press

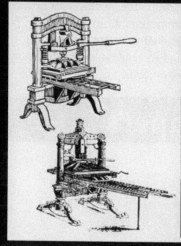

That was cool. But even that stayed pretty much the same until the early 1700's when we had the birth of the first successful daily newspaper, in Britain, in 1702, and the first daily American newspaper in 1784. In fact, one of the early American newspapers was called the Publick Occurrences Both Forreign and Domestick

Publick Occurrences Both Forreign and Domestick

New England News.

Numb. 1.

PUBLICK
OCCURRENCES

Both *FORREIGN* and *DOMESTICK*.

Boston, Thursday *Sept.* 25th. 1690.

IT is designed, that the Country shall be furnished once a moneth (or if any Glut of Occurrences happen, oftener,) with an Account of such considerable things as have arrived unto our Notice.

In order hereunto, the Publisher will take what pains he can to obtain a Faithful Relation of all such things; and will particularly make himself beholden to such Persons in Boston whom he knows to have been for their own use the diligent Observers of such matters.

from them, as what is in the Forces lately gone for *Canada*; made them think it almost impossible for them to get well through the Affairs of their Husbandry at this time of the year; yet the season has been so unusually favourable that they scarce find any want of the many hundreds of hands, that are gone from them; which is looked upon as a Merciful Providence

While the barbarous *Indians* were lurking

Right out of the gates, as you can see, newspapers communicated to people, not just local events, but global events as well. A huge breakthrough if your goal is to connect the planet! And of course, we know who that is! Today we have about 18,000 newspapers in 102 countries connecting all of us, all available right now at our fingertips anytime, thanks to another invention called the internet which we'll get to in another chapter. From newspapers, it went to radio, attributed to Marconi, but others would say, no it was Nikola Tesla.

Radio

This was a huge deal because now you could not only read what was going on around the world, but now you could hear what was going on around the world as well. Major improvement to unite the planet! In fact, the first transatlantic radio transmission occurred in 1901 with Marconi and from then on radio grew as a form of communication on a massive scale to a point where we now have 44,000 radio stations throughout the world broadcasting with over 15,000 of them just in the U.S.

Transatlantic Radio

Then that led to the development, all in our lifetime, of what's called Satellite Radio and Internet Radio.

Satellite Radio

So now anyone can basically have their own radio broadcast signal for people to tune in to, anywhere around the world, and communicate back and forth.

Television

Another major huge feat if you're going to connect the world! But then it went even further to television! And again, this was another huge breakthrough because now you can not only read and hear what was going on around the world, now you can see it! The first successful television signal occurred in 1927 buy a guy named Philo Farnsworth who is credited with the invention.

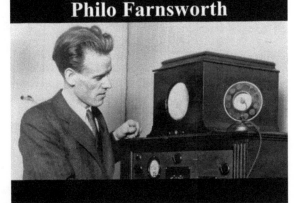

Philo Farnsworth

And this of course, as a form of communication, has gone ballistic. At first the reach of television didn't go too far. Remember the days of rabbit ears? Yes, kids there was life before cable! Then eventually came cable and satellite signals, and now TV can be broadcast anywhere in the world on a global basis to the tune of nearly 28,000 TV stations around the world. And now, even in recent years, again, all in our lifetime, television is morphing into APP based streaming technology via the internet, where you can customize and get just about any kind

TV Rabbit Ears

of TV channel you could ever think of, or want, on just about any kind of topic, anywhere in the world! You can see it all! Again, another fantastic leap forward

Streaming Television

if you want to connect the world! Again, I wonder who that might be? But again, all about the same time, we had the birth of another important invention called the Telephone!

Telephone

So, think about it. Now you can not only read and hear and see what was going on around the world, now you can speak to people around the world! Another huge communication breakthrough! The first successful telephone transmission occurred in 1876 buy Alexander Graham Bell who said the famous words to his assistant, "Mr. Watson, come here, I want you."

The very next year he started the Bell Telephone Company and within 10 years it went ballistic with more than 100,000 people in the United States getting phones and communicating all over the place. And today of course, phones have really gone crazy! In fact, let me show you how fast phone technology has advanced. How many of you remember the days of the rotary dial phones? Well, believe it or not, kids today have no clue what that is!

There is a box sitting on a table between two teenagers. The dad says "Ok, lift up the box." The boys take the box off the table and the dad gives them a tablet and says, "You have four minutes to dial that phone number." They stand there looking at the thing that is on the table. It is a yellow rotary dial phone that is connected not only to the wall, but the handset is connected to the phone. One boy looks at the number while the other one just stares at the phone. One kid asks, "Is that it?" "Yes," the dad replies. "With that phone." They both bend down to look a little closer at this thing they had never seen before. One says, "Push the number, push the button."

He puts his finger in the hole to push the number, but nothing moves. It doesn't work. They found out that the rotary does go around, so they put in one number and spin it a couple numbers and it goes back to the beginning. Well, that didn't work. The second kid realizes that the handset needs to be lifted or can be lifted but he sets it back in the cradle. So, then they go back to trying to figure out how to dial the numbers, but their time runs out."[1]

And they go on for like 4 minutes! Wow! But the reason why these kids are befuddled is because telephone technology has gone nuts in our lifetime! First it was the hanging wall phone, then the rotary phone as you just saw, to the cordless phone, to now, Cell Phones!

Cell Phones

Thanks to satellite technology, you now can communicate with anybody anywhere on the whole planet, mobile, as you walk around, drive around, go anywhere you want at any time on the whole planet!

In fact, cell phones are now even connecting both the technologies of speaking and seeing people at the same time through video chat, video phone, face time and all that other stuff! And now they're even coming out with 3D Hologram Phones![2]

And because of this explosion of cell phone technology they are now expecting this year the amount of cell phone users around the world to surpass the 5 billion mark! We're getting close to the whole planet having the ability to what? To communicate, see, hear! Where have I heard that before? And that's just cell phones! That's not counting regular phones or even internet phones that further increase our ability to communicate worldwide and it's all happening right now as we sit here!

So, maybe it's me, but it looks like somebody's uniting mankind once again into a universal common form of communication on a multitude of levels, how about you? And this isn't even counting computers, the internet, emails, which, again, we'll get to in another chapter. But the point is this. Never before, in the history of mankind can we communicate like we do now since the Tower of Babel, but now it's been reversed, just in time for the 7-year Tribulation, in our lifetime! But that's still not all. That's just step one.

The **2nd way** the enemy is recreating a last days global rebellious society is by **Connecting All Languages with Communication Technology**.

You see, you might be thinking, "Okay, that's cool and all, now we can read, hear, see, and speak with people anywhere on the planet for the first time in man's history, since the Tower of Babel. I'll give you that, but speaking of the Tower of Babel, wait a minute, we still don't speak the same language, so we're not at a full uniting." And you're right! That's a very good point! Because as we all know, even in our own English language we can have some serious language barriers!

On the Bill Cosby talk show, 'You Bet Your Life' some years back he had a guest come on from Pennsylvania.

Bill Cosby: *"How are you?"*

Lady Guest: *"I'm fine."*

Bill Cosby: *"Sheltonham, Pennsylvania."*

Lady Guest: *"That's right."*

Bill Cosby: *"Born."*

Lady Guest: *"No, I am originally from the North South Carolina."*

Bill Cosby: *"That's what I thought."*

Lady Guest: *"Yeah."* With a big smile on her face.

Bill Cosby: *"I don't know many people from Sheltonham."* In a fake southern drawl. *"That talk like that."*

Lady Guest: *"Well I was raised for 20 years down south."* She speaks with a very strong southern accent.

Bill Cosby: *"What was the name of the place?"*

Lady Guest: *"North."*

Bill Cosby: *"Noeth?"*

Lady Guest: *"No, NORTH."* She spells it out for him. North, it's in South Carolina. In South Carolina, there is a little town called Due West."*

Bill Cosby: *"Wait, Wait, slow down. In North Carolina?"*

Lady Guest: *"No, in South Carolina there's a little town call Due West and North is 90 miles southeast of Due West. North is South of the capitol. Columbia. You understand?"*

Bill Cosby: *"I was doing fine until you came out here. Then you started talking and I got lost and I'm not in a car and I don't care to go anywhere. Now you have me someplace where I have no idea where I am. I'm in a town North South of Due West. Well, where am I?"*

Lady Guest: *"No, no, it's North comma, South Carolina."*

Bill Cosby: *"I'm North, South Carolina."*

Lady Guest: *"Yes, it's North, comma, South Carolina. You put a comma between North and South Carolina."*

Bill Cosby: *"I'm in the state of South Carolina, but in city called North."*

Lady Guest: *"It's not a city, it's a town."*

Bill Cosby: *"Ok, let me ask you this. Where is the railroad?"*

Lady Guest: *"Oh, the railroad is right in the middle of the town."*

Bill Cosby: *"That's right! Now stop there. Where are the black people?"*

Lady Guest: *"I don't know, they are all around I guess."*

Bill Cosby: *"No, they are not all around."* As he stands up and looks at her. *"They are not all around."* He sits back down. *"They are either on this side of the tracks or that side of the tracks. Are they due north or south west?"*
Lady Guest: *"You're in North."*

Bill Cosby: *"I'm in North."*

Lady Guest: *"Yes, South Carolina."*

Bill Cosby: *"Here we go again."* As he shakes his head.

Lady Guest: *Anyway."*

Bill Cosby: *"No, no anyway. I'm sitting in my car and I'm lost. I want to find my people and you're trying to give me directions. OK, now let's put it this way. Where is the river?"*

Lady Guest: *"Which river?"*[3]

Now how many of you can identify with Bill Cosby's pain there trying to communicate to that lady? I've got relatives like that too! Wow! And again, that's just the English language! As you saw, just one language can have tons of different dialects that automatically create barriers to communication. We already saw there's around 6,500 different languages around the world with all their own dialects. And then add to that the reality of just the sheer amount of languages you would have to learn. Some people manually learn languages, and that takes quite a while, and you hear of stories of how someone throughout their whole lifetime actually learned 6,7,8,9, or maybe 10 different languages, but that's about it! So how in the world are you going to unite all 6,500 languages with all their different dialects? It's seems impossible, until now! Thanks to Modern Technology, the language barriers are coming down, all of them! First, we had an Automatic Language Translator invented by IBM in 1959 that automatically

converted Russian documents into English for the U.S. Military. Then IBM and other companies continued to further develop the technology through the 60's and 70's and then shortly after, the internet was invented in 1983 which allowed these translation technologies to get into the hands of the average Joe! This is when you began to see the development of what's called Internet Based Translation Services like Babel Fish which is now taken over as the Bing Translator. It automatically translated basically any language you type into the text box into another language of your choosing and vice versa at the click of a mouse! In fact, I remember using Babel Fish way back in the early 2000's when through the teaching ministry I would get emails from people around the world in different languages. I had no clue what they were saying! So I would copy their email into Babel Fish which then translated it into English for me and then I would type them back my English response, put that into Babel Fish, and it would convert it to their language, and then I would send that translation off to them and it actually worked quite well. And guess what? I didn't take one class and I didn't have to learn a language! It was all automatic and FREE!

In fact, the company admitted that the name Babel Fish, *"Refers to the Biblical account of the confusion of languages that arose in the city of Babel."* Not making it up! Direct quote!

But you might be thinking, "Well hey, that's all well and good but that's for the computer savvy people! How many people in the world today don't even know how to use a computer let alone own one, so that'll never work!" And you're right! That was a first huge step though! Now they're taking that same Universal Translation Technology and putting it into another communication device that we all basically have called the cell phone! And believe it or not, if you have a cell phone, right now you can translate just about any language you like, around the world, automatically, for free, right before your very eyes! Here's just one example!

"Word Lens from www.QuestVisual.com shows how it works. The person with the different language can hold up a paper with the language on it then the person with the cell phone can hold their phone like they are going to take a picture but instead the English language shows up on the cell phone screen, the translation of what the other person was holding up. And it also worked in reverse. Now she is holding up a paper that is in English but the person holding the cell phone is reading in the different language. It translates the text instantly. You only need the phone and word lens, without connection to internet or the cost of the network."[4]

This is just one of many app based automated translators for phones. The language barriers are coming down right before our very eyes! But again, you might be thinking, "Okay, that's cool and all, I can translate written text into a different language automatically, but that's still not speaking translation." At the Tower of Babel, they all spoke to each other. And again, you're right! And that's why thanks to Modern Technology, they now have ear buds that you can wear that will automatically translate yours and another person's different languages back and forth in real time! Here's just one example.

Sean Hollister, Senior Editor CNet: *"These are Google's Pixel Buds. The first wireless headphones and they are going to take on Apple's Airpods at the same $159.00 price. What they do that Apple's Airpods don't, is real time language translation.*

To show you how easy this experience is I'd like to invite Isabelle back on stage for a conversation in her native language, Swedish. So, Isabelle is going to speak Swedish into her Pixel Buds and I will hear the English translation on Pixel Two's front speakers, and then I'll respond in English and she will hear the Swedish translation in her Pixel Buds. To illustrate this today you will hear both sides of the conversation." At that point they conversed back and forth English to Swedish and Swedish to English."[5]

Wow is right! What you just read, whether you realize it or not, is the language barrier being removed for the first time in the history of mankind since the Tower of Babel! In fact, speaking of the Tower of Babel and languages, this just happened a couple of months ago, talk about creepy!

"Babylonian language is brought back to life nearly 2,000 years after the language died out." "Babylonian was the ancient language during the time of

the Mesopotamian Empire which dominated vast areas of the Middle East for two millennia, but it went extinct. However, a University of Cambridge professor has revived the deceased dialect and made a twenty-minute film, titled 'The Poor Man of Nippur.'

It tells the tale of a young man who sought revenge on a city Mayor who cheated him out of his prized possession – his goat. The movie is actually based on a Babylonian clay tablet they found telling of this story back then and they not only revived the dead language but made this film entirely out of the original Babylonian language.

The clip from the movie is all done in the Babylonian Language.

"Drive him away and throw him out through the gate!"

Tell your master thus the blessings of the gods: for one insult which you imposed on me, for that one, I shall repay you thrice!

He drove five pegs into the ground. For one insult which you imposed on me, I have repaid you thrice.

The Poor Man of Nippur.[6]

What are the odds of this? They not only just revived the ancient Babylonian Language that went extinct a long time ago, in our lifetime, but now even the language barrier that God set up to confuse the languages in Babel to keep mankind from rebelling against him on a global basis has also come down in our lifetime. It's almost like somebody's trying to set the stage for a last days rebellion in the 7-year Tribulation, with every tribe, people, language and nation!

And that's exactly what Revelation 13 says they're going to do in the last days. First the Antichrist and False Prophet do it with a Global Government, *"He was given authority over every tribe, people, language, and nation."* Then they establish a Global Religion. *"All inhabitants of the earth will worship the beast."* Coupled with Revelation 17, the Global Religious Harlot called, "Mystery, Babylon," and you have a Global Religion. And as we saw, modern technology has now removed all these barriers! Mankind could never have a true Global Government and a true Global Religion unless all peoples of the earth get connected globally, right? It's common sense, the planet *has* to be inter-connected! Think about it. If everyone is still on their isolated continents and they're still speaking their isolated languages, you'll never be able to unite them all. But for the first time in mankind's history, with all this travel and communication technology, we have the ability pull it off! We already have our world being governed by a single united global entity called the United Nations. It's been in function for many years representing 193 different countries. I was there last year. And how do all these heads of all these different nations get to the U.N. to discuss this One World Government in the first place? They get there with Modern Travel Technology. And when they do get together, how do they speak to each other? How do they remove the language barrier to discuss this Global Government? Modern Communication Technology devices.

But what about a Global Religion? If all religions are stuck in their own isolated countries from everyone speaking their own language, you'll never be able to unite them all. So, what do you do? Modern technology! First you get them connected and exposed to each other via Modern Travel Technology. Then you utilize the Modern Communication Technology to remove the language barrier to begin to dialogue on how to join hands together! And believe it or not, that's what Pope Francis and the Vatican have been doing for a long time now! Talk about shades of the False Prophet! If he aint't the False Prophet he's desperately trying to get the job! Pope Francis is out there right now telling the world we need to unite into a Global Government!

Pope Francis Statements Unifying World

- "The Vatican Calls for World Government" (Forbes)
- "The UN Launches A Blueprint For A New World Order With The Help Of The Pope." (Zero Hedge)
- "Pope to World Government Summit: There is no development without solidarity." (Vatican News)
- "Pope Francis Continues to Promote Globalism." (The New American)
- "Pope Francis Calls For 'One World Government' To 'Save Humanity'" (News Punch)

But that's just step one. Even previous popes have also been working at uniting the World's Religions for a long time!

Dave Hunt: *"The Vatican and the Roman Catholic Church. Its Pope is currently leading the greatest ecumenical movement in history in order to unite all religions under Rome's leadership. In 1986 Pope John Paul II gathered in Assisi, Italy, the leaders of the world's major religions to pray for peace. There were snake worshipers, fire worshipers, spiritists, Muslims, Hindus, North American witchdoctors.*

I watched in astonishment as they walked to the microphone to pray. The Pope said they were all praying to the same god. And that their prayers were creating a spiritual energy bringing about a new climate of peace. John Paul II allowed his good friend the Dalai Lama to put the Buddha on the altar at St. Peters church in Assisi and with his monks have a Buddhist worship ceremony there while Shintoist chanted, ringing their bells outside.

The prophesied world religion is in the process being formed before our eyes. And the Vatican is the headquarters for the movement. Is this not spiritual fornication?"[7]

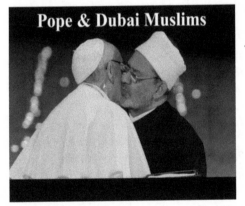

Pope & Dubai Muslims

Uh yeah! That's exactly what it is! But it didn't just stop there! Pope Francis is taking this behavior and putting it on steroids right now! Just recently he met with Muslim Leaders in Dubai encouraging them to unite with the Vatican.

And then he even more recently met with the Muslims in Morocco saying, "We're all brothers and sisters."

And he even recently met with the Mormons! Watch what the head Mormon Church said about the Pope!

Rome Reports.com: *"This is how Russell Nelson, President of the Church of Jesus Christ greeted Pope Francis. He and other*

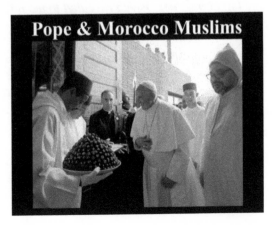

Pope & Morocco Muslims

Mormon leaders met the Pope on occasion of the dedication of their temple in Rome, Italy. The leaders then showed Pope Francis their new Temple. The first Mormon Temple in that city."

Russell Nelson: *"What a sweet, wonderful man he is. And how fortunate the Catholic people have him as their gracious, concerned, loving and capable leader."*

Rome Reports: "*It was a never before seen meeting of its kind that stroked some similarities instead of differences."*

Russell Nelson: *"So that is one of the many things we share in common with you."[8]*

Yeah! You're both false prophets and false teachers! And believe it or not, even so-called Christians are now calling the Pope a great guy!

Kenneth Copeland: *"You're going to talk about tonight for a long time. Brother Tony, come on up, would you please. Tony Palmer, some of you may know Tony, Tony and I go way back, but he is going to be telling you a story that I asked him to tell. He has a special message for us tonight."*

Tony Palmer: *"This brought an end to the protest of Luther. Brothers and Sisters, Luther's protest is over. Is yours? Tonight, I'm going to get a bit cheeky here because I challenge my Protestant Pastor friends if there is no more protest how can they be a Protestant Church? Maybe we are all Catholics again."*

KPRC 2 News Reports: *As we sat down and talked about the preparations for the big event, Joel Osteen revealed to me an incredible opportunity he just had to meet with Pope Francis."*

Joel Osteen: *"I felt very honored and very humbled by seeing the Pope give the mass to hundreds of thousands of people that day. You just see he has such a heart to help people. I love the fact that he has made the church more inclusive, not trying to make it smaller but to make it larger to take everybody in, so that just resonates with me."*

Rick Warren: *"The main thing is love always reaches people. Authenticity, humility, Pope Francis is the perfect example of this. He is doing everything* *right. You see, people will listen to what we say if they like what they see. And as our new Pope he was very, very symbolic in his first mass with people with AIDS, the kissing of the deformed man, his loving the children, the authenticity, the humility, the caring for the poor. This is what the whole world expects us Christians to do. And when they say, 'Oh that is what a Christian does! In fact, there was a headline here in Orange County that said, 'If you love Pope Francis, you'll love Jesus.'"[9]*

Yeah, real funny Rick! What Bible are you reading? Did you catch that? Our Pope? Us Christians? Christians do not have a Pope and Roman Catholicism is NOT Christianity! And lest there be any doubt as to why we need to unite ourselves with this Pope that everyone's enamored with, right now he is being pitched as a Global Religious Savior to save our planet and unite us all!

"No matter what divides us, his words unite us."

"For the first time in history the Pope opens his doors to address the questions and issues we face together as a leader whose faith inspires the world."

"I have the distinct honor of presenting to you Pope Francis of the Holy City."

"From the looks of this car, we are used to the huge American Limousine and this is a Mr. Bean car by comparison and yet it's going to take him around town."

Pope Francis: *"Families quarrel and sometimes plates fly. I won't speak about mother-in-law. In the family there are difficulties, but those difficulties are overcome with love. We need to learn to listen. Differences always scare us because they make us grow. Tenderness is not weakness, it's strength."*

"To bring us together."

"We have so much to do and we must do it together"[10]

And what's that? Oh yeah! Build a One World Government and a One World Religion, just in time for the last days! Folks, it's all being repeated! Revelation 13 is fast upon us! Our world is being united again into a One World Religion and a One World Government just like the Tower of Babel rebellion, with the Pope at the forefront! And that's precisely why, out of love, God has given us this update on **The Final Countdown: Tribulation Rising** concerning **Modern Technology & the AI Invasion** to show us that the Tribulation is near and the 2nd Coming of Jesus Christ is rapidly approaching. And that's why Jesus Himself said:

Luke 21:28 "When these things begin to take place, stand up and lift up your heads, because your redemption is drawing near."

People of God, like it or not, we are headed for **The Final Countdown**. The signs of the 7-year **Tribulation** are **Rising**! Wake up! And so, the point is this. If you're a Christian today and you're not doing anything for the Lord…shame on you! Get busy doing something for Jesus now! Stop wasting your life! We need you! Don't sit on the sidelines! Get on the front line and help us! Let's get busy working together doing something splendid for Jesus with what time is left and get busy saving souls! Amen?

But if you're reading this today and you're not a Christian, then I beg you, please, heed these signs, heed these warnings, give your life to Jesus now! Because when the Antichrist and False Prophet take control it won't be peace on earth, it will be hell on earth! Don't fall for the lie! Take the way out now, the only way out now, through Jesus Christ, before it's too late! Amen?

Chapter Five

The Increase of
Global Distribution

The **3rd** way that **Modern Technology** reveals that we're really living in the last days, is by the **Increase of Distribution**.

Believe it or not, that's exactly what needs to happen to our planet if we're going to see the fulfillment of several events recorded for us in Revelation 11 concerning the **Death of the Two Witnesses**!

But don't take my word for it. Let's listen to God's.

Revelation 11:3-9 "And I will give power to my two witnesses, and they will prophesy for 1,260 days, clothed in sackcloth.' These are the two olive trees and the two lampstands that stand before the Lord of the earth. If anyone tries to harm them, fire comes from their mouths and devours their enemies. This is how anyone who wants to harm them must die. These men have power to shut up the sky so that it will not rain during the time they are prophesying; and they have power to turn the waters into blood and to strike the earth with every kind of plague as often as they want. Now when they have finished their testimony, the beast that comes up from the Abyss will attack them and overpower and kill them. Their bodies will lie in the street of the great city, which is figuratively called Sodom and Egypt, where also their Lord was crucified. For three and a half days men from every people, tribe, language and nation will gaze on their bodies and refuse them burial."

Here we see the classic passage concerning the death of the Two Witnesses. And if we're going to get the prophetic significance of what's going on here with Modern Technology, we have to first look at this in its historical setting. Imagine what it must have been like when the Apostle John was writing this down nearly 2,000 years ago. It must have seemed like an incredible fantasy for the whole planet to simultaneously watch two dead bodies and rejoice over their death, right? That's what the text says! But guess what? As we all know, it's not a fantasy anymore! It's commonplace! Due to the advent of television and global satellite technology, you and I can simultaneously watch anything we want, anywhere we want, around the world, can't we? It happens every day! Which means, this passage can be fulfilled before our very eyes today! We have the technology right now to do this, to watch the death of the Two Witnesses for 3½ days for the first time in the history of mankind! But that's still not all. The text says one more thing. As they were watching this event, notice what they did. Let's go back to the text.

Revelation 11:10 "The inhabitants of the earth will gloat over them and will celebrate by sending each other gifts, because these two prophets had tormented those who live on the earth."

What's amazing about this is when you look at this from the Apostle John's perspective 2,000 years ago, this must have totally blown his mind! How could people not only watch the death of two guys from around the world simultaneously for three and a half days, but how in the world are they going to be able to celebrate and send each other gifts around the world within three and a half days? Because that's the timeframe there. I mean, they didn't even have the Pony Express back then! Well guess what? As we all know, it's not a surprise anymore! For the first time in man's history we now have a global distribution network! Thanks to this rise of Modern Technology we now have a global transportation system that's hooked up to a global communications system, that's linked to a global supply chain system, that's overseen by a global trade and commerce system that allows us to go down to our local store and get fresh crabmeat shipped to us from Thailand, or have a thoroughbred horse shipped to you from New Zealand. Or get fresh flowers all the way from South America, or have a New York City pizza delivered anywhere in the world, and send a package from Japan in the afternoon and have it arrive in Washington the next morning. As well as a celebratory package sent by someone who's gloating over the death of the Two Witnesses, within three and a half days. This is the first time in man's history, and it's being done in a couple of different ways that I wanted to show you.

The **1st way** we're seeing an increase of Distribution Technology fulfilling the Death of the Two Witnesses passage is the **Connection of All Delivery Routes**.

What I'm talking about is all the roads on which these celebratory gifts are going to travel in the 7-year Tribulation. Believe it or not, they're working on connecting all the roads on the whole planet! But before we get to that, let's deal with the history of delivering things so we can see the prophetic significance of the days we live in and see how it's ramping up exponentially so, just in time for Revelation 11 to be fulfilled. First of all, back in the day, they called them Trade Routes.

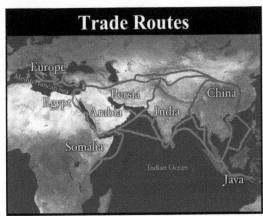

This was the term they used to identify various pathways and certain stops along the way that people would use, even back then, for delivering packages, cargo, and other commercial items. And it was a big first step in connecting huge sections of the planet in not just delivering goods, like salt or spice and other things, but it also exposed the planet to other cultures, religions, knowledge, and sometimes bacteria.

But let me share with you some of the more well-known influential Trade Routes in history. The most famous one was called, The Silk Road.[1]

The Silk Road

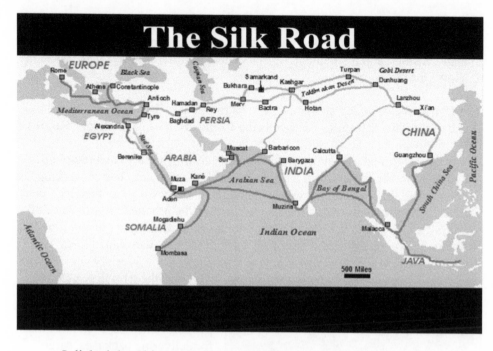

It linked the Chinese Empire to the Roman Empire, and they traded all kinds of things back and forth. Mostly what was considered luxury items, teas, salt, sugar, porcelain, spices, of course silk, cotton, ivory, wool, gold, and silver. In fact, some think it was the merchants traveling along that route that spread the plague bacteria that caused the Black Death. It was also on this route that Marco Polo was traveling when he went to China and this is also why they built the

Great Wall of China

Great Wall of China. It was built to protect and safeguard the Silk Trade Route. Then you had what was called the Spice Route which also linked the East to the West delivering spices like, pepper, cloves, cinnamon, and nutmeg which were all hugely sought-after in Europe. In fact, some say it was this spice trade that fueled the

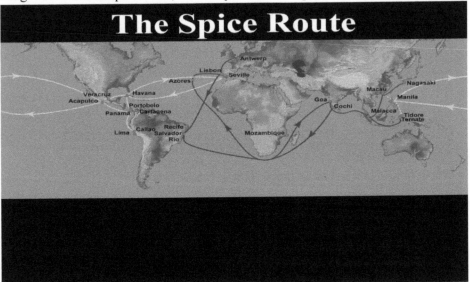

development of faster boats to get these spices to everybody faster. They really wanted them, chop, chop, hurry up, I can't get enough of them. This is also part of the reason why Christopher Columbus traveled his journeys, to find a trade route with these spices in mind. Then you had what was called, The Amber Road, that connected the Baltic area with the rest of Europe that was developed by the Romans.

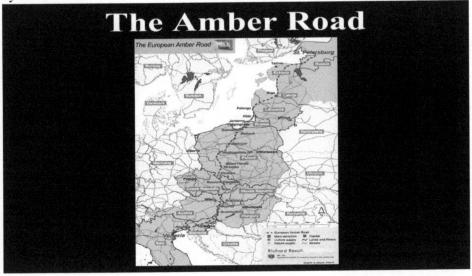

And speaking of the Romans, we also had the famous Roman Road system called Via Maris which is Latin for "the way of the sea," and was an ancient highway used by the Romans, as well as the Crusaders.

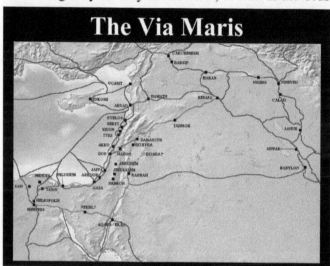

Not only for trade purposes, but to also collect tolls on people who traveled on their highway. So, if you're wondering why we have tolls and tolls booths today, blame it on the Romans! And then of course, we had what was called the Trans Saharan Trade Route that united Africa with Europe, even across the desert areas and traded things like gold, slaves, salt, and cloth. And speaking of slaves, this route is accredited with, being instrumental in the spread of Islam, which eventually led to the Crusades and other horrible atrocities. Which by the way was committed by the Catholics, not Christians! And there's many more trade routes throughout history, but you get the idea of the many, many attempts of people and countries around the world throughout history trying to establish universal delivery or distribution routes. In fact, historians say because of these trade routes, "Wars were fought over, lands were colonized, and fortunes made, but they also became the most significant developments in terms of globalization." In other words, a huge step in connecting our planet!

But here's the point. As you can see these various trade routes throughout history were wide and covered a huge area of the planet, but none of them had the ability to cover the whole planet, until now! This is wild! I couldn't believe I stumbled across this last year when I was flying on a plane down to Australia to preach at a conference. On the plane I was watching a documentary they had on the TV and it was all about how China is working on, right now, I kid you not, reconnecting our whole planet with one giant trade route to become a global superpower to handle all the distribution on the planet! In fact, their first big project being completed is recreating the Silk Road trade route with Modern Technology. Our own country is arguing over our own infrastructure, getting nothing done, and it will connect all of China with all of East Asia, Europe, Africa, even Russia.

Vox reports: *"There's a new highway in Pakistan and a new Rail Service in Kazakhstan, a seaport in Sri Lanka recently opened as well as this bridge in rural Laos. What is interesting is that they are all part of this one country's project that spans over three continents and touches over 60% of the world's population. If you connect the dots, it's not hard to see what country that is. This is China's Belt and Road Initiative. The most ambitious infrastructure project in modern history that is designed to reroute global trade. China plans to become the world's next superpower."*

"It's 2013 and Chinese President Xi In is giving a speech in Kazakhstan where he mentions the Ancient Silk Road, a network of trade routes that spread goods, ideas, and culture across Europe, the middle East and China as far back as 200 BC. President Xi In says 'We should take an innovative approach and jointly build an economic belt along the Silk Road.'"

"A month later he is in Indonesia and said 'The two sides should work together to build a new Maritime Silk Road in the 21st century. These two phrases were the first mentioned about the Xi legacy project, the multi-trillion-dollar project, the Belt and Road Initiative, or the BRI. There are also two components of the plan. There is an over land Economic Belt of six corridors that serve as new routes to take goods in and out of China. Like this railroad connecting China to London. And these gas pipelines connecting the Caspian Sea to China. And the high-speed train network from Southeast Asia."

"Then there is the Maritime Silk Road. A chain of seaports stretching from the South China Sea to Africa that also directs trade to and from China. The BRI also includes oil refineries, industrial parks, power plants, mines, and fiberoptic networks all designed to make it easier for the world to trade with China. So far over 60 countries have signed agreements for these projects and the list is growing because China promotes it as a win-win for everyone. In relationships and taking control of trade, China is well on its way."[1]

To what? Recreating the Silk Road and becoming a global superpower in trade, far surpassing the U.S. We better wake up and stop being distracted! In fact, many believe this is also leading to another prophetic development in the Bible with the Kings of the East in the 7-year Tribulation.

Revelation 16:12,14 "The sixth angel poured out his bowl on the great river Euphrates, and its water was dried up to prepare the way for the kings from the East to gather them for the battle on the great day of God Almighty."

In other words, the Battle of Armageddon. And so here we see at the end of the 7-year Tribulation, God draws the Kings of the East, you know China and the other countries over there, to the battle of Armageddon over in Israel's territory way to the West. And so, I wonder how are they going to get there? Well we may have just seen the actual roads they will be using! And not just any road, but with all this modern technology they're using on this New Silk Road they can get there in rapid fashion, just in time for the Battle of Armageddon in the 7-year Tribulation! Crazy stuff? But that's not all. China is also working at connecting the rest of the world as well with the help of Russia, another communist country, by going through Russia and crossing under the Bering Strait into America!

Youtube: Highestbridgecom: *"Having recently completed both the world's extensive expressway and the high-speed railway network, China is now looking beyond its borders for opportunities to keep building.*

China is considering building a high-speed rail line to the U.S. This rail line would start in North east China run through Siberia, cross a 125-mile underwater tunnel under the Bering Strait, then travel through Alaska and Canada before reaching the continental U.S. The good news is the high-speed rail from China to the U.S. is only one of four high-speed projects currently in the works.

Engineering High: *"Under the Bering Strait to feed a global appetite for goods and energy, the longest underwater tunnel in the world. But no matter what it takes the benefits of a permanent link between the continents could make it all worthwhile."*

CNN Live Reports: *"Let's look at the building site first because this is way, way up there, right at the edge of the Arctic Circle. The Bering Strait is what separates North America from Asia and as Sarah Palin says, you really can see Russia from here if you get high enough. The nearest point is about 53 miles high. How deep is this water? Not that bad. About 98 to 164 feet deep, depending on where you pedal your kayak.*

So, who would have to be involved in this project? Politically and economically, probably Russia and China and Canada and the United States. The Channel is what they would pattern this after in all likelihood. Let's look at the construction of this thing. Because that was built under the English Channel to connect the U.K. to France. Even at the narrowest point, which is twice as long as the Channel, the water is shallower here so essentially what they would have to do is start boring through and this is what they would probably aim for.

Something like this. Three tunnels, with one train going in one direction and one train going in another direction and in the middle sort of an access tunnel for emergencies and service and all sorts of ways to get back and forth. It is a big, big, big, project."

TOMO News: *"Russia plans superhighway that connects London to NYC. Driving from London to NYC would be possible if Russia succeeds in building a superhighway spanning across the country with links to Western Europe and Asia."*

"During a March meeting, head of the Russian Railways, unveiled the ambitious plan called the Transeurasian Belt Development which entails constructing a superhighway and an accompanying high-speed railway. If the plan is realized, motorists will be able to drive from London to New York. Russia hopes that the development will spur the economies of remote cities and towns."

"Suddenly, if you talk about continuing that rail that is being called the Eurasian Land Bridge, you are talking about connecting rail all the way from South Africa, up through the continent of Africa, through Central Asia, through Asia,

Russia, across the Bering Strait, down through North America, down through South America, once we solve the problem of getting across the Darien Gap, all the way down to Southern Argentina."[2]

In other words, you just connected the whole planet! Wow! Folks, that's not just wild and creepy, but it's really going down as we sit here! And we're all distracted wondering about the economy and who's going to win that game, while at the same time, for the first time in man's history, oh we've had many trade routes throughout history, but now they are looking at actually connecting the whole planet so you can drive from China to L.A. to New York, anywhere! And not just drive, but deliver things, including a celebratory package sent by someone in the 7-year Tribulation within three and a half days timeframe who's gloating over the death of the Two Witnesses for the first time in man's history!

The **2nd way** we're seeing an increase of Distribution Technology fulfilling the Death of the Two Witnesses is the **Computerization of All Delivery Routes**.

You see, it's not just about using Modern Technology to connect the whole planet with all these delivery routes, that's step one. You also need the speed of delivery, remember you have three and a half days to pull this off, deliver a package anywhere in the world, and believe it or not, they're doing just that with computers! Increasing the speed of delivery! And to give you an idea just how fast delivery speed has grown, in our lifetime, let's go back to our first delivery service, The Pony Express!

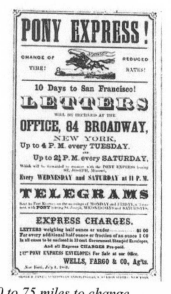

Courtesy of Brett Neilson: *"In January of 1830 the quickest way to send a letter from St. Louis, Missouri to Sacramento, California was by stagecoach. It took 25 days. The three men by the names of William Russell, Alexander Majors, and William Waddell came up with the idea to send mail by horseback non-stop from St Louis to Sacramento. They called this new business, Pony Express. The Pony Express hired riders that were young, brave, horsemen. These riders would stop every 10 to 15 miles to get a fresh horse and every 50 to 75 miles to change*

riders. The Pony Express riders would carry with them a mail bag called a mochila that had 4 pouches filled with mail. The first pony express rider with his mail bag left on April 3, 1860 traveling 2,000 miles and arriving in Sacramento 11 days later."[3]

What? See how good you guys have it? We whine and complain if we don't get our package in 2 days! Not to mention there was a time when the only delivery options were runners, horses, or even pigeons used to deliver stuff! But all in our lifetime, it's going crazy! We went from the Pony Express to the U.S. Postal Service, which was our standard for a long, long time. And then, again in our lifetime, privatized delivery companies began springing up making deliveries even faster and more reliable like, UPS and FedEx, which caused the US Postal Service to kick it into gear. You ain't the only game in town now!

And then around the world the same thing happened with the birth of all kinds of delivery services.

DTDC which is India's largest delivery service headquartered in Bangalore. Or Japan Post, obviously out of Japan, and one of the largest postal services in the world. PostNL servicing Netherlands, Germany, Italy and the U.K. Or Schenker AG out of Germany, or the Royal Mail, obviously out of England, one of the oldest delivery services in the world.

Then there's Blue Dart working together with DHL (German: Deutsche Post), that's not only popular in India and Southeast Asia, but they cover a total of over 220 different countries around the world. And of course, not to be outdone, China has their own delivery services with TNT and EMS International.

But here's my point. This not only opened up the ability for delivery around the world, but what came with it was *super-fast delivery* around the world! This all gave birth to what we have today, that we take for granted, not a week, but third day, second day, even next day air delivery, anywhere in the world, any package, anytime, all in our lifetime! It's going nuts! In fact, speaking of nuts, now the delivery services are going robotic. You don't even need people anymore. Here's just two options, one from Amazon called Scout and the other one called Starship!

Scout: "There is a little blue box-like robot on wheels, rolling down the street. It comes to a certain address and stops. The lady of the house comes out her front door and the lid of this little blue box opens, allowing her to take out her package that she had ordered from Amazon. On the side of the blue box is printed Prime. This is the new era in local delivery.

Introducing Starship: This is a self-driving robot, almost free on demand. When she initiated the delivery, the distance was 1.7 miles with an ETA of 10 minutes. It has zero emissions and can detect pedestrians or whatever else may be on the sidewalk in front of it. The packages are totally secure as only you can open the box with your cell phone."[4]

Oh, look there! I got my cake to celebrate the death of the Two Witnesses in record time! Isn't this wild? In fact, ordering stuff on your phone at the same time that all these computerized delivery services are going on, the method of ordering is also speeding up as well. First, we had mail order services like Sears & Roebuck, where you could get a genuine nose straightener or a bottle of hair

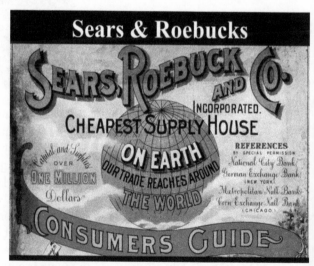

tonic. Then when I was growing up, we had those TAPE or CD of the Month

Tape of the Month Club

CLUB things! Remember them? You forever got stuck on their mailing and you ended up paying a billion dollars! You kids don't know how good you have it these days! Now you just download the music! But speaking of downloading, with the birth of the Internet, again, all in our lifetime, now you can order anything you want, anywhere in the world, at any time! Now you can, not just order things, but even food is available for delivery. Again, maybe a cake or something to celebrate some sort of event in the 7-year Tribulation, I wonder what that would be? But first it started off with just Pizza delivery or Chinese food delivery, and it pretty much stayed that way for a long time. But not anymore! All in our lifetime, as we sit here, just the last couple of years, we've had food delivery services going ballistic! In fact, here's a recent commercial of just one of them called, GrubHub!

Grubhub Commercial: *"It just takes a cell phone and an app. A person has his cell phone, looks at what is listed, hits the right option. The order goes directly to the one or many restaurants that prepare what you have ordered. The food is put in the Grubhub box, given to the delivery boy and it's on its way to your house. With the Grubhub delivery app, if you want it all you can get it all. Grubhub, restaurants you love, deliver."[5]*

But that's just the beginning! You not only have GrubHub to deliver any kind of food you want, but other companies are popping up like, UberEats, Eat24, Caviar, DoorDash and Postmates just to name a few. And then another company came along, and now they're offering not just restaurant food, but any kind of food. And that of course is the delivery service called Amazon Prime Now.

Today Show: *"We deliver is the boast of online companies that bring food, even entire meals to your home, so could this make the local grocer the thing of the past? Why go to the Supermarket when it can come to you? Seattle mom, Christine Holme gets groceries from Amazon on this day from the company's super-fast Prime Now service."*

Christine Holme: *"My husband and I both stay up late to watch TV after the baby is in bed and think, 'What ice cream can we order?' The items come to her in just one hour.*

Tech Insider: *"Here's what happens when you order Amazon Prime Now. Tucked inside this midtown Manhattan High Rise is an Amazon Prime Warehouse. Prime Now is a local delivery service. We put it to the test to see if they could deliver ice cream and other summer "essentials" in under an hour. There is a $20.00 minimum for Amazon customers to use it. Delivery for the 1-hour service costs $7.99.*

If you can wait 2 hours, its free. Items are randomly stored which Amazon determined to be the most efficient method for organizing the tens of thousands of items they stock. People working on the floor are either pickers or sorters. It took our sorter an incredibly short amount of time to gather our items even though every item was in a different aisle.

Once everything is bagged and labeled, it's handed off. A delivery person travels on foot, by subway or by truck depending on the distance. It took our delivery 15 minutes to travel from the warehouse to our office. It's available in 27 cities and if you opt for 2-hour delivery it's a pretty good deal."[6]

Yeah, good deal is right! I can get my food in 2 hours for free! Or pay a little extra and only have to wait 1 hour! Isn't this crazy? Which includes a celebratory cake for some event in the 7-year Tribulation! In fact, speaking of Amazon, they have now become the industry leader when it comes to delivering things, anything, including food, to the tune of becoming a multi-billion-dollar company that has now produced the richest man on the planet, Jeff Bezos, $131 billion dollars, or at least he was until he just got divorced and produced the richest woman on the planet! Amazon is at the forefront in these last days of not only delivery service options, but they are also radically improving delivery speed. Remember, we've got a three-and-a-half-day timeframe to meet here in the 7-year Tribulation. And Amazon is doing this in three different ways.

The **1st way** Amazon is different is they are changing the **Speed of Ordering**.

As you saw earlier, you can order just about anything you could ever want in the world online at Amazon.com. Now they're pushing their Amazon app so you can purchase anywhere you go on your cell phone or tablet. In fact, just in case that's too much work for you, they've now come out with just pushing a button!

Amazon Commercial: *"You are going through normal morning routine and you come to the chore of making coffee and you realize you are out. 'Don't let running out ruin your morning. Introducing the Amazon Dash button for Prime members. A simple way to order the important things you don't want to run low on so that you never run out. Set it up to order what you want, then press it when you are running low.*

Get an order alert on your phone. It's easy to cancel if you change your mind. And with Prime shipping you will get new products delivered to your door before you run out and never miss a beat. Prime members, request your free Amazon Dash button today.'"[7]

Wow! Talk about LAAAAAAAAAZY! But hey, it speeds it up, right? But that's not all.

The **2nd way** Amazon is changing the delivery service around the world in the last days is the **Speed of Delivery**.

First, it was for Prime members, free 2-day shipping, then as you saw with the food service, they offered free 2-hour shipping or pay a little extra and get it with 1-hour shipping or less. But now they're working on what's called Amazon Prime Air and you can get your stuff in 30 minutes or less!

Amazon Prime Air Commercial: *"This is the story of your not too distant future. It's the day of your daughter's big football match. To be clear, it's the kind of football you play with your feet. Anyway, she is missing a vital piece of her football equipment. To be specific, a size 3, yellow, Puma, power firm, soccer* *shoe. The left one. Some of it, sadly, is in the families 3-year-old Bulldog. So now what??*

Well, you could yell angrily at the poor dog, but what is the point? Because all he will hear is blah, blah, blah, blah. No, it's much more important to respond like a rational human being. Mind your temper and replace it with a pair of Puma, power firm soccer shoes and have them delivered in 30 minutes or less. And in a location not too far away a miracle of Modern Technology is dispatched.

It's an Amazon Drone and after rising vertically like a helicopter to nearly 400 feet, this amazing hybrid design assumes a horizontal intake and becomes a streamlined and fast airplane. In time there will be a whole family of Amazon Drones with different designs for different environments. This one can fly for 15 miles and it knows what is happening around it. It can sense and avoid obstacles around it, on the ground and in the air. Back at the house you get a message on your cell phone or tablet telling you that your package is delivering.

Then it goes back to vertical mode, scans the landing area for potential hazards, then lowers itself slowly to the ground, drops off the package, and flies straight back up into altitude. And moments later you are walking through the door with a brand-new pair of size 3, Puma, yellow, power firm, soccer shoes and a chocolate flavored chew for naughty, naughty Stewart."[8]

Whoa! Now can you imagine not just a cake, but any kind of celebratory gift a person could send to their friends or family in 30 minutes or less in the 7-year Tribulation, well within the three-and-a-half-day timeframe? But speaking of the Book of Revelation! That's still not all!

The **3rd way** Amazon is changing the delivery service around the world in the last days is the **Speed of Transaction**.

Now, as you already saw, through Amazon, you can not only purchase something with the push of a button, because it's all electronic, transactions that is, we are living in a cashless society. But even for you diehards out there who still want to shop outside your home, you can now, with Amazon, and complete your transaction with just a wave of the phone!

Amazon Go Commercial: "*Four years ago we started to wonder what would shopping look like if you could walk into a store grab what you want and just go.*

What if we could weave such an advanced machine in learning, computer vision, and AI into the fabric of the store, so you never have to wait in line. No lines, no check outs, no registers. Welcome to Amazon Go.

Use the Amazon Go app to enter, then put away your phone, and start shopping. It's really that simple. Take whatever you like. Anything you pick up is automatically added to your virtual cart. If you change your mind about that cupcake, just put it back. Our technology will update your virtual cart automatically. So, how does it work? We use computer vision, deep learning algorithms, and sensor fusion, much like you will find in self-driving cars.

We call it 'Just walk out technology.' Once you have everything you want you can just go. When you leave or just walk out, technology adds up your virtual cart and charges your Amazon account. Your receipt is sent straight to the app and you can keep going. Amazon Go...No lines, No check out, No seriously." [9]

Seriously is right! I mean, what's next? We just get an Amazon Prime Chip for "select customers" who "agree to do something" so they can "buy and sell" with the wave of their hand? Folks, that's exactly where it's headed!

Revelation 13:16-17 "He also forced everyone, small and great, rich and poor, free and slave, to receive a mark on his right hand or on his forehead, so that no one could buy or sell unless he had the mark, which is the name of the beast or the number of his name."

You see, there's only one drawback with all this convenience that Amazon is pushing for buying stuff. I mean we all know the dangers of a cell phone payment system are that you can lose it, break it, or have it stolen. Then what are you going to do? How can you "buy and sell?" Well, if you had a chip inside your body it would be totally secure, wouldn't it? And lest you think that would never happen as a form of payment, think again! It's already here as an option, and pretty soon, you might have to get one to keep your job!

The Now, Tampa Bay News: *"Some of us, the thing we have to do when we get to work is, swipe in with our key-card. When you sit down to start working and you need a password to log in here too. Here at our station if you want a snack for the break room, you must grab your snack, bring it over here with your card to be able to purchase it. But what if there was a way you didn't have to do any of this. Where you can be microchipped and that would work for the entire* *building. Well, dozens of people are doing it voluntarily. Next week, Three Square Market in Wisconsin will be the first company in the U.S. to give microchips to its workers. They are one of those businesses that put mini food markets, similar to ours, into business places. They expect more than 50 employees to opt for the microchip. It looks like the size of a grain of rice.*

It gets implanted in the hand between the thumb and the forefinger and it just takes seconds to do it. The chip implant uses the same technology as mobile payments like Apple Pay. The chip allows them to buy stuff in the break room, log into their computer and get into the building. The Wisconsin company got the idea from a company in Sweden who started putting chips in its workers recently."

Fox News: *"See that little microchip that you might put into your dog, so if he is missing you could find him? A Wisconsin company is putting it in 50 of its employees and they said, 'Yeah, let's do it.' It looks very painful. It goes between your thumb and your forefinger.*

So, if you buy a snack in the company breakroom, they track it, but oddly they say it also keeps your medical records there. Oh, they say they're not going to do that. (laughs).

So, if you have that chip, it allows you to open doors, use the copy machine, even log onto your computer, instead of that logging on things, just put your hand right there."[10]

Yup, just put your hand right there and make your payment, already here! And in the video, both talking heads were using their right hands as examples!

And that's precisely why, out of love, God has given us this update on **The Final Countdown: Tribulation Rising** concerning **Modern Technology & the AI Invasion** to show us that the Tribulation is near and the 2nd Coming of Jesus Christ is rapidly approaching. And that's why Jesus Himself said:

Luke 21:28 "When these things begin to take place, stand up and lift up your heads, because your redemption is drawing near."

Like it or not, we are headed for **The Final Countdown**. The signs of the 7-year **Tribulation** are **Rising**! Wake up! The point is this. If you're a Christian today and you're not doing anything for the Lord, shame on you! Get busy doing something for Jesus now! Stop wasting your life! We need you! Don't sit on the sidelines! Get on the front line and help us! Let's get busy working together doing something splendid for Jesus with what time is left and get busy saving souls! Amen?

But if you're reading this today and you're not a Christian, then I beg you, please, heed these signs, heed these warnings, give your life to Jesus now! Because this delivery and payment system won't lead to a life of ease or a party on earth, it will be hell on earth! Don't fall for the lie. Take the way out now, the only way out now, through Jesus Christ, before it's too late! Amen?

Chapter Six

The Increase of a Cashless Society

The **4**[th] way that **Modern Technology** reveals that we're really living in the last days, is by the **Increase of Electronic Transactions**.

I'm talking about a Global Cashless Society and believe it or not, that's exactly what the Antichrist and the False Prophet need to have to pull off the last days society and the Mark of the Beast system in the 7-year Tribulation!
But don't take my word for it. Let's listen to God's.

Revelation 13:11-17 "Then I saw another beast, coming out of the earth. He had two horns like a lamb, but he spoke like a dragon. He exercised all the authority of the first beast on his behalf and made the earth and its inhabitants worship the first beast, whose fatal wound had been healed. And he performed great and miraculous signs, even causing fire to come down from heaven to earth in full view of men. Because of the signs he was given power to do on behalf of the first beast, he deceived the inhabitants of the earth. He ordered them to set up an image in honor of the beast who was wounded by the sword and yet lived. He was given power to give breath to the image of the first beast, so that it could speak and cause all who refused to worship the image to be killed. He also forced everyone, small and great, rich and poor, free and slave, to receive a mark on his right hand or on his forehead, so that no one could buy or sell unless he had the mark, which is the name of the beast or the number of his name."

According to our text, there really is coming a day when all the inhabitants of the earth will be under the universal economy or monetary system of the Antichrist himself, right? He's literally going to control all the buying and selling. One day, believe it or not, the whole world will be unified into a One World Economy that is not only cashless, but it's actually satanically inspired! And whether you realize it or not, it's already happening right now before our very eyes! And they've done it in three different ways.

The **1st way** they've done it is by **Connecting All the Global Economies**.

Right now, there is already in place, the plans for absolute total economic control of the whole world. Unfortunately, for most of us, when it comes to the economy, we don't even know how the thing works! It makes no sense to us! Like these guys share!

ABC News Reports: *"Thanks for your time."*

"It's very good to be with you Bryan."

"Now you are a market economist?"

"Yes, well most economists are market economists."

"How do you think things are going at the moment?"

"Well there is a great deal of international concern. But things will work themselves out. This is what America does."

"Can you explain to me how it all works?"

"How the economy works?"

"Well, what is the problem at the moment?"

"Well there is an international credit crisis."

"Yes, how does that happen?"

"Well, I'm a bank, and I borrow money, and I lend it out. I charge more money to the people I am lending it to than what I pay to the ones I borrowed it from."

"Who do you borrow money from?"

"From depositors, Bryan, do you have a dollar? I borrow your dollar and I pay interest to you on that dollar. But I also charge you fees."

"But why do you charge me fees?"

"Because I am looking out for your money. Your money is secure with me at my bank. This is a very important amount of money, it's probably your nest egg. It's safe with us."

"And how much interest do you pay?"

"Probably the same amount as I am charging you in fees."

"That's not a good deal for me."

"Well, your money is secure. And then I lend that money to businesses and those businesses generate income."

"And they put that income into the bank."

"That they do Bryan and that builds the savings pool so we can invest more money."

"Well, who do you lend that to?"

"To the people that need credit, Bryan. You see money creates more money, so if we can create money to create more money, then we are broadening the economy. We are expanding it all the time."

"Shouldn't people just buy what they can afford?"

"You don't need to afford the things you buy, Bryan. You need to afford the interest on the money you need to borrow in order to buy them."

"And you are charging high rates for that."

"I do. We stick the hydraulics under that because it's a slightly high-risk strategy."

"Do people need to be buying these things?"

"Obviously they think so, Bryan. These things are advertised to people and they are very important and very deeply, deeply attractive.'

"Whose advertising things that people don't need."

"The companies that we are lending the money to."

"Then you bought into the U.S. subprime housing."

"We are so concerned in building a better Australia."

"You helped make a worse America."

"That was an accident, Bryan. What we were doing was investing in the international investment market."

"And that has been a disaster."

"Frankly, famously, that hasn't been a huge success."

"So, what are you going to do?"

"Ok, you give me Seven hundred billion dollars immediately."

"Why?"

"We need it, the system needs money. The economy is a body, it needs blood to run."

"You haven't got it."

"No, we haven't got it."

"Why not?"

"We lost it; I've just been explaining that."

"You've got mine. But that was the only money I've got."[1]

Now does that sound familiar or what? What a bunch of gobbledy-gook! But here's my point. Whether we understand it or not, for the first time in man's history our economies are already connected globally! Right now, there's already a universal bank called the World Bank which is the world's leader of lending money to the nations around the planet.

But wait a minute. If you're going to have a universal bank, then you need a universal lending institution to oversee the dispersion of loans, right? Well, what do you think is the function of the International Monetary Fund which oversees the whole world's financial system and even fixes the exchange rates? But, wait a minute. If you're going to have a universal lending institution then you need a universal money exchanger to funnel all this money to all the different countries, right? Well, that's why right now there's a Universal Electronic Banking System called SWIFT which automatically makes sure that all the different money transactions in the world match all the different currencies.

But wait a minute. If you're going to have a universal money exchanger then you need to have a universal strong arm to punish those who don't obey this world banking system, right? Well again, that's why, right now, there's the World Trade Organization which not only sets the trading rules for the world, but they punish all countries who do not obey with billion-dollar fines.

So, as you can see, the machinery for a One World Economy is already

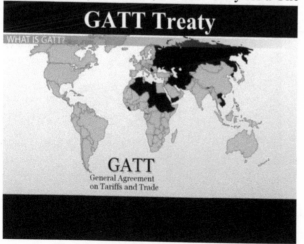

here! It's already in place! Not 50 years down the road, it's already here! Now for further proof, this is what all these treaties we keep hearing of are all about. They're all about tying together the world's economies! First, there was the GATT Treaty in 1944, the General Agreement on Tariffs and Trade to help, "Liberalize world trade." Then 50 years later in 1994 we had NAFTA or North American Free Trade Agreement. Then 10 years after that (2004) was CAFTA or the Central American Free Trade Agreement, combining Central American countries. And then the very next year, 2005, was the FTAA or Free Trade Agreement of the Americas, which proposes to encompass the whole Western Hemisphere and their economies and it's happening all over the world!

There's the AFTA, the ASEAN Free Trade Area, or APTA, the Asia-Pacific Trade Agreement, CAIS, the Central American Integration System, Or other proposed ones like CEFTA, the Central European Free Trade Agreement, COMESA, the Common Market for Eastern & Southern Africa, or GAFTA, the Greater Arab Free Trade Area or SAFTA, the South Asia Free Trade Agreement, and even TAFTA, the Transatlantic Free Trade Area, and on and on it goes! And the latest one out there is called TPP, or the Trans-Pacific Partnership which President Trump pulled out of, and Obama and Clinton were going headlong into. It encompasses 12 nations in the Pacific area, including Australia, Brunei, Canada, Chile, Japan, Malaysia, Mexico, New Zealand, Peru, Singapore,

Vietnam and the United States. And now they're freaking out because President Trump Trump pulled out of it!

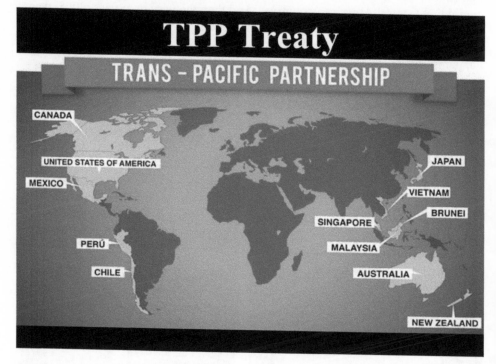

Fox News Reports: *At the Presidential debate, between President Trump and Hillary Clinton the following occurred:*

President Trump: *"Your husband signed NAFTA which was one of the worst things that ever happened to the manufacturing industry. You go to New England, you go to Ohio, Pennsylvania, you go anywhere you want Secretary Clinton and you will see devastation, where manufacturing is down 30, 40, 50%. NAFTA is the worst trade deal, maybe signed anywhere, but definitely in this country. But now, you want to approve the Transpacific Partnership. You were totally in favor of it, then you heard how bad it is and you said I can't win that debate but you know that if you did win, you would approve that and that would be almost as bad as NAFTA."*

CBSN reports: *We take you to the White House where President Trump has spent his first full week in office, he has signed three Executive Orders today with one withdrawing the United States from the Transpacific Partnership."[2]*

In other words, he kept his promise, unlike the other elites who wanted us to go along with this global treaty, TPP. Why? Because these global trade agreements are what they need to create a global economy for the last days society and the Mark of the Beast System in the 7-year Tribulation! And it's happening now right before our very eyes, which means, we're living in the last days! But that's not all.

The **2nd way** they've implemented a Global Cashless Society is by **Connecting All Global Commodities**.

Now, what I'm talking about here is the connecting of all actual products that people are going to be buying and selling all over the planet, now and in the 7-year Tribulation. Let's go back to our text.

Revelation 13:16-17 "He also forced everyone, small and great, rich and poor, free and slave, to receive a mark on his right hand or on his forehead, so that no one could buy or sell unless he had the mark, which is the name of the beast or the number of his name."

So here we see that the False Prophet and the Antichrist are not only going to have a global economy that they are going to control all over the world, they will also be controlling all the products people are buying and selling all over the world! You might be thinking, "Well, how in the world are you going to do that? It's one thing to connect all the economies on the planet, but how do you connect every single product that people buy and sell on the planet?" Ah! Can you say Modern Technology? They're already using Modern Technology to connect literally everything on the planet! All things, all people, you name it! First, they built the matrix that ties all the portals to get these products to all these people over the world. It's called the Internet.

And think about it. This new invention which was developed in our lifetime now connects all information, all knowledge, all forms of media, and even all finances, including what we buy and sell. The key word there is *net*, because I believe the *net* is closing in on us! It's not just in existence right now, but they've already, in just a few short years, got us conditioned to using it, accepting it, and relying upon it for almost all of our needs, including financial needs. You can buy online, you can sell online, you can bank online, you can do all your studying and research online, you can shop online, you can watch TV online, you can register online, you can make your appointments online, you can do just about anything and everything online! Everything is going online. Have you noticed the matrix they've built? Now here's the point. This giant matrix system is not only connecting the information, including financial information, all over the world, it's also being used to connect all products to all the people all over the world! And that's being done right now through the NEW 5G Network.

Tom Chitty, CNBC Reports: *"That is 4G, the new mobile network used around the world to make calls, send messages, and surf the web. Now there are plans to replace 4G with, you guessed it, 5G. A new faster network that has the potential to transform the internet. 5G is a software defined network. It means that while it won't replace cables entirely it could replace the need for them. Largely operating on the cloud instead.*

It means it will have 100 times more capacity than 4G which will dramatically improve internet speeds. For example, to download a 2-hour film on 3G would take about 26 hours, on a 4G you would be waiting about 6 minutes, and on a 5G you will be ready to watch your film in about 3.6 seconds. But it's not just internet capacity that will be upgraded. Response time will also be much faster.

Our 4G responds to our commands in just under 50 milliseconds, the 5G will respond in about 1 millisecond, 400 times faster than a blink of the eye. Smart phone users will enjoy a more streamlined experience. That for a world that needs the internet just to function. A reduction in time delay is critical. Some experts predict that by 2020 nearly half of the internet users in the U.S. will be 5G, a greater percentage than any other country or region."[3]

In other words, this new 5G Network is going all over the world very soon! And you might be thinking, "Well, so what? What's the big deal about having faster internet downloads, speeds, and times? I could care less."
Well, you should care more because this will enable them, for the very first time in man's history, to create what's called IOT or the Internet of Things, where, all products, and all people can be connected to this Global Matrix! Through microchip technology embedded in every single product and person, that is then connected to the Global 5G Network Internet System. It will allow them to connect every single product and every single person on the face of the earth all

at the same time continuously in a non-stop monitoring system they say will lead to a life beyond your wildest dreams! Here's just one video promoting it! The new internet of things!

What is the IOT, the internet of things? *It makes life more simplified with cloud-based automation. When you come home, your garage door opens for you automatically. You walk into your kitchen in the morning at 7:00 am, with a flick of your hand when you add sensors with open door alerts, a notification comes on that the bathroom is occupied and someone is in the shower, and it sets the temperature of the shower.*

In the other bathroom the daughter just walks in and the lights come on. When going into the refrigerator a notification comes on of what is in the refrigerator. A list of the inventory. Then when it is time to replace anything it sends a notification that it is time to go to the store. The music is set all through the house in case someone is late getting up, a great alarm clock. When it's time to go to work you are safe because you are sent a notification of the vehicle diagnostics to let you know the condition of the car. If you are low on gas, if the tires need air or if all is okay.

A notification will be sent to you to leave early so you can stop to get gas and you won't be late for work. The system will also send you a notification if there are any toxic fumes in the garage and to open the doors. Whoops, someone got something out of the refrigerator as they were running out the door. The door didn't close completely so a notification goes out that the door is open. IOT knows when everyone is gone, and it adjusts the thermostat to be more energy efficient.

When you get to work IOT automatically turns on your computer, opens the window shades and notifies you of any meetings that you need to be attending. When driving down the street IOT will tell you if you are going too fast. It also keeps track of your children and monitors where they are at all times. IOT will notify you when someone is at your front door and if they are supposed to be there or not, you have the option to say yes or no for the gardener or pool man.

When the family members are in the yard IOT controls whether the sprinklers are to come on or not. Also, it keeps score while kids are playing ball in the back yard. IOT will tell you when your garden doesn't have enough water in the soil and will identify anyone at the front door to see if they are approved to enter the house or not. At the end of the day you can depend on IOT to lock all the doors and turn out all the lights so you can have a peaceful night."[4]

Wow! So, everything is microchipped and connected to this Global Matrix. Who wouldn't want to live in that paradise, right? Yeah right! Who wants to be a rat, is what's going on! Your Smart Home is connected with your Smart Car that connects to your Smart Office and Smart Watch and Smart Phone and all your Smart Devices including your Smart Appliances, even Smart Shoes that monitors, you, your family, your health, and everyone's every move! It's paradise! It's wonderful! No thank you! What it leads to is a life of slavery and constant monitoring! I mean, gee what's next? A Smart Chip you put in your hand or your head just in case you lose your Smart Watch or Smart Phone and get disconnected, heaven forbid, from this Giant Matrix System you built? Yeah, that's exactly where it's headed, pun intended!

Which leads us to the **3rd way** they've implemented a Global Cashless Society is by **Connecting All Global Currencies**.

Once again, let's go back to our text and pull out another nugget.

Revelation 13:16-17 "He also forced everyone, small and great, rich and poor, free and slave, to receive a mark on his right hand or on his forehead, so that no one could buy or sell unless he had the mark, which is the name of the beast or the number of his name."

Now think about it, its common sense. If the Antichrist and the False Prophet are going to pull off this One World Economy system and the Mark of the Beast System, you are not only going to have to combine all the world's economies into one system, and you not only have to combine all the world's products into one global matrix system to control all the buying and selling, but you have to combine all the currencies into one, right? In other words, they have to, at some point, make the money around the world electronic or cashless, right? Why? Because as we saw, he controls all the buying and selling with a what? A mark in the right hand or forehead, right? And so, this tells us it has to be some form of "electronic" payment system. Because you don't tape a dollar bill to your hand to make a payment here in this passage, or slap 20 bucks on your forehead to pay for your groceries. Obviously, you've got to have some sort of electronic capability to make a financial transaction with the Mark of the Beast system either in your right hand or forehead, right? It's common sense! It's right there! And so, here's the point. Good thing we see no signs whatsoever of us ever going to some sort of cashless system even here in the U.S. let alone around the world that enables us to make electronic payments, with our body parts. Uh, yeah, it's already here! For the first time in mankind's history we have already, slowly but surely, been conditioned to move into a cashless society, something that the Bible predicted would come in the last days, in the 7-year Tribulation! And let me show you how fast it's sped up just in our lifetime!

"The concept of currency ultimately boils down to trade. As far as historians know barter economy was the only form of trade until 3000 BC when the shekel started being used as the first standard unit of currency. Money as we know it today started taking shape around 600 BC when the first national currency was created. Coins were standard in civilizations around the world. Until the Jioazi printed the first paper backed by gold, silver, and silk. Paper currency was lighter and more convenient to carry. In the middle ages the concepts of banking and commercialized debt emerged.

While lending occurred throughout history, Italian merchants started turning a profit by financing the sea voyages of other traders. In the centuries that followed the Industrial Revolution allowed people and ideas to move more freely and moving the money wasn't far behind. Money wires made it smoother and easier to send money across the world. Lending took on a new, more convenient form when the Diners Club began giving out credit cards to be used at multiple locations unlike the single store cards before that.

The advent of the internet with digital payments, like online transfers and ecommerce: In the last 20 years our phones have become extensions of our wallets. Even to this day money continues to evolve. In 2008 anonymous coders released bitcoin. The first decentralized virtual currency on the internet."[5]

Ooh! There's the internet and there's your electronic currency! But notice how currency didn't change for the longest time until the 50's when we saw the birth of the card instead of a cash payment system! It's all going down in our lifetime! In the last century alone, we have gone from paper currency to electronic cash and it's happening very fast! For instance, if we didn't have any money on us, don't worry, just write a check. Then if we didn't have the money to write a check, don't worry, just charge it to a credit card. But if we didn't want to pay the interest on a credit card, don't worry, just take it out of your checking account with a debit card.

And then not long after that, debit card spending overtook cash which led to all these features being combined into one card called a Smart Card. That's a card about the size of a regular credit card only this one has a tiny microchip in it that can store and receive information and make financial transactions as well. And then, all these convenient payment features were transferred to another microchip device that everybody on the planet carries around in their hands called the cell phone to buy their stuff with.

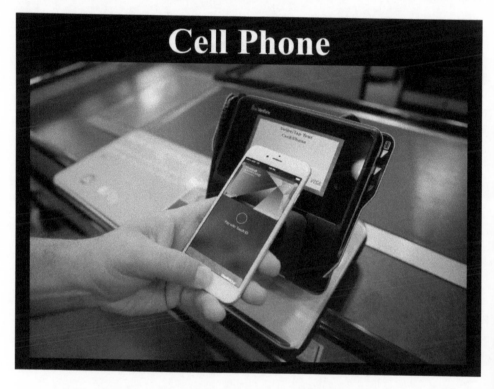

Cell Phone

And so much so has this step by step conditioning process worked, that even here in America, we are now basically a cashless society!

NBC News Reports: *"When Breann Kimmel gets ready to go in the morning cash is not in the equation."*

Breann Kimmel: *"I think the last time I went to an ATM was 2 years ago."*

NBC Nightly News: *"She streamlined to credit cards only. Cash she feels is inconvenient and dangerous."*

Breann Kimmel: *"There are a lot of times that I feel if I had cash on me, I would feel a little bit anxious."*

NBC Nightly News: *"Between 2000 and 2013, non-cash payments grew by almost 400%."*

Breann Kimmel: *"I haven't really needed cash, to be honest. It's either my credit card or if I'm out with my friends I will use Venmo."*

NBC Nightly News: *"The mobile app where people can pay each other on a smart phone now processes $2 billion per month. This year Apple added similar payment capabilities on I-message. These free services are so popular that 30 major banks launched a similar competing product called Zelle. Doing away with paper money has been a big boom for small businesses."*

TRT World News Reports: *"Washington's family run deli Bozelli's has been in business for five decades. At their newly opened downtown location they have taken a radical step to remain competitive. No more cash. If you want to eat your lunch here, you have to pay with plastic."[6]*

In other words, no cash accepted in the United States of America! We're going cashless, right before our very eyes, in our lifetime, just in time for the 7-year Tribulation! And it wasn't just individuals preferring this, but businesses demanding it! But you might be thinking, "Well that's all good and all, but that's just the United States. There's no way the whole planet is going cashless, are they?" Uh, yeah, they are! In fact, so much so, that much of the world is further along than we are, including Sweden who is now only 1% cash transactions in their whole country. 99% of all transaction are electronic!

"In Sweden almost all transactions are done digitally. Notes and coins are gone, and Sweden is leading the race to become the first cashless society.

Patrick Jenkins, Financial Editor, Financial Times: *"Sweden is becoming the king of the card. There's not much you can't buy these days with a card in fact many stores don't take cash at all.*

On the street he asked some passerby's: *'When was the last time you used cash?' She answered, 'The last time I used cash was maybe last year. In the summer.'*

Lukas Berg, CEO, Insight Intelligence: *"People talk about when will we be cashless. For me, I have believed in a cashless society for 5 years. I haven't used cash for 5 years."*

Tomas, Swedish Church Member, Uppsala: *"The banks, they have stopped handling cash."*

Ali Withers, NBC Left Field: *"Sweden has become one of the cashless places in the world. So much so that banks will not handle your cash. In fact, it's hard to find any business that will take cash. You have to pay with a card or a mobile app on your phone. The most common is Swish."*

"Only about 1% of cash is used in Sweden and at the present decline it can be completely cashless by 2025."[7]

In other words, for the first time in mankind's history, a whole country will be completely cashless in just a few years' time, right on time for the Mark of the Beast System in the 7-year Tribulation! In fact, so much so that this cashless society is catching on globally and many other countries are following Sweden's lead. They too are going cashless, including seemingly insignificant countries like Peru and Nigeria!

CBS This Morning Reports: *"The day of overstuffed wallets in your back pocket or purse might be coming to an end by 2020. Mobile wallets in our smart phones are expected to surpass the use of credit and debit cards in the U.S. It has already happened in China. Ben Tracy is in Beijing to show us what a cashless society actually looks like. Ben, good morning."*

Ben Tracy: *"When I moved here a couple of months ago, I would get funny looks every time I would pull cash out of my wallet to pay for things. Then I got one of these. A code on my phone and now I can buy just about anything here in China.*

Ben on the street: *"When you pay for something, how do you pay for it?"*

On the streets of Beijing, cash is definitely not king. "What do you think of people that pay cash for things?" He answers, "That is rare and weird. Only the elderly and people who don't know how to use a phone pay cash."

CNBC @eschulze9 reports: *"If you were looking to buy coffee a year or so ago here in London it might have been normal to ask, 'Do you take cards?' Now it is becoming more frequent, 'Do you take cash?'*

Ross Brown, Browns of Brockley: *"We probably have customers in here now that don't even know that we don't accept cash because they just tap their card and go."*

CNBC @eschulze9: *"Ross stopped accepting cash at his London café more than a year ago after a trip to Sweden. He said paper money was nowhere to be found."*

Global Business Reports: *"From groceries, to bus fare, to fuel you don't get far without a handful of cash. Have you ever imagined a world without cash? It just takes these (cards) and this (cell phone). A company in Tanzania believes that we should all be paying with digital payments. The challenge right now is that hardly any Tanzanians have bank accounts or credit cards. A bit do have mobile money. Jones is one of the one of the group of campaigners that say mobile money would give East Africa the unique opportunity to get ahead of the rest of the world."*

CCTV-American Reports: *"Only 29% of Peruvians have bank accounts, one of the lowest uses of financial services in Latin America. To bring in people you have to look at their uses in their everyday life. They found that no matter how humble the person or remote the area, cell phones were ubiquitous. Mobile phones are a great leveler in Peru. At least one for every person in the country. Most people use pre-pay where you go and shop and credit over the counter. An e-wallet works in much the same way. You don't need a smart phone to send and receive money. In fact, you don't even need a bank account, just a 4-digit key."*

Akiko Fu NBC Reports: *"If you walk around Delhi, you see digital cell phones payment platforms everywhere. Samsung, American Express, Novia. The number of digital transactions in India have quadrupled since last year. Welcomed by the government to reduce India's reliance on cash. The prime minister of India* *pulled nearly 90% of their money out of circulation last year and this has proved to be a big boost to India's digital economy."*

Viet Nam News: Jan 2017: *Vietnam's deputy prime minister has signed a policy to dramatically reduce cash transactions by 2020. The policy aims to turn Vietnam into a cashless economy and change the payment habits of the Vietnamese. It seeks to reduce cash transactions to less than 10% in all supermarkets, malls and distributors by 2020."*

DW News: *"Paying without cash is fast becoming the norm." 'I pay even tiny amounts with my card,' says one man passing by. A lady tells us, 'It's just easier.' 'It's easier,' another one tells us. Will cash soon be a thing of the past? 'When I think about it, I pay more without cash than with.' Around the world financial corporations, politicians, and leading economists, are working to do away with cash."*

"I see a future where you will be able to hold digital euros, digital dollars, directly at the Central Bank. Who stands to profit from a world without money? And who will be the losers?"[8]

Well, let me answer that for you. The losers will be those people who rejected Jesus Christ as their Lord and Savior and got left behind at the Rapture. And thus, they were thrust into the horrible 7-year Tribulation and will have to deal with accepting or rejecting this Mark of the Beast Cashless Payment System and being sent straight into HELL! But the winners of course will be the Antichrist and the False Prophet who are working so feverishly, as you can see, behind the scenes, all over the world, in our lifetime, as we sit here, putting this whole system into place! In fact, this is so obvious that this sudden push for a cashless society around the world is part of the prophesied Mark of the Beast system warned about nearly 2,000 years ago. Even the news is picking up on it! These guys aren't even Christians that I know of!

RT News Reports: *"Many Economists believe the future will be cash free. You are already seeing it everywhere you go. At your baseball game or your local deli. Now Sweden is getting there faster than anywhere else according to a New York Times report. And 4,000 Swedes have a micro-chip implanted in their hand so they can pay for products with just the wave of their hands. Makes the Apple watch look obsolete.*

So, on top of that, many Swedish companies are asking their employees to get this implant to pass through access points and to pay for conveniences. Now the red flag starts going up. So, now for our red flag analyst, Lionel. Lionel, thank you for joining us, I know you have something to say about this red flag and I feel like I am reading out of the Book of Revelation. So, what comes to you about the humans microchipping themselves?"

Lionel: *"It's the mark of the beast. I'm no Biblical scholar here, but it's amazing, the parallels made. Now listen, let's get down to brass tacks. I wish they would stop this. 'We're going cashless.' We've been cashless. Where's this cash? Have you ever bought a house with cash? Or a car? I don't know where this comes from. I have a couple of bucks. We've been cashless.*

But that's not the issue. One of these days these kids, I think you call them millennials, they are going to take these little RFID chips, about the size of a grain of rice, and they are going to be cool, oh they are going to be waiting in line overnight to get implanted. And they are going to say 'Look at this, I can go to the drugstore, I can call a cab, how cool am I. Look I have this little embedded chip' and they will say they have medical records. They are going to do this to grandma or grandpa in case they have some kind of dementia, they're walking off... After all we have it for our dog, why not for humans, OnStar for human beings. But here's the catch. One of these days when they find you guilty of something, and you go before a court, and they say we are going to sentence you. To prison? No, we're going to turn your chip off and you don't exist."[9]

In other words, you can no longer buy or sell! Where have I heard that before? Even the secular news can put two and two together! Step by step we have been conditioned, yet how many Christians even know about it? But notice how they also mentioned how the Swedes have already jumped from the cashless system to the implant system so now they're paying with a wave of the hand with a microchip inside of them! What do you think that is? We'll get to that in the next chapter!

But that's precisely why, out of love, God has given us this update on **The Final Countdown: Tribulation Rising** concerning **Modern Technology & the AI Invasion** to show us that the Tribulation is near and the 2nd Coming of Jesus Christ is rapidly approaching. And that's why Jesus Himself said:

Luke 21:28 "When these things begin to take place, stand up and lift up your heads, because your redemption is drawing near."

People of God, like it or not, we are headed for **The Final Countdown**. The signs of the 7-year **Tribulation** are **Rising**! Wake up! If you're a Christian today and you're not doing anything for the Lord, shame on you! Get busy doing something for Jesus now! Stop wasting your life! We need you! Don't sit on the sidelines! Get on the front line and help us! Let's get busy working together doing something splendid for Jesus with what time is left and get busy saving souls! Amen?

But if you're reading this today and you're not a Christian, then I beg you, please, heed these signs, heed these warnings, give your life to Jesus now! Because this cashless payment system won't lead to a life of convenience or a great joy, it'll lead to great sorrow and hell! Don't fall for the lie! Take the way out now, the only way out now, through Jesus Christ, before it's too late! Amen?

Chapter Seven

The Increase of
Mark of the Beast Technology

The **5ᵗʰ way** that **Modern Technology** reveals that we're really living in the last days, is the **Increase of Electronic Marking**.

And of course, I'm talking about the Mark of the Beast and believe it or not, the technology needed for that kind of marking system set up by the Antichrist and the False Prophet on a global basis, is here as well! But don't take my word for it. Let's listen to God's.

Revelation 13:11-18 "Then I saw another beast, coming out of the earth. He had two horns like a lamb, but he spoke like a dragon. He exercised all the authority of the first beast on his behalf and made the earth and its inhabitants worship the first beast, whose fatal wound had been healed. And he performed great and miraculous signs, even causing fire to come down from heaven to earth in full view of men. Because of the signs he was given power to do on behalf of the first beast, he deceived the inhabitants of the earth. He ordered them to set up an image in honor of the beast who was wounded by the sword and yet lived. He was given power to give breath to the image of the first beast, so that it could speak and cause all who refused to worship the image to be killed. He also forced everyone, small and great, rich and poor, free and slave, to receive a mark on his right hand or on his forehead, so that no one could buy or sell unless he had the mark, which is the name of the beast or the number of his name. This calls for wisdom. If anyone has insight, let him calculate the number of the beast, for it is man's number. His number is 666."

Now, according to our text, the Bible clearly says there really is coming a day when all the inhabitants of the earth will not only be under the authority and economy of the Antichrist, but what? They're going to receive the Mark of the Antichrist. They will actually be deceived into receiving some sort of mark on their bodies, either in the right hand or forehead, to connect themselves to the Antichrist system so they can "buy and sell" and escape the threat of death! But again, as always, the question is: Could this really happen? Could the whole world really be deceived into receiving The Mark of the Beast and is there any evidence that it's really going to take place just like the Bible said? AND more importantly, do we have the technology for this to happen in our lifetime? Uh, yeah! In fact, it's happening as we sit here!

The **1st way** we know the planet is ready for the Mark of the Beast is **The Technology is Already Here**.

That's right, what I'm talking about is a global emerging technology out there called R.F.I.D. Radio Frequency Identification.

And believe it or not, it's already gone global, and it's the exact kind of technology the Antichrist needs to pull off his Mark of the Beast system. It's a tiny microchip that can be implanted or embedded in, or on, just about anything that you can think of and it stores and receives information. It can be used as a tracking device, and of course, can make financial transactions. All in one device, it's very convenient. But it's not just being put in all the products on the planet, as we saw before, those things that people "buy and sell," but it's also being put into people across the planet in order to "buy and sell." All things including people are being marked with this R.F.I.D. technology. The one's they're using for people is called a Biometric Implant. It's a tiny little microchip implanted into people about the size of a grain of rice that is implanted just beneath your skin.

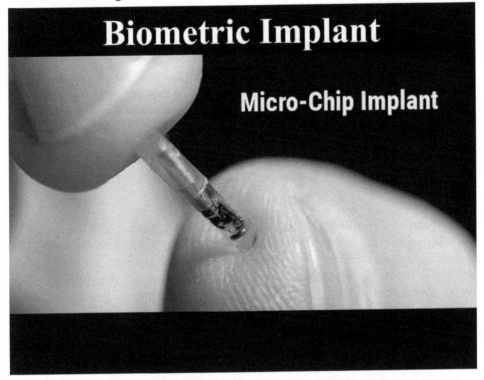

And its benefits, they say, are that it can't be stolen, and you can't lose it, because it's implanted inside your body which means it's with you wherever you go. Isn't that great? Isn't that convenient? And for those of you who might be a little bit squeamish, don't worry. It's already been approved by the FDA as far back as 2002. But if you who think this would never catch on, it's already being done! Here's just one example of RFID Biometric Implants.

KPIX 5 News Reports: *"Microchip implants are a popular way to keep track of pets. Now some people are getting them, but for a different reason. The microchips can unlock doors or log into a cell phone. Consumer reporter Julie Watts explains."*

Julie Watts: *"Tim uses it to open his front door and manipulate his smart phone. Crissy uses hers instead of a key card at work. Crissy says, 'It's just a little glass* *piece the size of a grain of rice.' They are among a growing number of people implanting technology under their skin."*

Zoltan Istvan: *"We don't want to carry devices. We want devices built into us."*

Julie Watts: *"Zoltan Istvan, belongs to the Transhumanist Party. The Party seeks to radically improve humans through digital implants and even genetic manipulation. For now, the common procedure is implanting programmable RFID chips under the skin. But instead of a doctor's office now they are turning to tattoo and piercing shops."*

Tattoo Shop owner: *"We are doing the procedure from start to finish just like we would do a piercing, nose ring, belly button ring, it's just a little piece of glass."*

Julie Watts: *"The online company called 'Dangerous Things' sells the device and the injection kit for $57.00, but they are not alone. A San Francisco company is developing tiny implantable digital tattoos. They will authenticate credit cards, track your location, even collect health data. But the next big thing does present an age-old tech problem." 'I have the older chip, now I have to get the upgrade.' Constantly being forced to upgrade the implanted technology can mean more than just a pain in the pocketbook."*[1]

Yeah, the pain is that it's setting you up for the Mark of the Beast! Now notice a couple things. First of all, who would have thought we would see people in our lifetime willingly receiving a microchip implant into their bodies under the guise of coolness or convenience? Secondly, notice the technology can be implanted in or on, so it covers both bases depending on your translation. And third, notice the industry who was promoting this. Not only the media, but those who are in the Tattoo Industry, (i.e. Body Art, Body Piercing.) It's all the rage right now! Have you noticed? I mean, back in my day nobody got a tattoo! But look at today, everybody's got to have one! And to me, that's not by chance! It's the logical progression of getting people used to eventually getting a microchip implant, in or on their body! I mean think about it. The entire Body Art industry continues to push the envelope and they're willing to do all kinds of things to their bodies!

New Body Art

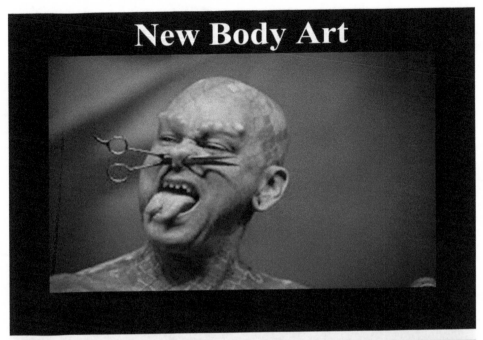

New Body Art

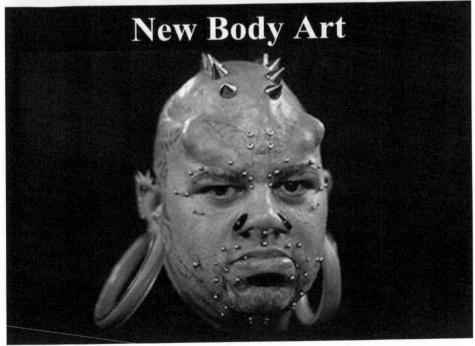

New Body Art

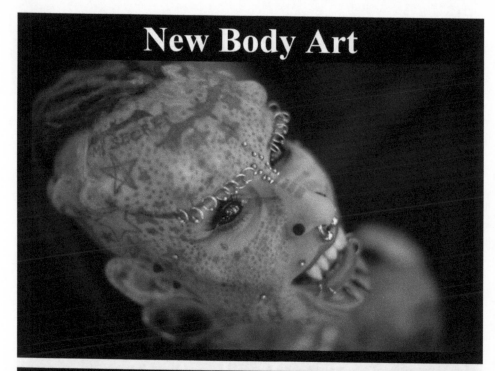

New Body Art

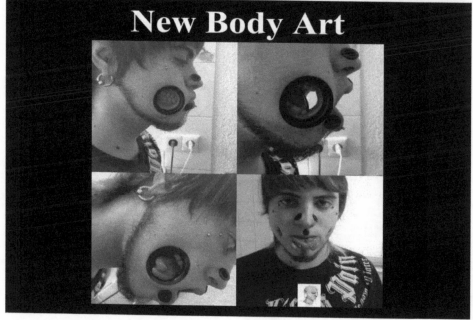

New Body Art

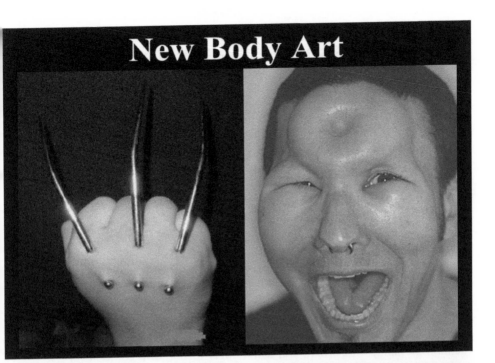

New Body Art

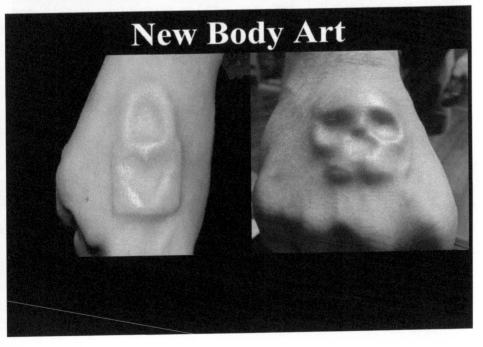

Now here's the obvious question, "Do you think those people will have a problem getting a mark in or on their right hand or in or on their forehead in the 7-year Tribulation?" Are you kidding me? A microchip is chump change compared to what they're doing right now! But as you can see, the Technology is here for the first time in mankind's history to pull off this Mark of the Beast system in the 7-year Tribulation, and people are already doing it!

Which leads us to the **2ⁿᵈ way** we know that the planet is ready for the Mark of the Beast, **The Willingness is Already Here**.

You see it's not just the Body Art industry that's willing to get a microchip implant, again, a device that not only stores and receives information, acts as a tracking device, unlocks doors, computers, all kinds of devices for you, but it can make financial transactions as well. And believe it or not, for those already hooked on cashless payment systems, this is the next logical step as well. As we saw in the last chapter on a Cashless Society, there's only one problem with all these cashless payment systems. You can lose it, or it can get stolen. The cell phone, the card, etc., then what would you do? You're shut out of the system! Oh no! Well hey, wouldn't it be great if you put that same microchip technology inside you, where you could never lose it, or it could never get stolen? I mean, you carry your body parts with you wherever you go, right? And lest you think that's some wacky conspiracy theory, it's already being done in Sweden. Remember the last chapter, Sweden is the country that's 99% cashless. Only 1% of their transactions use physical money and that's going away very soon. But it just so happens, those who are on the forefront of a total cashless society, i.e. Sweden, is also now marking themselves with microchip implants to do the same thing. In fact, so much so they are throwing microchipping parties!

Local 4 News Reports: *"Thousands of people in Sweden have opted to trade in their I.D. and their credit cards for tiny microchips that will be implanted underneath their skin.*

'These chips are supposed to take the place of key cards, rail cards, credit cards.' 'Yes, these chips are the size of a grain of rice and they are implanted just under the skin between the thumb and the forefinger.' 'So many people are lining up to get these microchips. The country's main chipping company says they can't even keep up with the number of requests.' 'Really, no way would I do that!'

'It's the Illuminati, mark of the beast, witchcraft, and it's going on over there in Sweden. Haven't they heard of a wristband. Everybody wears a wristband or an Apple watch?' 'I'm sure it was tested for safety but I'm not even feeling comfortable. Although there are microchips in pets, so I guess it's not unheard of."[2]

Yeah if you're going to put a microchip in Sparky, why not Johnny & Susie? But here's the point. This is not by chance! It's a setup, a step by step process. First get people, even a whole country, to go cashless, then get them to convert to microchip payments, to mark their bodies with this. Not to just unlock doors and copiers and the like, but to make payments! Who would have thought, in our lifetime, we'd not only see people, but literally whole countries of people willingly receiving a microchip implant into their bodies to make financial transactions when they buy and sell? Where have I heard that before? It's not coming, it's already being done! The willingness is here, for the first time in mankind's history, on a global scale, to pull of this Mark of the Beast system in the 7-year Tribulation!

Which leads us to the **3rd way** we know the planet is ready for the Mark of the Beast is **The Propaganda is Already Here**.

You see, you might be thinking, "Well hey man, there's no way in the world that this marking system to make financial transactions with a microchip implant for 'buying and selling' is going to go global. I mean maybe in the Body Art Industry, maybe the Swedes and even the rest of Europe, but not here in America, nosiree, we know better, right?" Actually NO! Not even close! And it's because of two things. One, the Church refuses to teach on it. So, people even in the Church have no clue about the Mark of the Beast, let alone the technology and how far advanced it is, or what it looks like. They're left in the dark! In fact, I'll even say this. I speak at a lot of Bible Prophecy conferences every single year, and I'm not saying that to boast, but to share with you a strange trend I've noticed even with those who do teach on prophecy. You know how many speakers ever speak on the Mark of the Beast at these conferences? Virtually none! They talk about all different kinds of topics, and that's great, but not the Mark of the Beast! I never hear messages on it! At a time when it's never been so prevalent! Now, is that by chance? But two, the reason why America is also falling for the Mark of the Beast technology is propaganda. Think about it, the enemy knows what he's doing…he knows that the Bible says those who receive the Mark of the Beast are going straight into hell!

Revelation 14:9-11 "If anyone worships the beast and his image and receives his mark on the forehead or on the hand, he, too, will drink of the wine of God's fury, which has been poured full strength into the cup of His wrath. He will be tormented with burning sulfur in the presence of the holy angels and of the Lamb. And the smoke of their torment rises for ever and ever. There is no rest day or night for those who worship the beast and his image, or for anyone who receives the mark of his name."

You can't get any clearer than this! The Bible says if there's one thing you never want to do, it's what? Don't take the Mark of the Beast, right? Why? Because you go straight into hell, right? Says it right there! Forever and ever and ever and you ain't getting out! And so, the question then is, well, how does the Antichrist and the False Prophet get people to risk this horrible destiny by receiving his mark in the 7-year Tribulation? We know they do. But how does he get them to do it? Well, first of all, he does what he always does. He lies, and he twists the truth, and he makes the bad look good! And that's being done through propaganda and the modern media system. Think about it! If you're going to get people, even here in America, warmed up to the idea of getting a microchip implant into your body, then you have to repeatedly encourage them do so over and over again in a multitude of ways. Year after year after year, and that's being done in a multitude of ways!

The **1st way** they're using Propaganda to condition people, even here in America **right now**, to receive the Mark of the Beast is with **Prisoners**.

You see, put yourself in the enemy's shoes. You can't just come full force and announce in plain language your goal of microchipping the whole planet. People will freak! So, here's what you do. You start at the end of the spectrum, then work your way to your final goal, where everybody is chipped. Start off with those fringe people and then work your way in. And speaking of fringe people, we all know those prisoners, those "bad people" deserve to be microchipped, right? And lest you think we're not being encouraged to think that way, it's already being pitched in the media!

CBS New York Reports: "*With the two fugitives on the loose a lawmaker from upstate, has a high-tech plan to prevent another prison break. She is proposing microchipping prisoners. CBS News political reporter Marsha Cramer here with that proposal.*"

Marsha Cramer: *"Well Dana, bloodhounds and expensive man hunts are so yesterday when it comes to hunting escaped prisoners. That is the opinion of one upstate Senator who says the state should explore implanting tiny GPS devices under convict's skin. Others say microchipping criminals could have multiple uses."*

Kathy Marchione, NYS Senate – Saratoga: *"If you have got convicted murderers that are the type of people that these two men are, it would make some good sense at that level that we should have something that we could track them."*

Marsha Cramer: *"With 800 law enforcement officials still unable to pick up the trail of escaped murderers, the suggestion from Kathy Marchione to microchip people convicted of serious crimes with tiny GPS devices under their skin is picking up steam. They already microchip pets."*

Man on the street: *"It wouldn't do any harm, I guess. They do dogs."*

Another man on the street: *"I think that would be a good idea. Maybe it will work."*

Woman on the street: *"I heard about it in other parts of the world and I would say yes."*

Another man on the street: *"After we go down this path, they are going to microchip all of us which is what I think some people would like to do."*[3]

As well as the Antichrist and the False Prophet. But as you can see, it's a step by step process. They're already doing it with pets, cats and dogs, so hey why not those people in society who they say deserve to be treated like dogs! You know, those prisoners, they deserve to be microchipped! Not like the rest of us "good citizens" in America who don't do anything wrong. We have nothing to be afraid of, they'll never chip us. Really? As the man mentioned, it's a slippery slope! If you'll microchip a prisoner against his or her own will, then why not the rest of the population in another government-controlled institution called Healthcare?

Which leads us to the **2ⁿᵈ way** they're using Propaganda to condition people here in America to receive the Mark of the Beast technology and that's with **Medical.**

You see, they not only control the prison population, but they now control the medical population or industry and believe it or not, they're already using propaganda to condition us non-prisoners to receive a microchip as well!

Dr. Oz: *"This show is all about the latest breakthroughs. Turns out the biggest discovery is this tiny chip. See how small that is? This little chip may be the next big thing. Sounds like it is right from a Sci-Fi movie but people all over the world are implanting these in their wrists. So, I asked my producer Dean to find out more about this cutting-edge technology and what it could mean for your health."*

Producer Dean: *"Whether it's our smart phone, our watches, our fitness trackers, or our blue tooth headphones it's clear that technology is not just part of our lives, it's running them. It's how we buy things, watch things. how we date, stay safe and even how we travel. We are so attracted to our devices that they are basically becoming a part of our bodies. But what if they really could become part of our bodies?*

Well, guess what? They can. Meet the RFID Microchip. This tiny chip which can be implanted into your wrist. Yes, I did say wrist. It uses a short-range radio frequency identification similar to the tech to track your pets or your phone. Once implanted in your body it can identify you as you pass through the airport, open the door to your home, it can even be used to buy groceries at the supermarket.

Now your driver's license, passport, keys and wallet are all inside your body. It's inside something the size of a grain of rice. I know it might sound like science fiction but it's not. 10,000 people have already been chipped and the number is growing. The possibilities are limitless. Especially when it comes to your health. Imagine you are rushed to the hospital without any identification but with just one scan of your chip doctors know your name, date of birth, medical history, insurance, blood type, allergies, even the medications you are taking. This chip in your wrist won't just change your life, one day it just might save it. And that is why this tiny microchip is the next big thing."[4]

Yeah, if you want to promote the Mark of the Beast system! But hey, if it's good for Dr. Oz, surely, it's good for us! I'll say it again, aren't you glad the Government took over the Healthcare System? I'm sure it's a coincidence that the Medical Industry is promoting microchipping people just like prisoners, hopefully not against our will. Speaking of which…

The **3ʳᵈ way** they're using propaganda to condition people in America to receive the Mark of the Beast technology is with **Alzheimer's.**

You see, not only are the prison and medical industries promoting microchipping people, but both are also recommending microchipping people against their will, including Alzheimer's patients! I mean, who cares, right? It's not like they know the difference anyway! Just microchip them for their own good, like a dog!

WTHR 13 News Reports: *"A company is developing a microchip that could be used to help people with dementia. This Wisconsin company got a lot of attention last year when they put microchips in their employees. They use the chips like other companies use I.D. badges. Now they say they are working on a more advanced version. That they have gotten requests from people with relatives who have Alzheimer's or dementia. The new device will have GPS technology."*

A daughter speaks: *"Every time my mom would call panicked. 'I just got out of the shower and dad is nowhere to be found.' Immediately my mind went to a bad place."*

WTHR 13 News: *"It's why she was intrigued to hear about a piece of technology made by Three Square Market, a company in River Falls. Someone with Alzheimer's or dementia, time is your biggest enemy. Patrick McMullen is the President of the company that you may remember offered hand inserted microchips to their employees to scan to get into the building or buy things from the breakroom. The developers of the microchip now believe it could save lives, especially those suffering from dementia or Alzheimer's."*

Patrick McMullen: *"It's a low powered GPS device."*

WTHR 13: *"If a person with dementia or Alzheimer's has the microchip inserted in a hand and gets lost, the microchip would send their location or a map of where they had recently been back to the persons caregiver or loved ones notifying them in real time, where the person is."*[5]

So much for not being a tracking device! But hey, don't you see? See what peace of mind you can have with your loved one? Wouldn't it be great to never worry again about their whereabouts ever again if they wander off with Alzheimer's? Just put a chip in them and be at ease! Which leads us to....

The **4ᵗʰ way** they're using propaganda to condition people in America to receive the Mark of the Beast technology is with **Children**.

You see, if you're an adult taking care of your parent or loved one with Alzheimer's and you microchip them for their own good and your own personal peace of mind, then hey, why not do that with other people who are under your care that might get lost, like your children? Believe it or not, that too is being pitched as well! Watch this propaganda!

NBC News reports: *"It happens in seconds, moms and dads, you know that feeling. Your child gets lost in a store, just wanders off for a second or two, your heart stops and panic sets in, and you think the worst. It's happened to most of us, but what if you had a secret weapon? That extra layer of protection so to speak. How far would you go to keep your children secure? Would you be willing to microchip them? Experts tell us the technology already exists. Turns out one Bay area mother is all for it and she shares her story with our Melanie Michael."*

Melanie Michael: *"Good morning to you both. You know chances are if you have a 4-legged family member at home it's already been microchipped. The technology exists to save Fido in an emergency, but what about microchipping your child? Before you say, no way, I'd never do that, here is one mom's story."*

Steffany Rodriguez-Neely: *"It's the longest two seconds of your life. And it's absolute panic."*

Melanie Michael: *"We have seen it in movies. Over and over again, children gone missing. For Steffany Rodriguez life is busier than ever with 4 children and a newborn. She knows scary situations can happen in an instant. And for her it has."*

Steffany Rodriguez-Neely: *"It's terrifying. If it would save my kid, there is no step that is too extreme."*

Melanie Michael: *"Steffany's teenage daughter is a special needs child. Prone to wonder off and trust strangers. For that very reason Steffany whole-heartedly welcomes microchipping."*

Steffany Rodriguez: *"If a small chip the size of a grain of rice could have prevented a tragedy, I think most parents would have done it."*

Melanie Michael: *"A well-known technology expert out of Boston tells us microchipping poses little to no health risks and would act as a bar code of sorts."*

Stuart Lipoff, Electronics Engineer: *"It could save a life, reunite a family, find a missing Alzheimer's patient."*

Steffany Rodriguez: *"I always tell people that as long as you feel that is best for your child, you're not really wrong."*

Melanie Michael: *"Guys, this is what we are talking about. The Microchip. I don't know if you can see it in my hand, it's the size of a grain of rice. Very, very small. And the expert we spoke with actually told us that bar-codes were introduced in the late 1960's and people thought that this was way too invasive and too weird and now bar-codes are so commonplace that we don't even think about them anymore. The experts tell us this will happen sooner rather than later. Somewhere, someday, someone is going to pull this off and we will see these microchips in everyone."*[6]

Yeah that's interesting, and that someone is the Antichrist and the False Prophet! Can you believe this? On the news! Talk about propaganda! I mean, wouldn't you feel better? Now you've got both ends of the spectrum covered. If your parent wanders off or your kid wanders off, both are protected by being microchipped, nothing to worry about, have a great day! Isn't life great with a microchip implant? But that's right, just in case that's still just a little too much for you, enter our next propaganda technique, to put you over the edge.

The **5th way** they're using Propaganda to condition people in America to receive the Mark of the Beast technology is with **Hollywood**.

Shocker! Because we all know Hollywood has no effect on us! Yeah right! Most of America looks at Hollywood celebrities as their gods, their idols, and whatever they say is good as gold. It's called star power in the industry. And believe it or not, they're using Hollywood celebrities right now to push for microchipping people, including our children. I mean, haven't you heard? Brooke Shields says it's a good thing to do, and so should you!

Today Show: *"Ok, the next one is a little creepy. Let's see what you guys think. Brooke likes this idea."*

Brooke Shields: *"It is, and it isn't."*

Today Show Host: *"So you forgot your ticket to a soccer game? In Argentina it's not a problem because you can use the microchip that has been embedded under your skin. The Argentinian soccer team is planning experimentally at this point to offer supporters to implant a microchip in their skin that lets you walk through an easy pass, to walk right into the stadium."*

Brooke Shields: *"I'm not really thinking of it in terms of sports as much as I would love to put one into my kids. I know it's creepy and futuristic, but my dog has one and she ran away and somebody did deliver her to a facility that could scan her, and they found us. I honestly am not completely against chipping my children. I thought I would do it in their sleep. Mom what was that? It was a mosquito. There is something about it, I don't know about the scanning and it will help you in the subway."*

Ryan Eggold: *"Then you will be programing them to eat their vegetables, just flip a button."*

Brooke Shields: *"We are scanning things with our eyes, it's not just a thumb print any more, I wouldn't put it past us being done."*

Ryan Eggold: *"Can't we just put it into our phone and swipe the phone or something."*

Brooke Shields: *"How do you find your children if they somehow get kidnapped?'*

Host: *"Alright."*[7]

A baby low-jack! Real funny Brooke! Can you believe this? Promoted right now on television! But hey, come on! This is Hollywood! If microchips are good for Brooke Shields, why not the rest of us? I mean, surely she knows what she's talking about, after all, she's a Hollywood icon, she knows what's best for us.

But, here's my point. Put all this together, this propaganda of microchipping prisoners, the Medical industry, Alzheimer patients, children, you name it, and Hollywood backing all this, and you end up with this: For the first time in man's history, people even in the United States are now willing to get microchipped just like the rest of the world so they can be tracked, store, and receive vital information, and make financial transactions. Where in the world have I heard that before? All this "buying and selling" with the wave of a body part, including the "wave of the hand" is being implemented right now in our own country!

Restaurant worker: *"I can't believe he just paid with his hand, like you just literally put your hand up and you're good to go. Like that's crazy."*

Charlie Warzel: *"Hi, my name is Charlie Warzel, I'm the Senior Writer for Buzz Feed News and in order to see what the future of money would look like, I decided to live for a month where I just paid for things with my phone. Somewhere along the line I ended up getting a microchip implanted inside my hand to see if I can be the first person in the world to pay for something out in the real world using just my hand.*

I basically wanted to try to download as many apps on my phone as possible to be sure I could use alternative currencies and try to secure cash and credit cards anyway possible. A couple weeks into my experiment I ended up going to Sweden. Sweden happens to be way far ahead of the United States when it comes to getting rid of cash. I ended up meeting with some people that are really active in the Biohacking community and I found that you can really plant an RFID chip in your hand.

So, I figured if I put it in my hand then maybe I could pay for something with my hand. It definitely hurt more than they said it would. It looked sort of like a grain of rice. So, once everything was healed, I decided I needed to start focusing on how to make this chip work. I really wanted to be the first person to ever pay for a meal at a restaurant with their hand. At the restaurant it took a second, but I was good to go. After doing that experiment, I can bet that in about 10 years it's kind of abnormal to carry around a wallet stuffed with cash. My hand paid for everything."[8]

Just like the Bible warned about nearly 2,000 years ago! Who would have thought that in the United States of America, in our lifetime, a country that boasts of having way more supposed Christians than any other country in the world and thus should know better than anyone else about the Mark of the Beast Technology, would be marking themselves with it in order to buy and sell right now! We're living in the last days and it's time to get motivated!

That's precisely why, out of love, God has given us this update on **The Final Countdown: Tribulation Rising** concerning **Modern Technology & the AI Invasion** to show us that the Tribulation is near and the 2nd Coming of Jesus Christ is rapidly approaching. And that's why Jesus Himself said:

Luke 21:28 "When these things begin to take place, stand up and lift up your heads, because your redemption is drawing near."

Like it or not, we are headed for **The Final Countdown**. The signs of the 7-year **Tribulation** are **Rising**! Wake up! And so, the point is this. If you're a Christian today and you're not doing anything for the Lord, shame on you! Get busy doing something for Jesus now! Stop wasting your life! We need you! Don't sit on the sidelines! Get on the front line and help us! Let's get busy working together doing something splendid for Jesus with what time is left and get busy saving souls! Amen?

But if you're reading this today and you're not a Christian, then I beg you, please, heed these signs, heed these warnings, give your life to Jesus now! Because this Mark of the Beast System won't lead to a life of coolness or convenience, it'll lead to your greatest sorrow and throw you straight into hell! Don't fall for the lie! Take the way out now, the only way out now, through Jesus Christ, before it's too late! Amen?

Chapter Eight

The Increase of Big Brother Information Gathering

The **6ᵗʰ way** that **Modern Technology** reveals that we're really living in the last days, is by the **Increase of Electronic Monitoring**.

Of course, now we're talking about the Big Brother Society and the Global Technology needed for the Antichrist and the False Prophet to literally micromanage the whole planet. Because that's another thing they do in the 7-year Tribulation! But, don't take my word for it. Let's listen to God's.

Revelation 13:11-17 "Then I saw another beast, coming out of the earth. He had two horns like a lamb, but he spoke like a dragon. He exercised all the authority of the first beast on his behalf and made the earth and its inhabitants worship the first beast, whose fatal wound had been healed. And he performed great and miraculous signs, even causing fire to come down from heaven to earth in full view of men. Because of the signs he was given power to do on behalf of the first beast, he deceived the inhabitants of the earth. He ordered them to set up an image in honor of the beast who was wounded by the sword and yet lived. He was given power to give breath to the image of the first beast, so that it could speak and cause all who refused to worship the image to be killed. He also forced everyone, small and great, rich and poor, free and slave, to receive a mark on his right hand or on his forehead, so that no one could buy or sell unless he had the mark, which is the name of the beast or the number of his name."

Now as we saw before in this text, we saw how the Bible clearly says that the False Prophet in the last days is not only going to dupe the whole world into worshiping the Antichrist, but he's what? He's going to make them, he's going to order them, he's going to cause them, he going to force them to do whatever in the world he says to do, otherwise they will what? They will die, right? Now again, focus on the words there, "make" "order" "cause" and "force." This implies that we have some serious global enforcement going on here! Because again, that's the context. It's global. He forces the whole planet to do whatever in the world he wants them to do, or they're going to die! But hey, good thing we see no signs of anybody having the technology to monitor everything we do on the planet all at the same time, how about you? Yeah, right! It's already here! They're already monitoring our every move! What we do, where we go, and what we think!

The **1ˢᵗ type of big brother surveillance system** they've already put into place is in the **Information System**.

You see, whether you realize it or not, there is already in place a massive number of databases to identify who you are and literally everything about you. In fact, they're so big they're called mega-databases. Let me give you just one example. A company in the U.S. is called Acxiom and it operates one of the world's largest databases on ninety-five percent of all-American households.

CNN Money Reports: "*They've been called the Cyberotzie. Largely unknown companies that buy and sell personal information on virtually everyone in the country. Data marketing is now a three hundred-billion-dollar industry.*"

Don Jackson, Security Researcher: "*They know more about us than we know about ourselves and they can actually predict what we will do in the future with a high rate of accuracy.*"

CNN Money Reports: "*There are hundreds of Data Brokering companies in the U.S. and one of them is Acxiom in Little Rock, Arkansas. In case you missed it, this company reported its sales last year of more than one billion dollars. This is the first TV interview Acxiom's chief executive has ever granted.*"

Chief Executive: "*So we collect data and we use that data about people to give them more relevant advertising and help businesses make better decisions about marketing to those people.*"

CNN Money: *"The raw data about individual people is run through complex algorithms, tracking purchasing, lifestyle patterns, then you are grouped into a life stage cluster. There are about 70 different groupings with names like Savvy Singles and Apple Pie Families. It's all perfectly legal but pinpointing how it is all done and what they have isn't easy."*

CNN Money: *"Do they know the numbers to my bank account?"*

Chief Executive: *"Well let me tell you what I know. (laugh) We collect things like contact information, demographics, and your preferences on things."*[1]

First of all, notice how he laughed about whether or not they had our bank account information. Now let me share with you just some of those personal preferences he was talking about. Right now, 24 hours a day, they are gathering and storing information on us from credit card transactions, magazine subscriptions, telephone numbers, real estate records, car registrations, fishing licenses, you name it. And because of all this information, they can provide a full profile on each one of us, right down to whether we own a dog or cat, enjoy camping or gourmet cooking, read the Bible or other books, what our occupation is, what car we drive, what videos we watch, how much gas and food we buy, and even where our favorite vacations spots are. And that was just one of what? Hundreds of these kinds of companies making billions of dollars tracking our every move! And did you catch that phrase? "They know so much about us that they can even predict what we'll do in the future with a high degree of accuracy!" You know, like worship the Antichrist! And this is all legal??

In fact, it's estimated that, right now, each adult in the developed world is already located, on average, in three hundred different databases with an average of 1,500 data points on you. That's a huge file! In other words, Big Brother is already here, even in the U.S. for the first time in mankind's history, to do what the Antichrist and the False Prophet need to do in the 7-year Tribulation, micromanage the whole planet! And so, the question is, "Good thing they're the only one's doing this!"

Yeah, right! Believe it or not, even the U.S. Government has massive databases on us! Under the guise of national security and terrorist threats, thank you 9/11, the Government now has full authority to monitor and intercept all this information, collect it, store it and analyze it. Including our cell phone conversations, emails, faxes, TV viewing, you name it, it's all being monitored right now as we sit here! And one such government institution that collects and stores all this information is called the NSA or the National Security Agency, which is the U.S. intelligence agency that is responsible for the global monitoring, collection, and decoding of information and data for foreign intelligence. Now, the problem is, it's not just for foreign intelligence, it's being used on even you and I here in the United States of America. Here's just one of their databases. The Utah Data Center.

CCTV News Reports: *"The biggest U.S. Department of Defense construction project isn't an aircraft carrier or a U.S. missile site. It's a massive data storage facility in Utah. What will be stored there is raising some serious questions. CCTV's Jim Spillman has that story."*

Jim Spillman: *"In a field in Utah, about a half hour south of Salt Lake City, a massive construction project is wrapping up. When it is completed in a few months it will be the world's largest repository of digital information. The owners, the U.S. National Security Agency, the NSA. James Bamford has been writing about the NSA for more than 30 years."*

James Bamford: *"All the information will be stored there and then people like NSA headquarters or their listening posts from around the world will be able to dip into it."*

Jim Spillman: *"It's called the Utah data center. Sprawled over 450,000 square meters with its own power plant, water pumping station to cool the servers, and intense security. It's a key part of the NSA strategy. Gather as much information as possible, from as many sources as possible, and use it to stop terrorist attacks and create strategic advantages over rival countries."*

Alan Friedman, Brookings Institution: *"What this is really about is the ability to take a lot of data and learn things that you otherwise can't. So, to do that you need to throw mountains of information at very powerful computers."*

Jim Spillman: *"Where the data is coming from is what is concerning privacy advocates. So, if I make a phone call or send a text message, do a Google search on my phone, that information could end up at that data center in Utah?"*

Alan Friedman: *"Oh definitely. Any kind of communication."*

Jim Spillman: *"The NSA is one of the most secretive agencies in the U.S. Government with little oversight from Congress. Even its budget is not publicly released. So what data is stored here and where it came from will likely never be known. But there is no sign that any intelligence agency or the NSA in other countries are slowing down this hunt for data and information. Is this an arms race for data?"*

Alan Friedman: *"Yes, it's very much an arms race for data."*

Jim Spillman: *"And this data center in Utah is soon to be the United States' biggest weapon in its information arsenal."*

CCTV News: *"And the NSA won't say how much the Utah mega center will be able to hold but experts say it will be a Yoda bite. To put that into perspective an iPhone can hold 16 gigabits, the NSA's new facility will be able to hold the same amount as 64 trillion iPhones. Laid end to end that number could stretch to the moon and back over 10,000 times."[2]*

Whoa! And that's just one! And did you catch the U.S. isn't the only one doing this? "It's a global arms race for data!" A bunch of other countries are doing this around the world. And gee, I wonder why? Maybe somebody's building the infrastructure needed to micromanage the whole planet in real time during some horrible time frame. I wonder who that might be? It rhymes with the Antichrist! This is not make-believe, it's not a conspiracy theory, it's really going on! They're monitoring all of our information on a global basis even here in the U.S., even the news is reporting on it! But we're all distracted, wondering how the economy's doing, who's going to win that game, and that's right, did you see on social media that sandwich somebody posted or that cat playing piano again on YouTube? Yet the point is once the Antichrist rises to power in the 7-year Tribulation, the technology is already here to turn this planet into one big giant global Big Brother society, just like that! He can micromanage the planet now!

But apparently, that's not enough, they want even more information just to make sure! And with recent technology birthed in our lifetime, they've tricked us into giving it to them voluntarily. How? Not only through the loyalty cards, but also through credit cards, ATM cards, Credit Rating Agencies, Search Engines, and even Social Media! You see, we just thought it was about fun and entertainment, and staying in touch with each other. It's all about gathering an unbelievable amount of information on us. More than you could ever dream of!

Social Media, like Facebook, Twitter, Instagram, you name it, builds massive amounts of database information on us from all of our photos, our friends, our communications, our contacts, everything you can think of we give it up for free! And because of that, they know everything about us, who we are, where we are, what we're doing, who we're hanging out with at any given moment, building huge massive data profiles on us down to the intimate detail! Here's just a teaser of what they're getting from us!

"What does Facebook know about you? Facebook can take all the data you submit and combine it with other users and outside information to construct a profile of you. Facebook uses nearly 100 different data points to classify your interests and activities. This would include basic stuff like your age and gender but also more complicated like whether you own a motorcycle, or you recently went on vacation, or if you're a gadget geek. Researchers have found that by using signals like your likes and interactions, Facebook can tell if you are in a relationship or going through a breakup.

Where you go ... Facebook doesn't just know who you are, it knows where you are. If you have location tracking turned on Facebook collects enormous data about where you are going, where you came from, where you live, where you work, restaurants and businesses, and they use this information to target ads to you. The location data can reveal other people who live in your house, even if you're not connected to them on Facebook.

What you buy ... now obviously Facebook knows its users buy when they click on ads on Facebook, but what most people don't realize is that they have ways of knowing your offline purchases as well. For many years Facebook has had partnerships with data brokers that collect information about people's purchases. So, for an example, if you buy a burrito with your credit card, Facebook could know about that transaction, match it with the credit card you added for Facebook or Facebook messenger, and start showing you ads for indigestion medicines.

Who do you know ...? One of the most controversial parts of Facebook data collection is a feature called 'People you may know' and this is where Facebook uses many different signals of what it knows about you to determine who else you may be connected to. This is not always things that you may share with Facebook. It might be contacts in your phone, it might be people that have been in the same room as you, Facebook was using location data to recommend friends. So, it might be recommending people that you shared a doctor with you or work in the same building.

What you do ... Facebook can also compile data about your political activity. Like protests or marches you go to. In one case in 2016 the ACLU found that 500 police organizations had signed up for a service called Geopedia, which takes data from Facebook, Twitter, and Instagram to help officers look for users who may be in a specific location or attending a specific protest.

Your Future ... Facebook doesn't just know who you are, where you are, and what you buy, it figures out what you might do in the future, to predict life outcomes. Like if you will become addicted to substances or if you will change political parties, whether you are physically healthy or physically unhealthy."[3]

And of course, whether or not you'll physically worship the Antichrist! Is this crazy or what? And you wonder why I call Facebook, Tracebook! And we voluntarily give it to them! Talk about slick! No wonder the devil's called cunning! But you might be thinking, "Well hey, that's precisely why I will never get a Social Media account. They can't get me!" Really? It's already come out that Facebook has figured out a way to track you even if you don't have a Facebook account!

RT News Reports: *"What is Facebook up to and why does it even effect people? Web developers expert Sander Venema joins me via Skype from the Netherlands. Sander, welcome back from going underground. So, what effect has Facebook done to trample on your European privacy laws?*

Sander Venema, Founder, Asteroid Interactive: *"Well, there was a report that was published by the Belgian Privacy Commission about Facebook's tracking behavior and more specifically the social pluckings that they use. These are the 'Like' buttons and 'Share' buttons that see millions of sites across the internet and these are loaded in from Facebook's domain that basically places a cookie, Facebook places a cookie on your computer, whenever those buttons are loaded in."*

RT News: *"So if you press 'Like' or one of the 'Like' buttons, which doesn't even have to be on your Facebook site, it can be anywhere, it could be asking your ideology or your political persuasion, it all gets stored on your computer and this is what the European regulators are worried about."*

Sander Venema: *"Actually, before you click 'Like", before the button is loaded in. You open a website, the 'Like' button is loaded in, before you even click on it the information goes to Facebook. Then Facebook places a uniquely identifying cookie on your computer which they subsequently use on all of their other sites with Facebook 'Like' buttons to map the sites that you visit."[4]*

So now I don't even have to have a Facebook account, I just have to run across any webpage that has a Facebook like button on it, which is basically everywhere, and I don't even have to click on it! Just being on a page with it…they're tracking me! So much for being anonymous! And whether you realize it or not, here's my point. I believe all this Social Media Technology is what the Antichrist and the False Prophet need to fulfill what they do in the 7-year Tribulation.

And the 1st **way** it does that is it **Prevents You From Running and Hiding**.

Revelation 13:15 "He was given power to give breath to the image of the first beast, so that it could speak and cause all who refused to worship the image to be killed."

So again, here we see the penalty for the people who choose not to worship the Antichrist in the 7-year Tribulation and notice what it was. You're going to die, right? Says it right there, plain as day! But my question is: Well, how in the world are you going to find these people? I mean we're talking on a global basis here. You know they're going to run and hide so how do you find them anywhere on the planet? Can you say Facebook? They're not only getting all this information on us with all this social media stuff, but it's called FACEbook for a reason! They're using our faces to not just market us, but to find us, even in a crowd!

Juju Chang, ABC News: *"Science Fiction almost got it right. Face recognition technology has become part of daily life. But instead of controlling security access to top security facilities, the knowledge is being used to identify them in that crazy picture from last week at the beach party. It all happens of course on Facebook, which has been quietly using face recognition software on every photo you upload."*

"Facebook knows me, it knows my friends, it tracks what I like, where I live, and knows my sisters are Christy and Laura, but now Facebook also knows my face

and everyone else's. Not just mine, if you are on Facebook, Facebook can recognize your face too. Here's how... While we keep uploading more than 20 billion photos, Facebook has been making file metric fingerprints of all our mugs and now Facebook has a massive collection of our faces, probably the largest collection in the world. Kinda cool, kinda creepy. Here's how it works. That's our intern, Brenda Williams."

Brenda Williams: *"I'm going to upload some photos of myself."*

"She's one of millions of people using this feature already. When Brenda uploads photos, Facebook recognizes her and her friends and says, 'Hey, that's you right?' Most of the time it is and tagging becomes almost automated. Face recognition technology has been around for awhile, mostly used by police. They even scanned people walking into the Super Bowl and caught 19 criminals. The guys at Face.com, in Israel, showed us how Facebook's technology works. They are the largest facial recognition company online. And once they had my photo the computer recognized me, no matter where I was every time.

Which got us at Nightline thinking. We would trick Facebook. We tried one other way to confuse the computer. I put on a fake mustache, hat and sunglasses and sent that photo to Face.com. And, yes, they recognized me in my cover-up. Which just goes to show, a disguise may fool your friends, but it probably won't fool Facebook."[5]

And it won't fool the Antichrist or the False Prophet in the 7-year Tribulation! Did you catch that one part, "Once they had my photo, the computer recognized me no matter where I was, every time." Which means...you can't run and hide!

Oh, but it gets even worse than that! So much so are they scanning our data and photos from us that they might not even wait for you to run and hide. Just like in the Tom Cruise movie, *Minority Report*, they can now even predict when you'll run and hide with a Pre-crime Unit and get you before it ever happens!

RT News: *"Most people are familiar with the plot of the Tom Cruise movie, Minority Report, the concept to have the ability to prevent a crime before they happen. Well, there is a new software system attempting to do something very* *much like that. Like forecasting the highest risk times and places for future crimes.*

'Accessed through any browser (fixed or mobile) on any internet-enabled device including tablet, smartphones, laptop and desktop computers, 'Beware' from Intrado searches, sorts and scores billions of commercial records in a matter of seconds, alerting responders to potentially deadly and dangerous situations while enroute to, or at the location of a call.'

Officers already have a lot of this information at their disposal, be it in their cruiser, on their laptop or a number of different data bases. What is unique about this particular technology?"

Derek A Smith, *Dir. Cybersecrity Initiatives, Excelsior College: "Well, with this, we've been doing this for years, data collection, intelligence gathering for years. Now we have the new technology to get it done much quicker and we have that technology right here at our hands. Right here at our hand so we can act quickly with it, to be more proactive with it instead of reactive as in the past."*

RT News: *"I was reading on 'Beware' today, about this particular technology and one thing that is unique and stood out to me is that the technology is actually scanning commercial, criminal, and social media information as well as any, quote, comments, that could be construed as offensive in order to be able to determine the threat score, then each suspect that the police are responding to is assessed through this technology, a threat score on different levels. Green, Yellow and Red, based on comments they made and the algorithms not only telling you the crime could exist but actually who is going to commit that crime."*

Derek A Smith: *"That is correct. They are trying to forecast on maybe your past behavior or what is seen on your social media and a change of behavior or things you are boasting about, and they say maybe this person is going to perpetrate a crime in the future. Then they want prevention from the police officer."[6]*

In other words, they come and round you up because they know you're not worshiping the Antichrist and you plan on running and hiding! This is crazy! Go back to our text in Revelation 13. For the first time in man's history, I believe the question is solved! How in the world are you going to find people all over the planet who refuse to worship the Antichrist and how are you going to find these resisters and take them out and kill them? Simple, the technology is already here through social media to know where you run and hide and if you even plan on running and hiding! There is no chance to escape, just in time for the 7-year Tribulation!

The **2ⁿᵈ way** this Social Media Technology helps the Antichrist and the False Prophet fulfill what they need to do in the 7-year Tribulation is **You Can't Buy or Sell**.

Revelation 13:16-17 "He also forced everyone, small and great, rich and poor, free and slave, to receive a mark on his right hand or on his forehead, so that no one could buy or sell unless he had the mark, which is the name of the beast or the number of his name."

So now we see the penalty for those who not only choose not to worship the Antichrist, but who choose not to receive the Mark of the Beast. And notice the penalty. You're not going to be able to buy or sell. You're going to be shut out of the system. Says it right there, plain as day! And so again, that's the question: How in the world are you going to shut people out, all around the world, of this system you built that controls all the buying and selling? Again, we're talking on a global basis here. Can you say Facebook? They're not only getting all this information on us to know who we are, where we are, what we're going to do, but they're also using it to determine if we can get a job! You know, the thing we need to buy and sell!

CTV News: *"We live in an information age and many people comment and put photos on social media daily. If that is you or someone you know, you should know about a new survey.*

Yes, 60% of employers say they check a person's social media background before hiring and what you post could prevent you from getting a job. Pat Foran has the story on Consumer Alert."

Pat Foran: *"The new survey from 'Career Builder' found that 60% of employers will not hire someone until they research how they appear on social media sites like Facebook and Twitter. The findings are similar to a recent study made by Workopolis, Canada's largest online job board that connects companies and job seekers. Marsha Forde says many people don't realize that what they put on the web is often there for everyone to see."*

Marsha Forde: "*You would be surprised at the number of people who don't put restrictions high on their Facebook profile allowing just about anybody to see details of their social media life.*"

Pat Foran: "*Workopolis found 63% of companies check social media before hiring and 48% of the companies saw something that caused them not to hire.*

Reasons they didn't hire:

Excessive Drinking or drug use; Profanities, racist or sexist comments; Suggestive/provocative photos; Negative comments about previous employers.

Always think before you post.

Marsha Forde: "*Be mindful for today. Be mindful of what you are posting. Because it will have an impact on your career if you don't.*"

Pat Foran: "*And many employers are turned off of a person if they look angry in the profile picture. They are more receptive to a someone who is kind and smiling. So, a picture is not just worth a thousand words it could help you get a job too.*"[7]

In other words, you won't get that job to buy and sell unless you smile, real big, look happy at all times, obey! Can you believe this? Talk about George Orwell 1984! I mean what's next, you not only get a threat score with all this social media database information, but a social score to determine whether or not you can buy or sell in the first place? Exactly! And believe it or not, China is already implementing that!

CBS This Morning: "*By 2020 China plans to give all of its 1.4 billion citizens a personal score on how they behave. So, some people with low scores are already being punished if they want to travel. Nearly 11 million Chinese people could no longer fly and 4 million are barred from trains. Next week the program will start expanding nationwide. Ben Tracy is in China with what is behind the governments scoring system. Ben, this sounds like scary stuff. Good Morning.*"

Ben Tracy: "*Good Morning, the government here said they are trying to purify society by awarding those who are trustworthy and punishing those who are not. So, like the credit score Americans get for how they handle their finances,*

Chinese citizens are now getting social credit scores based on whether they pay their taxes on time or how they cross the street."

When Leo Hu recently tried to book a flight, he was told he was banned from flying because he was on the list of untrustworthy people. Leo is a journalist who was ordered by court to apologize for a series of tweets he wrote and was then told that his apology was insincere.

Leo Hu: *"I can't buy property, my child can't go to private school, you feel like you are being controlled by the list all the time.*

Ben Tracy: *"And the list is now getting longer as every Chinese citizen is being assigned a social credit score. A fluctuating rating based on your behavior. It's believed that community service and buying Chinese made products can raise your score. Fraud, tax evasion, and smoking in non-smoking areas can drop it. If a score gets too low a person can be banned from buying plane and train tickets, real estate, cars, and high-speed internet.*

Now there are upsides for people that the Chinese government consider trustworthy. They can get better interest rates at banks, they can get discounts on their energy bills, and China's online dating site reportedly even boosts the profile for people with high social credit scores."[8]

Wow! So, I can get an extra super-duper spouse if I just do what I'm told, not to mention I can buy and sell a car, or house, or have a bank account from people who are monitoring everything I do, on a massive scale. Not coming in the 7-year Tribulation, but already here on a nationwide scale, the largest populated nation on the planet, China! Do you think that's by chance? No way! I believe China is the testing ground to bring this type of totalitarian regime across the whole planet! You put all this together and it sure looks to me like we have the ability for the first time in mankind's history, for one man and his cohort to not only monitor everything and everyone on the whole planet, but to also force them anywhere on the planet to do whatever they say to do. Otherwise they will be rounded up and killed or not be able to buy or sell without their permission. Where have I heard that before? Oh yeah, Revelation 13 warned about that 2,000 years ago as a sign you're living in the last days!

That's precisely why, out of love, God has given us this update on **The Final Countdown: Tribulation Rising** concerning **Modern Technology & the**

AI Invasion to show us that the Tribulation is near and the 2nd Coming of Jesus Christ is rapidly approaching. And that's why Jesus Himself said:

Luke 21:28 "When these things begin to take place, stand up and lift up your heads, because your redemption is drawing near."

Like it or not, we are headed for **The Final Countdown**. The signs of the 7-year **Tribulation** are **Rising**! Wake up! The point is this. If you're a Christian today and you're not doing anything for the Lord, shame on you! Get busy doing something for Jesus now! Stop wasting your life! We need you! Don't sit on the sidelines! Get on the front line and help us! Let's get busy working together doing something splendid for Jesus with what time is left and get busy saving souls! Amen?

But if you're reading this today and you're not a Christian, then I beg you, please, heed these signs, heed these warnings, give your life to Jesus now because this Monitoring System of the Antichrist and the False Prophet is not going to lead to a life beyond your wildest dreams, Jesus said it's going to become mankind's greatest nightmare! Don't fall for the lie! Take the way out now, the only way out now, through Jesus Christ, and avoid the whole thing, before it's too late! Amen?

Chapter Nine

The Increase of Big Brother Satellites

The **2nd type of big brother surveillance system** they've already put into place is the **Satellite System**.

That's right, I'm talking about the Big Brother Eye in the Sky that's watching us all the time, 24/7! You see, apparently, just to make sure that we're always under the careful, ever watchful eye of Big Brother, they're not only storing a massive amount of database information on us right now as we speak, but they're even monitoring our every move with cameras from above, and unfortunately, it's going to lead to a horrible slaughter in the 7-year Tribulation! But don't take my word for it. Let's listen to God's.

Matthew 24:15-22 "So when you see standing in the holy place the abomination that causes desolation, spoken of through the prophet Daniel – let the reader understand – then let those who are in Judea flee to the mountains. Let no one on the roof of his house go down to take anything out of the house. Let no one in the field go back to get his cloak. How dreadful it will be in those days for pregnant women and nursing mothers! Pray that your flight will not take place in winter or on the Sabbath. For then there will be great distress, unequaled from the beginning of the world until now –and never to be equaled again. If those days had not been cut short, no one would survive, but for the sake of the elect those days will be shortened."

168

Now, according to our text, the Bible clearly says that during the 7-year Tribulation, after the Antichrist shows his true colors and goes into the rebuilt Jewish temple to declare himself to be god, the abomination of desolation that was spoken of by the Prophet Daniel, and that's what Jesus is referring to here, what's going to happen at that time? What does Jesus tell the people to do? He said you need to be fleeing, right? You need to get out of there in quick flight, right? Why? Because other passages tell us that Antichrist is going on a hunting spree at that time! He's going to be hunting people down and killing them! It's going to lead to another horrible Holocaust, starting with the Jewish people.

Zechariah 13:8-9 "In the whole land, declares the Lord, two-thirds will be struck down and perish; yet one-third will be left in it. This third I will bring into the fire; I will refine them like silver and test them like gold. They will call on my name and I will answer them; I will say, they are my people, and they will say, The Lord is our God."

So here we have some good news/bad news going on in this text. The good news is that the Jewish people finally turn back to God at this point. But the bad news is that it comes at a horrible price! Just the Jewish people alone, two-thirds of them are going to die at the hands of the Antichrist and only one-third are going to be left. Another horrible Jewish Holocaust is coming, the Bible is unfortunately very clear about that. But that's just the tip of the iceberg when it comes to the slaughter that the Antichrist is going to be a part of during the 7-year Tribulation. A massive amount of people are going to die during that time frame!

Revelation 6:3-4,7-8 "When the Lamb opened the second seal, I heard the second living creature say, 'Come!' Then another horse came out, a fiery red one. Its rider was given power to take peace from the earth and to make men slay each other. To him was given a large sword. When the Lamb opened the fourth seal, I heard the voice of the fourth living creature say, 'Come!' I looked, and there before me was a pale horse! Its rider was named Death, and Hades was following close behind him. They were given power over a fourth of the earth to kill by sword, famine and plague, and by the wild beasts of the earth."

So here we see after the first seal is opened, the second seal is opened, and a global war breaks out that the Antichrist is a part of. Just to give you an idea of how big that number really is, if this war were to break out today, the death toll would be over 1.8 billion people! Nearly 2 billion people are going to die in this war in the first half of the 7-year Tribulation! How many of you would say that's pretty bad? But that's still not all! The Bible says another third of the planet is going to be wiped out after that in the second half of the 7-year Tribulation.

Revelation 9:15 "And the four angels, who had been prepared for the hour and day and month and year, were released, so that they would kill a third of mankind."

So here we see yet another slaughter! One third of the earth is going to die in this battle! And if you subtract this number from the first slaughter, this is going to be another 1.8 billion! Interesting math, when you bust out the calculator! So that means, just in these two judgments alone, 3.6 billion people, about half of our current planet, are going to die, not even counting the second unfortunate Jewish Holocaust. And here's the point. No wonder Jesus said it's going to be the worst time in mankind's history! And no wonder there's an urgency to accept Him now so you can avoid the whole thing. And no wonder Jesus said for those who unfortunately rejected Him and found themselves in this horrible timeframe, in the 7-year Tribulation, that your only option is to flee, right? Remember what He said? You better make flight, you better run, you better flee, and you better do it fast! Don't go back into your house, don't go to your workplace, don't get anything, just get out of there now, right? Why? Because a horrible slaughter's coming! Half the population of the planet is going to be annihilated!

And here's my point. I believe this satellite system that they've already put into place is going to help them get the job done! Whether you realize it or not, right now, Big Brother not only knows everything we do, everything we say, everything we think with this information system we saw last time, but they've even developed a system that monitors everywhere we go with satellites. Right now, we are "secretly" being monitored anytime, anywhere, on the whole planet, 24 hours a day, 7 days a week, with satellites! And I'm not talking just about the military satellites that have been going on for a long time, many decades, from a multitude of countries, including our own! I'm just talking about the plethora of satellites orbiting our planet right now from businesses, private entities, scientists, you name it, 24 hours a day, 7 days a week, they're monitoring our planet live! In fact, here's one system they put together called Live Earth!

"Live Earth is a real time mapping platform for visualizing time series data and live data streams. Live Earth delivers real time situational awareness to help organizations make time critical data driven decisions leveraging information from different sources. Live Earth helps correlate events and uncover patterns and trends by synchronizing weather radar, traffic conditions, connecting cars, transportation sensors, video management systems, shock detection sensors, and more.

This touch screen software is built with an intuitive interface that requires little or no training because it borrows concepts from your smart phone and tablet like pinch and zoom maps in an interactive timeline like you used to record and play your favorite TV shows. Live Earth also provides instant replay which lets you play, pause, and rewind that special data over time. To quickly reconstruct recent scenarios.

Live Earth is configurable and extensible allowing you to add and remove data sources, live feed, and app players to suit your operational needs. Live Earth's advanced visualization delivers the right information at the right time helping you make the right decisions. With Live Earth you can see all your streaming data in one place to quickly understand what's happening and act fast when it matters most."[1]

Yeah, you know, like when somebody tries to run and hide when an order's given to worship the Antichrist…anyone feeling like a caged rat? But how many of you had any idea that this was going on as you read this? As you saw, the whole planet is being watched live in minute detail! And did you catch that one part, apparently it's being recorded live as well because you can even stop, fast forward, rewind, just like a DVR from the sky and see what went on at any time just in case you missed it! In fact, and again, I'm not just talking military satellites, but we have so many satellites monitoring our every move from the sky, that they even have apps to see just how many are monitoring you at any given time!

All about Android Reports: *"So summertime calls for warm nights out back yards, hopefully not too much light pollution, and while you are just looking up at the stars, to see what's going on up there, what you see might not be a star but actually a satellite. And if you want to figure out what satellite is flying over you, there's an app for that. This app is called 'Satellite Tracker.'*

You select how you would like to search for a satellite. You can search by radius, you can search by a globe mechanism, you can search by satellite name, if you know the name of the satellite you would like to find, or you can do a map search. It will search wherever you want it to. So, we are going to use that one. We are going to figure out what is flying over us right now. If anything. As you can see this is a map of the world. If I zoom into the United States and zoom in just above San Francisco, Santa Rosa, there are several overhead and I will just pick this one. As I confirm this point a large circle shows the coverage. You can expand how much of the radius you want, confirm the category and all those satellites are above us right now.''[2]

And notice they're moving in real time, tracking your every move, and most people have no clue this is going on, and there's a ton of them! In fact, that's still the tip of the iceberg. Here's a photo from the ESA or European Space Agency showing just how many satellites are up there! It's a little crowded, don't you think? It's crazy!

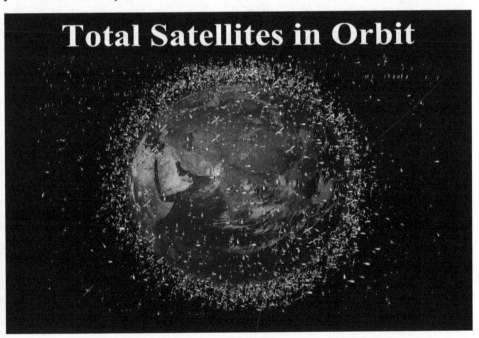

Again, are you starting to feel like a caged rat being watched? The satellites I'm talking about today are not even the military ones. But it's now common knowledge, as we've seen in previous chapters, that this kind of tracking system is already being used to monitor the locations of, yes, of military personnel, but also boat traffic around the world. Garbage men in England are being watched right now from the sky on their jobs in order to make sure that they don't linger in one spot too long! In fact, England is even using satellites to measure the speed of motorists from space! You don't have a radar detector on earth for that one! They're also monitoring farming land in Australia, not to mention around the world, right now, for food production and crop yields. And even here in America, satellites are being used by state governments to search for unreported improvements that might increase property taxes, to check for water-use permits, find improper tree cutting and even seeing whether or not you turned your lights off on your house to conserve energy. Yeah, Go Green Deal! In fact, many of these different companies have launched satellites around the earth that specifically pick up and track signals from the chips in your phones, not to mention other kinds of microchips. For instance, Motorola a couple decades ago launched 66 low-orbiting satellites that have that capability.

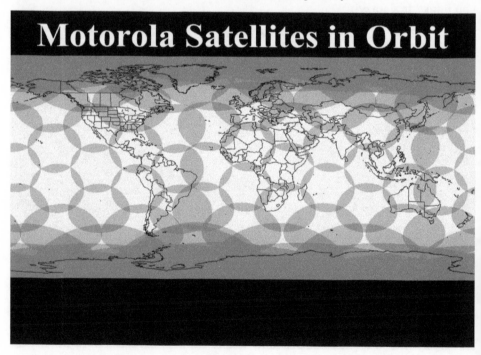

This is their live animated satellite coverage photo of not just a single satellite, but all 66 satellites that as you can see provide continuous coverage of the whole planet all at the same time! They call them satellite constellations.

Groupings of satellites that cover the whole planet simultaneously! So, think of this scenario. Here you have a system of satellites that continuously monitor the planet all at the same time for microchips, and imagine in some horrible future timeframe scenario like the 7-year Tribulation, and for those who unfortunately take the Mark of the Beast, which might also be some type of microchip device, then can you imagine what the Antichrist could do with all this? If you ever tried to disobey or flee, there's no place to hide on the whole planet! These satellites are tracking the whole planet all at the same time in one continuous feed, they'll find that microchip! And again, that's just Motorola's setup! That's not all the companies. That's not even counting the military's!

There's not just one satellite that you can avoid for a short period of time while it does its flyby and you're free and clear. It's a continuous monitoring from a multitude of satellites. There is no gap in monitoring! There is no way to escape this satellite system already put into place! And so, you might be asking the question, "Well how in the world did we get into this kind of monitoring system? Are we literally being monitored from the sky like a bunch of caged rats?" Well once again, like with any other Big Brother type technology, we've been conditioned to accept it slowly but surely.

The **1ˢᵗ way** we've been conditioned to accept this Big Brother monitoring from the sky with satellites is they say **It's For Our Own Good**.

Yeah, right! But speaking of our own supposed good, of all people, Bill Gates, Mr. Population Control himself is funding a Satellite System called Earth Now that watches the whole planet now, all at the same time!

"Imagine ... you can see Earth like an astronaut and have the freedom to look where you want, when you want. Introducing 'EarthNow.' A constellation of 500 satellites viewing Earth in real-time, all the time. Equipped with extensive on-board processing to intelligently observe Earth with spot view imagers, four high resolution cameras, and a global view imager, capturing ultra-wide-angle video. Real-time monitoring of high-value assets.

You can follow migrating whales, catch illegal fishing in the act, observe and measure volcanic eruptions and constantly watch hurricanes. You would be able to detect fires the instant they start, enhance news reporting, help cities be smarter and assess crop health on demand. We will connect you visually with your Earth now. Download the app on your smart phone, your tablet, your laptop, use it in the educational system, or as you drive in your car. Earth Now. "[3]

Yeah, Earth Now, being monitored 24 hours a day 7 days a week from the sky with 500 satellites in real time! Thanks Bill Gates! Of all things for you to work on! What are you up to? But don't worry, this is all for your good! It can find those whales lost in the ocean, capture those illegal poachers, detect those forest fires, and of course, watch over your city for your own good. And just to prove this is really for your good, we'll give you access to it! Who cares! So, what! That's like giving a rat in the cage its own webcam to watch himself! Yeah, he's free alright! Free to watch himself not be free! But that's not all.

The **2nd way** we've been conditioned to accept this Big Brother monitoring from the sky with satellites is they say **It's For Our Own Convenience**.

I mean, haven't you heard of GPS? Isn't that convenient? Everybody uses it! And depends on it! In fact, here's a list of all the different uses for it!

1. Location - determining a position
2. Navigation - getting from one location to another
3. Tracking - monitoring objects or personal movement
4. Mapping - creating maps of the world
5. Timing - bringing precise timing to the world

And that's really needed if you're going to run the Rat Race in your rat cage of life. But isn't this great? With all these GPS satellites monitoring us at all times we can never get lost, always find that loved one no matter where they are, have a map of the whole earth, and of course have accurate time! And that's just one way companies are pushing this satellite coverage under the guise of personal convenience. Another one is Google. Google has already gone on record saying, "We want to be like the mind of God," but apparently, when you look at their other technologies, they also want to, "Be like the eye of God!" Watching everything! Google is not only buying up satellite companies right and left, but they've been doing so for many years, and supposedly it's to provide us with great personal conveniences like Google Maps. Let's see how that works.

Trace Dominguez D News Reports: "*Hey you, I can see you over there. 'Where' you ask. Everywhere, because I can just pull it up on a satellite.*

Hey gang, it's me Trace here from D News, there was a time when satellites were conspiracy talk. Only available to high level government officials, like spies. But thanks to Google Maps and Apple Maps, and Bing Maps, and Map Quest, and dozens of others out there we can see satellite images every day for free. I use it to find the nearest Thai restaurant usually.

When Google acquired their satellite imaging company in 2004 that changed the whole game. Anyone could look down on the planet and make comments. Today the actual satellite images are taken by companies like Tele-Atlas, Digital Globe, Earth Sat, Skybox and others. They are then sold or licensed to governments and companies for geology, mapping, urban planning, and shipment tracking. The applications are pretty much endless.

A few months ago, regulators loosened restrictions on U.S. based digital globe so last week they launched the new World View-3 satellite. Their highest resolution satellite ever. Which means, in a few weeks, maps could see resolutions as high as 25 centimeters. Basically, they will be able to see a piece of paper you are holding. They want to launch satellites with a 10-centimeter resolution, about the size of your phone screen."[4]

Well hey, wait a second, I thought you told me this was for my own personal convenience to provide maps. Why would you want to have that kind of resolution? You're not doing something sneaky, are you? Yeah, their true colors come out in another service they have called Google Earth. Not just Google Maps but Google Earth, what does that tell you? And now they not only want to monitor and map all the streets on the Earth, but the whole Earth itself, all at the same time, in 3D!

This is Earth, all 196.9 million square miles of it. Google Maps is for finding your way. Google Earth is about getting lost. Google Earth is the biggest repository of GO imagery, most photo realistic digital version of our planet. We're trying to create a mirror world and go anywhere. From mountains, to cities, to the bottom of the ocean, the imagery has been getting better and better. I was really curious to know how Google Earth was created. How many images actually make it up. And where do they come from.

So how did we build Google Earth? The way it starts is we look at places that we want to collect imagery. And we collect it through a variety of different ways. One is satellites, satellites give you the global views. That's all 2D imagery that is wrapped around the globe. When we get close to the ground, we get 3D data that we collect from planes.

Yes, you heard right, planes. I had always assumed that every overhead photo of the earth, that I had seen was taken by satellite. I learned creating 3D imagery required special conditions. So, Google fly's planes, or as I like to think of them, street view cars with wings. A typical flight to take photos is around 5 hours except the planes aren't going around the country they are making little zig-zags over the area.

So, it's north, then south, sort of like mowing a lawn. This pattern helps the photos overlap and multiple cameras help to capture a place from different angles. There might be five different cameras, one looking down, and the other four looking forward, right, back, and left. This allows them to make a definite map. And that is just our understanding of how far the things are from the camera. We take all these various apps from the different cameras, stitch them together for what's called a mesh which is a big 3D reconstruction of the place, we texture it, the texture is applied to the photography that we took to the sides of these 3D buildings. We did a collection of Yosemite National Park and we were able to capture that in high-fidelity with all the bends that a rock face might have.

We use this product called Earth Engine that allows you to look at all of this data and using computer vision, draw out insights from the things that are changing so we can track deforestation in the Amazon because we can see how the trees are changing, shrinking and growing, and then from that we can generate a heat map of the most logged places on the planet. We can also do that with fishing to see the most over fished areas.

And you can keep multiplying this, all the different levels of zoom that exist in Google Earth which are over twenty. Using Earth feels like one seamless world that you are just zipping around. Think about it as a health monitor for the planet"[5]

What? What's that got to do with maps? A "Health Monitor" for the planet? Who do you think you are Google? God? You not only want to be the mind of God, but you really want to be like the eye of God apparently. In fact, they've already gone on record saying, they have intentions of "surveying the globe by taking pictures of the entire planet three times a day" Including video footage. "We'll be counting the ships, cars, shipping containers and trucks that move around our world on a daily basis." Not to mention people. In fact, here's a screenshot of just one article exposing this. "Google's Satellites Could Soon See Your Face from Space."

Google will soon have an unprecedented ability to spy on you from space with hyper-detailed photos and videos of the globe. Now here's the point. So much for fleeing in some horrible timeframe like the 7-year Tribulation when an order is given to worship the Antichrist who just declared himself to be god. You

Google Sees Face from Space

Google's Satellites Could Soon See Your Face from Space

Google's hired eyes in the sky will soon be able to make out "manholes and mailboxes." What else?

have no place to hide! And we just thought it was about personal convenience, you know, maps!

Which leads us to the **3rd way** we've been conditioned to accept this Big Brother monitoring from the sky with satellites is, they say **It's For Our Own Protection**.

Now, did you catch that part about Google using planes? We've already been conditioned to see those Google street cars everywhere taking photos of us.

Google Street View Car

But who knew about the planes? Well, believe it or not, they're not the only ones using planes to monitor us! A lot of agencies have been doing it for years including with drones! Buy hey, don't worry, it's all for your protection! Yeah, right! In fact, this is not only going on, but they're using drones and planes to monitor whole cities from the sky all at once. They call them Persistence Surveillance Systems and they monitor whole cities from the air. From Dayton, to Compton, and even Baltimore.

Ross of Persistent Surveillance Systems: *"There was a shooting on Gilmore Street yesterday. Lawrence and Preston, there was a shooting on that. I think there was a murder just one street over."*

Reporter: *"Ross is not a morbid news junkie. The reason he knows about all these shootings is because he saw them happen. In fact, he can bear witness to almost 18,000 crimes over the past few months. Right now, he is pulling into a parking lot in West Baltimore to show us how he sees it all."*

Ross: *"They got us."* As he walks across the parking lot looking at his phone.

Reporter: *"What, you just got a text?"* "That text had come from Ross's office, miles away in downtown Baltimore."

Back at his office he asks, *"Hey, Alek, what's going on?"*

Alek shows him on the screen, *"This is where you were in the parking lot."*

Reporter: *"It was taken from a plane we could just barely see off in the distance while we were there. The camera wasn't pointed at us specifically. The plane was taking a picture of the entire 30-mile-wide radius of West Baltimore. That is one 30-mile image every second, all day, every day. And that is what it takes to witness 18,000 crimes."*

Ross: *"We do wide area surveillance; we watch cities at a time and assist law enforcement in lower crime rates. We are essentially Google Earth Live with TEVO capabilities that allows us to follow people to and from crime scenes."*

Reporter: *"Here's how it works. Ross and his team listen to emergency calls and police scanners to find the time and place of reported crimes. They go to the live feed that their plane is sending down and start to scroll back and forth through time to actually see the crime take place."*

Ross: *"So right here you can actually see two cars that match the description from the 911 calls. We are going to follow those cars and see if we can find the final location that they go to. We will also follow them backward in time to see if we can figure out where they came from."*

Reporter: *"When Ross has enough information, he compiles a report, hands it off to the Baltimore Police and then it's off to the next crime."*

Ross: *"We started off in Philadelphia, at one point we did operations here in Baltimore, previously, we had operations in Indianapolis and Compton, Nogales (Mexico) Torreon, (Mexico) Charlotte, and we hope to be here forever."*[6]

Excuse me? Forever? Well, that's certainly enough time to make it into the 7-year Tribulation where this is going to come in handy for the Antichrist. Especially when people try to run and hide during some horrible timeframe!

But hey, don't worry, it's all for your protection! They say, "It allows them to catch criminals in the act." and "track crimes." For instance, in one case, "We tracked a criminal as he approached a woman, grabbed her jewelry, and then ran to a getaway car. This technology watches 10,000 times the area that a police helicopter could watch." And we've all been conditioned to accept that too! What's the big deal? It's for our protection! They're using it to catch those bad guys! But that's just it! What if you became the bad guy, and who gets to define that anyway? That's the problem! But again, this monitoring from the sky is not only being done with planes but drones, including those little drones we saw before called Micro Aerial Vehicles or MAV's. Those tiny little drones that can not only be miniaturized but made to look like nature so you'd never know it was a drone! Including a bug! In fact, Hollywood is already helping us to see what this technology can do.

Movie clip from 'Eye in the Sky"

"The soldier takes out his cell phone and opens it up, then he takes out a pack of what looks like cigarettes. But when he opens the pack there is a big black bug inside. He takes the bug out and places it on the cell phone, closes the cigarette box and proceeds. He pushes a button on his phone and the bug, which looks like a beetle, starts to spread its wings and fly. The soldier is watching what is going on across the street.

There are people walking back and forth and a lady is selling bread out of her wagon. He pushes another button on his phone and the beetle flies towards the window of the building across the street. While this is going on a person at headquarters is watching this on the screen. She can see everything through the camera that is inside the beetle. The beetle is a drone, a very small drone. There are other top officials also watching from another location.

They are waiting to see if a wanted terrorist is inside the building. The beetle flies through the door and lands on a beam in the ceiling of the building and faces who is in the room. At this point they know who is there and what they are doing without any of the occupants having the slightest idea that they are being observed."[7]

Doesn't that bug you? It bugs me! Actual technology that Hollywood is depicting, not coming, but already here! And as we saw before, carries a payload that can take people out as well! Now here's my point. Stir all this together and here's what you get. Go back to our opening text. The Bible says in the 7-year Tribulation, after the Antichrist shows his true colors and declares himself to be god, the abomination of desolation, that was spoken of by the Prophet Daniel, there's going to be a horrible slaughter. He's going on a hunting spree! And Jesus says don't go back to your house, don't worry about your cloak, just get out of there now, quick, flee, run, just get out of there in hurry! Why? Because a massive amount of people are going to die! They're not going to make it! Maybe it's because of all this satellite technology that scours the planet monitoring people, including people with microchips, combined with this drone technology. And I think you might have your answer for the first time in the history of mankind! That slaughter might look something like this!

Clip from "Slaughterbots'

"Pilots directed almost three thousand precision strikes last year. We are super proud of it. It allows you to separate the bad guys from the good. It's a big deal. But we have something much bigger. Your kids probably have one of these, right?" He is talking about the tiny drone that is flying around his head.

"Not quite. Skill of a pilot? No, that skill is AI. It's flying itself. Its processor can react one hundred times faster than a human. The stochastic motion is an anti-sniper feature. Just like your mobile device these days, it has camera and sensors, and just like your phones and social media apps it does facial recognition. Inside here are three grams of shaped explosive. This is how it works." He turns it loose out over the audience and it flies back to the manikin that is standing on the stage and flies right into the head causing a big hole and the death of the manikin, if it were alive.

"Did you see that? That little bang is enough to penetrate the skull and destroy the contents. They used to say, guns don't kill people, people do, well, people don't. They get emotional, disobey orders, aim too high. Let's watch the weapons make the decisions. No trust me, these are all bad guys." The video shows some guys breaking into a car to steal it. But they didn't get very far because the drones saw what they were doing and took them all out.

"Now that was an airstrike of surgical precision. It's one of a range of products. Trained as a team they can penetrate buildings, cars, trains, invade people, bullets, pretty much any counter measure. They cannot be stopped. Now I said this was big. Why? Because we are thinking big. Watch... a twenty-five-million-

dollar order now buys this." On the screen you see a plane that opens the back-cargo door and thousands of these drones fly out.

"Enough to kill half a city. The bad half. Nuclear is obsolete. Take out your entire enemy. Virtually risk free. Just characterize them, release the swarm, and the rest is easy. These are available now. We have a distribution network taking orders from military, law enforcement, and specialist clients."

DN Reports on the latest attack on the Senate, *"The nation is still recovering from yesterday's incident which officials are describing as some sort of automated attack which killed 11 U.S. senators in the Capitol Building."*

One Senator reports: *'They flew in from everywhere and attacked just one side of the aisle. It was chaos, people were screaming.'*

DN Reports: *"You can see high windows, precisely small punctures to gain entry to the building."*

Another Senator: *"I just did what I could for him, the things weren't even interested in me. They were just buzzing around."*

DN Reports: *"Sources have admitted that the intelligence community has no idea who perpetrated the attack." "Relaxing fire legislation would be useless against these so-called 'slaughterbots." "Stay away from crowds, when indoors, keep your windows covered with ... protect your families, stay inside,"*

While the kids are in school, they start to hear some noises hitting the walls outside. The slaughterbots are flying right through the walls and into the classrooms. The students start running to try to get away, calling their parents to say good-bye.

DN News: *"Authorities are still trying to make sense of an attack on 12 university campus's worldwide of which 8,300 students have been killed, and why they targeted some students and not others."*[8]

You know, like those who will worship that Antichrist and those who won't. This technology is not coming, but already here, just in time for the horrible slaughter Jesus warned about in the 7-year Tribulation! But that's precisely why, out of love, God has given us this update on **The Final**

Countdown: Tribulation Rising concerning **Modern Technology & the AI Invasion** to show us that the Tribulation is near and the 2nd Coming of Jesus Christ is rapidly approaching. And that's why Jesus Himself said:

Luke 21:28 "When these things begin to take place, stand up and lift up your heads, because your redemption is drawing near."

Like it or not, we are headed for **The Final Countdown**. The signs of the 7-year **Tribulation** are **Rising**! Wake up! And so, the point is this. If you're a Christian today and you're not doing anything for the Lord, shame on you! Get busy doing something for Jesus now! Stop wasting your life! We need you! Don't sit on the sidelines! Get on the front line and help us! Let's get busy working together doing something splendid for Jesus with what time is left and get busy saving souls! Amen?

But if you're reading this today and you're not a Christian, then I beg you, please, heed these signs, heed these warnings, give your life to Jesus now because this monitoring system of the Antichrist and the False Prophet is not going to lead to a life of good times & personal convenience but a system that allows them to have targeted assassinations! Don't fall for the lie! Take the way out now, the only way out now, through Jesus Christ, and avoid the whole thing, before it's too late! Amen?

Chapter Ten

The Increase of Big Brother Cities & Streets

The **3rd type of big brother surveillance system** they've already put into place is the **Camera System**.

That's right, we're now talking about the Big Brother eye on the ground that's watching us as well, all the time, 24/7! Believe it or not, they're not only storing a massive amount of database information on us right now as we speak and monitoring our every move with cameras from above, but now even cameras down below. And I mean everywhere! And I believe it's the same kind of "secretive" behavior the Bible says the Antichrist is going to use in the last days. In fact, the Bible says it's already at work behind the scenes. But don't take my word for it. Let's listen to God's.

2 Thessalonians 2:1-8 "Concerning the coming of our Lord Jesus Christ and our being gathered to Him, we ask you, brothers, not to become easily unsettled or alarmed by some prophecy, report or letter supposed to have come from us, saying that the day of the Lord has already come. Don't let anyone deceive you in any way, for that day will not come until the rebellion occurs and the man of lawlessness is revealed, the man doomed to destruction. He will oppose and will exalt himself over everything that is called God or is worshiped, so that he sets himself up in God's temple, proclaiming himself to be God. Don't you remember that when I was with you, I used to tell you these things? And now you know what is holding him back, so that he may be revealed at the proper time. For the secret power of lawlessness is already at work; but the one who now holds it back will continue to do so till he is taken out of the way. And then the lawless one will be revealed, whom the Lord Jesus will overthrow with the breath of His mouth and destroy by the splendor of His coming."

So here we see the Apostle Paul comforting the Thessalonians from a misconception going around apparently at that time by some false teachers saying these Christians missed the Rapture. That the Day of the Lord had already come, which starts at the 7-year Tribulation. But Paul says No! Christians are not going to be around during the 7-year Tribulation and he's emphatic about it! He says the Day of the Lord does not come until the rebellion occurs and the Antichrist is revealed which happens the moment he makes a covenant with the Jewish people, the very event that starts the 7-yearTribulation, **Daniel 9:27**. That's why he says: "Don't be deceived." Don't you remember I already told you this? Why are you falling for this? Hello! You can't be there! Christians are nowhere around in the 7-year Tribulation! We leave prior at the Rapture! So, don't freak out and listen to these false teachers! But he does mention something about the Antichrist that is already here, right now today! And that's the phrase, "The secret power of lawlessness of the Antichrist, is already at work." In other words, the wicked intent of the Antichrist to overthrow God in the future, during the 7-year Tribulation, is already here. The machinery is already being put into place. Now, the embodiment of the Antichrist hasn't come yet, as he says, but the machinery behind the scenes, if you will, is being built as we speak. And I believe the key word there is "secret power." It's the Greek word, "musterion" which means, "a secret or something hidden from us."

And believe it or not, much of this Antichrist's Big Brother global monitoring system is doing just that. It's being "secretly" worked on behind the scenes and "hidden from us," "secretly" being put into play and monitoring us. Again, not just Big Brother Eye in the Sky with satellites, but the Big Brother Eye on the Ground with cameras. It's called CCTV, which you might as well call it Antichrist TV, but it's the term they use to speak of the constant non-stop 24/7 video monitoring of us or video surveillance of you and I whether we realize it or not! Why? Well, thanks in part to Executive Orders, under the guise of "terrorism" and other so-called "bad guy" reasons, the government now has full authority to utilize all kinds of new surveillance technology on us. Not a foreign entity, us! And one of the biggest ways they're doing that is by installing cameras literally wherever we go! And I mean everywhere!

And the **1ˢᵗ way** they're doing that is in **Cities**.

Whether you realize it or not, right now, cities across the world are secretly being monitored with video cameras watching our every move, starting with the UK. Right now, in the UK, there are around 6 million cameras in the government, private sector, businesses, you name it, they're everywhere. ATM's, elevators, hospital rooms, hotel rooms, just about everywhere you can think of. It's called a virtual "surveillance canopy" and it's pretty much common knowledge to the average Britain. One person said this:

"So dense is the network that in many urban areas people may be monitored from the moment they step out of their front door and be kept under observation on their way to work, in the office, and even in a restaurant if they choose to dine out. Over the course of a day they could be filmed by 300 cameras. The latest figures show that, in cities, people are captured on film at least once every five minutes."

In fact, this system has been in place for so long and the people have rolled over and accepted it, that now they want to take it to the next level and now even monitor your every move including other forms of media.

RT News Reports: *"Did you ever feel like someone's watching you? Well, if you are a U.K. citizen the government is attempting to step up its public surveillance policy and snooping on your own personal emails. Despite CCTV cameras already a major fact in U.K. life there, it now plans to store personal data including information from social networking."*

"Soon you could be watched everywhere you go in the U.K., even where the camera can't see you. All your emails, texts, and phone calls will be monitored under a new Terrorist Spy Plan. The government will know which web sites you visit, and it will even sneak on your private Facebook messages. No matter who you are, all your personal data will be stored for a year in a massive surveillance operation privacy campaign.

Britain is already one of the most watched societies in the world. Now the government wants to monitor all communication as well, including social media. Taking surveillance to a level never seen before. The government will know exactly who you speak to, when you do it and where you are. Security services will have real time access at the click of a button. Secretly living your life with you. "[1]

Well, that's exciting! Talk about a rat in a cage. What did he say? Secretly (there's your word again) living your life with you? But at first you accepted cameras, did you really think it was going to stop there? Not even close! You opened up Pandora's Box! Or should I say Big Brother box! But hey, maybe that's just the UK. I mean surely, that would never happen here in the U.S., would it? I mean, we love freedom. Well, guess what? It's already here! The UK has an estimated 6 million cameras, we have an estimated *30 million cameras*, shooting 4 billion hours of footage a week. "Americans are being watched, all of us, almost everywhere." That's from Scientific American. Why? "Following the September 11 attacks, the use of video surveillance in public places became more common to deter future terrorist attacks." How? "Under the Homeland Security Grant Program, government grants were made available to cities to install surveillance camera networks." In other words, we're paying for it in virtually every major city in the U.S. And the biggest one so far is Chicago! Their Homeland Security System is called "Operation Virtual Shield."

AP News Reports: *"Watchful police cameras like these have some people thinking Big Brother."*

Edwin Yohnka, American Civil Liberties Union: *"You have the right to privacy in that you have the right to not have government watch what you do."*

AP News Reports: *"To others it's a dazzling new crime fighting tool. No city in America has a surveillance system this vast and sophisticated as the one here in Chicago. Cameras, big and small seem to be almost everywhere. The footage is watched around the clock at the city command center. Police, Fire and people on the lookout for threats of terrorism. Hundreds of privately-owned cameras on office buildings, shops, and restaurants are also looped into the system. Now more cameras are going in. Police say, so-called covert cameras may be next, as small as a box of matches."*

Edwin Yohnka: *"And here is the amazing thing. Citizens of the city of Chicago have never got a chance to vote on it, any of this. "[2]*

In other words, it's being done behind the scenes in secret. (There's your word again.) And notice it wasn't just cameras everywhere, small or big, but they even tap into existing cameras from businesses and private entities. Who gave you that right? In fact, Chicago's Operation Virtual Shield consists of 600 miles of fiber optics stretching across the whole city and it captures and processes camera feeds in real time, including 4,000 cameras installed in public schools alone, and at least 1,000 at Chicago O'Hare International Airport. Former Mayor of Chicago Richard Daley called it, "The next best thing to a police officer on every corner." It's worth it! Really? What city has the worst crime rates in the whole country? Chicago! "The city's overall crime rate, especially violent crime rate, is higher than the US average and Chicago was responsible for nearly half of 2016's increase in homicides in the U.S. being named, 'America's mass shooting capital.'" So much for working! How could that be with all these cameras? It's a bunch of baloney! These cameras are having no effect on crime, it's all about monitoring us secretly! In fact, so commonplace is this constant 24/7 video surveillance in virtually all major U.S. cities, not just Chicago, that:

"Whether as motorists or pedestrians; as visitors to convenience stores, banks, ATMs or the post office; as shoppers with credit cards or telephone users; even at leisure, in parks, playgrounds and golf courses, we're constantly on candid camera. Full-time surveillance is a reality of modern life."

Yes, even here in America! All in the name of supposedly reducing crime, or terrorism, or traffic concerns, or a whole list of other supposed excuses. Millions of cameras right now are going up right here in America, and all over the world! Now the biggest one to date is, China! Shocker! The communist totalitarian country, that I believe is a testing ground for much of the Antichrist behavior and technology we see in the 7-year Tribulation, is leading the way towards a Total Surveillance Society! "China has built the largest camera surveillance system in the world. With 170 million CCTV cameras and 400 million new cameras expected to be installed in the next couple of years."

"About 65% of all CCTV cameras in the world are now being installed in Asia to: 'Look at everything about its citizens.' 'A single image is all it takes to identify someone's face, age, gender, and ethnicity.'

And they're coupling it with facial recognition technology which means, no matter where you try to run or hide, they will find you, like this reporter found out!

BBC News Reports *"In your face, China's all-seeing state. China is building the world's largest and most sophisticated camera surveillance system. In the city of Guiyang, the police are about to demonstrate how it works. Their vast digital catalogue contains the image of every Guiyang resident. And now, one more."*

John Sudworth, BBC Correspondent: *"Well, let's see how long it takes you to find me. Thank you very much, let's go."*

"Across China, cameras with artificial intelligence are in widespread use. Some can read faces, others can estimate age, ethnicity and gender. We can match every face with an ID card and trace all our movements back one week in time. We can match your face with your car, match you with your relatives and the people you're in touch with. With enough cameras, we can know who you frequently meet."

John Sudworth: *"Well here we are, and I just got out of the car, close to the City Centre, and for the purposes of this exercise, the plan is for me to start walking in the direction of the bus station. My image is already being flagged to the authorities as a suspect and in theory it should only be a matter of time."*

"When the system recognizes a face the control room raises the alarm."

John Sudworth: *"Right behind me you can see, over my left shoulder there"* 'Hello guys, I've been expecting you. Maybe these guys aren't in on the joke.'"

"The exercise took just seven minutes."[3]

Seven minutes to find somebody in a giant city with a population of about 4.5 million people! So much for running and hiding in some horrible timeframe like the 7-year Tribulation, from a guy named the Antichrist! That's just the **Cities** right now!

The **2ⁿᵈ place** they're installing Big Brother Cameras on the ground right now is in **Streets**.

Right now, you can go to tons of web sites to "monitor" traffic and "monitor" people, "just for fun" not only here in America but around the planet. Which means for the first time in history we can monitor anyone, anywhere on the planet, whether they realize it or not! And if you don't believe me, check it out for yourself! This week, again, I was on this website called "Earth Cam," again just one of many like it. I was hopping all over the world with the click of a mouse, watching people live, and it wasn't just video footage, it was audio!

"Alright here we are at Earth Cam, and this is just one of many sites that you can visit and tap into just about any place around the world. Let me give you a little tour here. This is in Dublin outside of a pub. And what you need to understand is that this is not just video, this is live and if you turn up the volume you hear these people. This is audio. These people we are watching in Ireland, have no clue that they are being monitored and listened to. In fact, you can not only listen to them, but you can zoom in. To get a closer look you can pan to the left or pan to the right, and on and on it goes. These people have no idea they are being watched.

In America, this is Times Square. Let's check it out and see what these people are doing. It's daytime there and again, notice it's not just video, its audio that you can listen to as well. But hey, something more tropical. This is the Aruba cam. Looks like the tourists stayed up too late last night and they are still sleeping. How about Niagara Falls, I use to live there, but hey, I don't have to live there anymore, I can just go on the Earth Cam, type in there live and see what they are doing anytime I want.

How about Hollywood. If you don't get a chance to go there just tap into the web cam and check it out, see how they are doing. But again, what I wanted to show you, it's not just the populated places around the planet. It literally is in the little tiny places. Here's a live camera from Enid, Oklahoma. Look at this, these people have no clue we are watching them. And again, it's not just video, it's audio. They are being monitored and they have no clue. Here we have Hyden, Kentucky and that guy in the red truck has no clue they are being watched from Las Vegas.

This one really got to me. This is in North Dakota. There's not much action there as you can tell, they still have their Christmas lights up. But if you ever lived in a small town, they stay up there all year around. The person backing out the white car there, has no idea they are being watched and I'm telling you this is anywhere, everywhere around the world, we are just barely scraping the surface."[4]

Now that's not just freaky, but I'm sitting there watching and listening to people "live" from around the world and I was wondering…"Gee, I wonder if those people walking by on the streets have any idea that a Pastor from Las Vegas is watching them in his office!"

But that's not all. Do a web search for "traffic cams" or "online traffic cameras" and you'll see just about every street around the world is being "monitored" and "watched." But just for traffic, right? It's to help improve the traffic. Wrong! Let's go back to Chicago! They're using their Traffic Cams to not only watch all cars but watch and zoom in on people! And they admit it!

Aljazeera Reports: *"In the windy city, Big Brother is busier than ever. Chicago's traffic cameras are now doing double duty. Catching red light runners and performing surveillance."*

Ed Yohnka, American Civil Liberties Union: *"What we don't know is, are we tracking a terrorist or are we just tracking someone else? Are we tracking someone that we don't like because of their political views?"*

John Hendre: *"Chicago's traffic cameras are nothing new. For years you could walk from one end of downtown to the other without ever being out of range. What's new with the new cameras is they can pivot to follow an individual or zoom in for a positive I.D."*[5]

In other words, have fun trying to run and hide! But that's not all. They've also turned the light posts on the streets into Big Brother viewing and listening devices. They're called Smart Streets or Intelli-Streets. And as I've said before, anytime you see the word "smart" in front of something, just supplant it for what it is, it means Big Brother, because that's what it is. But these Big Brother Light Posts not only emit light, but they've got cameras and intercoms and speakers to warn people of inappropriate behavior and to give public service announcements, all kinds of stuff. So, imagine walking down the street and hearing all of a sudden, "Hey! Stop that! Knock it off! We see you!" Or, "Stay tuned for this very important public service announcement" and a video starts playing from a light post! It's not only crazy, it's already being done here in Las Vegas!

NBC3 News Reports: *"If you have paid attention to all the downtown redevelopment over the past few years you know a lot of progress has been made. One more upgrade currently in the works is a brand-new street lighting system. The lights are capable of all sorts of fancy features, and they may save the city* *money. But there is a concern. Gerard Ramalho joins us for this special report. Gerard, these new streetlights are also capable of recording not only video but sound."*

Gerard Ramalho: *"It's amazing. They are also adaptable, and the streetlights are being tested in Las Vegas and they could soon be positioned throughout the city"*

Neil Rohleder, Las Vegas Public works: *"We wanted to develop more than just the streetlight, we want to develop an experience for the people that come downtown."*

Gerard Ramalho: *"Neil Rohleder is with the City of Las Vegas Public Works Department. His latest project involves the testing of a new streetlight system called Intelli-streets. They look like ordinary street poles."*

Neil Rohleder: *"We have one here on Main Street and another two over here at the traffic signal."*

Gerard Ramalho: *"But they are actually capable of a wide variety of features. Illuminating Concepts, the company that is behind Intelli-streets is based in Philadelphia."*

Illuminating Concepts: *"The Intelli-Street Processors store and analyze data, soundtracks, announcements, commercials and video files."*

Gerard Ramalho: *"According to their own marketing video, the lights they manufacture are adaptable, capable of adding cameras for surveillance, security and even recording devices. Yes, these same streetlights being tested in Las Vegas could someday be set up to record conversations of everyday passersby. Another big concern here is these systems run on wireless technology. Wi-Fi of course is something that could be hacked."[6]*

Oooh! Which means, someone can hack into the whole system and hijack it for some nefarious purpose, and we'll get to that in just a little bit. But notice this is all being done in secret whether you want it or not! But speaking of being listened to, they've not only installed hidden microphones on these streetlamps, but just about every corner you can think of just to make sure we're watched and listened to at all times!

KPIX 5 News Reports: *"We are exposing a new surveillance program operating all around the Bay area. Federal agents planting microphones that secretly record conversations. Jackie Ward is at the Courthouse. Jackie, can they do that?"*

Jackie Ward: *"Yes they can and that may surprise you. Imagine standing at that very bus stop having a conversation with your friend and having no idea that your conversation was being recorded. It happens all the time and the FBI said that they don't even need a warrant to do it."*

Man on the street: *"They put microphones under rocks, they put microphones in trees, they plant microphones in equipment, I mean there are microphones planted in places that people don't think about because that's the intent."*[7]

In other words, it's being done in secret, there's that word again. But notice it's everywhere. Microphones not only on streetlamps but on rocks, trees, equipment, basically everything else on the street where you walk. And again, they're doing this all over. They've already installed hidden microphones on utility poles and rooftops in most major cities across the U.S. to "monitor strange noises" or "gun shots" for our supposed protection. And what's concerning about all this technology is it's not only being done, and done around the whole world, but it's being done "in secret" which is exactly what the Antichrist is going to do. The secret power of lawlessness is already at work! The Antichrist is working to create his Big Brother Surveillance Society that he needs in the 7-year tribulation right now before our very eyes! And speaking of which, lest you think he won't be able to tap into the whole system and use it for his nefarious purposes, they already admit it's all being tied together!

W News Reports: *"Surveillance cameras, car cameras, cell phone cameras. They record countless hours of video, huge amounts of data. Much of it ends up on servers.*

Jeng-Neg Hwang, Professor: *"All this information, how are they going to take advantage of it?"*

W News Reports: *"Now, University of Washington Researcher, Jen Neg Hwang, has developed a way to tap this resource. Hwang can track individuals as they are recorded on unrelated cameras. Then even with variation of color, angle, and lighting, they can follow a subject across cameras."*

Stacy Sakamoto, University of Washington: *"With this new technology anyone searching the videos would be able to spot me and as I move from camera to camera to camera."[8]*

Not in China, but in the Unites States! And notice it wasn't just CCTV cameras, but cameras in your car, cameras in your cell phone, basically any camera! All being tapped into to create a seamless net for anyone, someone, to hijack and utilize for some nefarious purposes just in time for the 7-year Tribulation. I wonder who that will be? Rhymes with the Antichrist! Good answer! In fact, speaking of the Antichrist, I wonder if this is how he will also make his global announcement that he's god and people are to worship him. Maybe he'll just tap into this giant global video system and make a global announcement and then watch to see if people obey him. And thanks to Obama, he already pushed for that when he was in office!

Fox News Reports: *"President Obama may soon have the ability to speak to everyone in our country with just the flip of a switch. Today the FCC will propose an overhaul to the Emergency Alert System. The President will be able to appear on every television channel immediately. Right now, if the President wants to address the nation, he has to get in touch with each local broadcaster and they have to agree to pick up the message. The new system will cost between 7 and 13 million dollars so they wouldn't have to ask, we wouldn't have to agree to it, it would be put up any time he would agree to it."*

"So, if he wants to talk about immigration reform, he would just have to flip the switch on all the channels including the Food Network?"

"If it was considered an emergency, yes."[9]

Wow! So, if some global figure wanted to make some global announcement like he's god, worship me, he can do it! He can tap into the global video system and do it with the flip of a switch, for the first time in the history of mankind, not to mention see who obeys the announcement as well!

Folks, we are that close! And this is precisely why, out of love, God has given us this update on **The Final Countdown: Tribulation Rising** concerning **Modern Technology & the AI Invasion** to show us that the Tribulation is near and the 2nd Coming of Jesus Christ is rapidly approaching. And that's why Jesus Himself said:

Luke 21:28 "When these things begin to take place, stand up and lift up your heads, because your redemption is drawing near."

People of God, like it or not, we are headed for **The Final Countdown**. The signs of the 7-year **Tribulation** are **Rising**! Wake up! And so, the point is this. If you're a Christian today and you're not doing anything for the Lord, shame on you! Get busy doing something for Jesus now! Stop wasting your life! We need you! Don't sit on the sidelines! Get on the front line and help us! Let's get busy working together doing something splendid for Jesus with what time is left and get busy saving souls! Amen?

But if you're reading this today and you're not a Christian, then I beg you, please, heed these signs, heed these warnings, give your life to Jesus now because this monitoring system of the Antichrist is not going to lead to a life of good times and personal safety but a system that allows him to monitor your every move! And if you don't obey, you die! Don't fall for the lie! Take the way out now, the only way out now, through Jesus Christ, and avoid the whole thing, before it's too late! Amen?

Chapter Eleven

The Increase of Big Brother Buildings & Transportation

The **3ʳᵈ place** they're installing Big Brother cameras on the ground right now is in **Buildings**.

Once again, they're doing even this in "secret" by and large. That is exactly what we saw last time that the Antichrist is going to do. Let's go back to that text that exposed this "evil" behavior.

2 Thessalonians 2:1-8 "Concerning the coming of our Lord Jesus Christ and our being gathered to Him, we ask you, brothers, not to become easily unsettled or alarmed by some prophecy, report or letter supposed to have come from us, saying that the day of the Lord has already come. Don't let anyone deceive you in any way, for that day will not come until the rebellion occurs and the man of lawlessness is revealed, the man doomed to destruction. He will oppose and will exalt himself over everything that is called God or is worshiped, so that he sets himself up in God's temple, proclaiming himself to be God. Don't you remember that when I was with you, I used to tell you these things? And now you know what is holding him back, so that he may be revealed at the proper time. For the secret power of lawlessness is already at work; but the one who now holds it back will continue to do so till he is taken out of the way. And then the lawless one will be revealed, whom the Lord Jesus will overthrow with the breath of His mouth and destroy by the splendor of His coming."

So again, as we saw last time, the Apostle Paul comforts the Thessalonians from a misconception going around at that time by some false teachers saying they missed the Rapture and we're in the 7-year Tribulation. Paul says No! Christians are not going to be around during the 7-year Tribulation, we leave prior at the Rapture, and he's emphatic about it! He says the Day of the Lord does not come until the rebellion occurs and the Antichrist is revealed, which happens the moment he makes a covenant with the Jewish people, the very event that starts the7-yearTribulation; **Daniel 9:27.** That's why he says "Don't be deceived." Don't you remember I already told you this? Why are you falling for this? Hello! You can't be there! Christians are nowhere around in the 7-year Tribulation! We leave prior at the Rapture! So, "Don't freak out and listen to these False teachers!" But again, as we saw, he does mention something about the Antichrist that is already here, right now, today! And that's the phrase, "The secret power of lawlessness of the Antichrist, is already at work." The embodiment of the Antichrist hasn't come yet, as he says, but the machinery behind the scenes, if you will, is being built as we speak. And it's being done in "secret."

Again, not just Big Brother Eye in the Sky with satellites, but Big Brother Eye on the Ground with cameras in the cities and streets, and again, as I just mentioned, even in the buildings. The Antichrist is not dumb. He's got every base covered! He's knows there's going to be resisters in the 7-year Tribulation. He knows not everybody is going to obey. So, he's developing a system to make sure nobody can get away. Including those who might say something like this, "Okay, so maybe they'll find me in the cities and in the streets, but I'll show them! I'll just stay inside buildings and hide out and they can't get me! Ha! Ha! Ha!" Really? Have you noticed just how many cameras are being installed in just about every building in existence for the past several years? They're all over the place!

And the **1st place** they're putting them in is **The Workplace**.

That's right! Just to make sure you are a so-called productive worker, millions of cameras and other devices are being installed and utilized in businesses around the world, even here in the United States. In fact, here's just one news report explaining the rationale for this constant monitoring of you and I in the workplace.

CBS This Morning: *"Some companies this morning are starting to monitor their employees more closely than ever. A recent New York Times article highlights the technology that allows your performance to be tracked in real time. Nick, I kind of have to say this, it gives me the heebie-jeebies. Explain the technology here. How does this work?"*

Nicholas Thompson: *"There's a lot of technology going on but what these companies are doing is they are tracking their employees when they come in, when they leave, when they take breaks. That's sort of the most basic level. A lot of companies are tracking their employees through apps on their phones. When they leave, they can be aware of where they go. If they are in sales it can be very helpful, which can be creepy. Some companies are tracking all the sites they are visiting on their browser, see their stroke as they type it in. And then other companies are having real time feedback on employees, for example at Amazon, if you want to say something to one of your employees, as their manager, either praise or criticism, you can immediately do that, this technology is set up to allow you to do that. It's constant monitoring all the time."*

CBS Good Morning: *"They're not putting a chip behind my ear."*

Nicholas Thompson: *"Nobody has done that but in due course, once the technology does exist, it will be used."*[1]

Yeah, real funny! First you monitor us like a rat, as he said, constant monitoring all the time, but an implanted chip is coming next! It's called soft disclosure, getting you used to the idea of what's coming! But listen to all the different ways they're currently monitoring us at work!

"Every action is recorded as an information block with subtitles that explain the performed operation. This helps track the actions of workers, especially when they are making critical financial transactions, such as correcting or cancelling a sale, withdrawing money or altering personal information."

In fact, here's a list of other actions an employer might want to monitor you.

- Scanning of goods, selection of goods, introduction of price and quantity.
- Input and output of operators in the system when entering passwords.
- Deleting operations and modifying existing documents.

- Implementation of certain operations, such as financial statements or operations with cash.
- Moving goods, revaluation, scrapping and counting.
- Control in the kitchen of fast food restaurants.
- Change of settings, reports and other official functions.

In other words, monitoring everything! And lest you think that's not their plan, listen to this, *"Each of these operations is transmitted with a description, allowing the detailed monitoring of all actions of the operator,"* and *"Some systems allow the user (i.e. the employer or whoever) to search for a specific event by date, time, text description and evaluate operator behavior and predict deviations from the standard, and record behavior."* In other words, everything you do! Like the guy said, constant monitoring all the time! Welcome to Rat World! In fact, this isn't just being done to adults but even young adults!

The **2nd place** they're putting cameras in buildings is in **The Schools**.

And one of the countries taking this to an extreme level is, of course, China!

MegaFun: *"A high school in Hangzhou City, Zhejiang Province located on the eastern coast of China, has employed facial recognition technology to monitor students' attentiveness in class. At Hangzhou Number 11 High School, three cameras at the front of the classroom scan students' faces every 30 seconds, analyzing their facial expressions to detect their mood, according to a May 16 report in the state-run newspaper 'The Paper.'*

The different moods, surprised, sad, antipathy, angry, happy, afraid, neutral, are recorded and averaged during each class. A display screen, only visible to the teacher, shows the data in real-time. A certain value is determined as a student not paying enough attention. A video shot by Zhejiang Daily Press revealed that the system, coined the 'smart classroom behavior management system' by the school, also analyzes students' actions, categorized into reading, listening, writing, standing up, raising hands, and leaning on the desk.

An electronic screen also displays a list of student names deemed 'not paying attention.' The school began using the technology at the end of March, vice principal Zhang Guanchao told The Paper. Zhang added that students felt like they were being monitored when the system was first put in place but have since gotten used to it. On Sina Weibo, a social media platform similar to Twitter, one user from Beijing said, 'this is more frightening than being in prison.' Many users felt the school was violating these students' basic rights with such monitoring. [2]

Yeah, a non-stop electronic prison! Better not get out of line! One student stated this, *"Since the school has introduced these cameras, it is like there are a pair of mystery eyes constantly watching me, I don't dare let my mind wander."* Mystery eyes! Of all terms to use. The same Greek word "musterion" used to describe the "secret" workings of the Antichrist in the last days. Where have I heard that before? In fact, China is also enforcing, in their schools what's called Smart Uniforms that students have to wear with GPS tracking to surveil the students! (First on the outside, then maybe on the inside.) Then they go on to say, "The Chinese regime has championed a nationwide system of security cameras, called Skynet, that uses facial recognition and other artificial intelligence features to gather personal information on passersby in real time, with plans to cover the entire country by 2020." Wow! Have fun trying to run and hide in China in the 7-year Tribulation. You ain't going nowhere! You better get saved and avoid the whole thing!

In fact, it's so bad there that: *"People have had their dogs taken away for not being on a leash. Announcements are being made on public transit to not misbehave or it will affect their social score, and of course never complain about the government."* But hey, good thing it's only being done in China. Yeah right!

"In Britain, New Zealand, Australia, and even in the United States, CCTV is widely used in schools right now to prevent bullying, vandalism, monitoring visitors and maintaining a record in the event of a crime."

"Cameras are generally in hallways, parking lots, front offices where students, employees, and parents come and go, gymnasiums, cafeterias, supply rooms and classrooms."

Again, just about everywhere, and it's increasing, just like China!

"According to the National Center for Education Statistics, more than 80% of public schools—and more than 94% of high schools—in the U.S. use security cameras to monitor students, doubling the number of schools using cameras a

decade earlier," and, *"They have become the cornerstones of school safety and security plans."* In other words, it's all here to keep you safe! Yeah, right!

But that's not all. The **3rd place** they're putting cameras in buildings is in **The Public**.

I'm talking about just about every place you can think of is being monitored with cameras. Nowadays even in places you wouldn't even think of. Again, not just in China but here in the U.S. Here's just a quick list of places.

- Sporting Events
- Restaurants
- Hotels
- Fast Food Chains
- Shops
- Grocery Stores
- Restrooms
- Lounges
- Hallways
- Businesses
- Exits/Entryways
- Warehouses/Docks
- Loading/Unloading Areas
- Reception Areas
- Waiting Rooms
- Work Environment
- Customer Interaction Points
- Banks/ATM's
- Even Secluded Areas – such as Parking Lots, Back Alleys, Dumpsters, you name it!

All being monitored, and a lot of it being combined with facial recognition technology, just like China, to be able to recognize you wherever you go. Give it up for Facebook, they've got a lot of photos to choose from! In fact, there are so many cameras out there in the public arena, right now, including hidden cameras that other companies are now selling Hidden Camera Detectors that you can buy to see just how many different ways we're being spied upon **secretly**. Where have I heard that before? Here's just one of them they offer!

SpyFinder Pro Commercial: *"Now, more than ever our privacy is under attack because there are tiny hidden cameras watching and recording us all the time everywhere, even in our most intimate moments without our knowledge. These tiny cameras are found all the time in dressing rooms, hotel rooms, public bathrooms, apartments, locker rooms, and places you didn't think possible. This SpyFinder Pro puts an end to privacy concerns and invasion by instantly uncovering all hidden camera lenses that are spying on you.*

This easy to use pocket size detector can go along with you anywhere. To use this SpyFinder Pro, look through the viewfinder while pushing the button on top to activate the 6 super-bright LED strobe lights. These special red lights are specifically engineered to bounce off the reflective surface which all camera lenses have, no matter how big or small they may be. In a slow sweeping motion, scan the room, look at all surfaces until you are confident the room is clean and clear of potential hidden cameras. Even if the camera is turned off, you'll clearly see that the camera lens is blinking back at you at 45 feet away. Put a stop to the invasion of your privacy before it starts. Get your SpyFinder Pro now."[3]

And find how many ways you're being spied upon in the public wherever you go secretly with hidden cameras on coffee cups, speakers, alarm clocks, you name it, they're all there watching you, just in time for the 7-year Tribulation! The secret power of lawlessness is already at work! Have fun trying to run and hide! You might want to get saved and avoid the whole thing!

The **4th place** they're installing Big Brother cameras on the ground is in the **Transportation**.

You see, you might still be one of those resisters out there thinking you don't need Jesus and you're the ultimate survivor and you're just going to hide out in the 7-year Tribulation, and you don't need God, saying something like this, "Okay, so maybe they'll find me in the cities and in the streets and even in the buildings. But I'll show them! That's why I bought my piece of property out in the middle of nowhere and built my own Bug Out Shelter! I'm just going to go hop in my car or jeep or whatever and hide away! Ha! Ha! Ha! They can't get me!" Really? You really think that Antichrist hasn't thought of that? You ain't going nowhere! They're also installing cameras in just about every piece of transportation you can think of!

And the **1st place** they're putting them in right now is **Public Transport**.

Starting with Taxis and Buses!

RT News Reports: *"Big Brother is set for a ride in Oxford in Taxi's if local authorities have their way and install audio surveillance in every cab in the British city."*

In Oxford, surveillance cameras are everywhere and now in a city council scheme, taxis will become the latest target of state bugging operations. Over the next few years licensed cabs will be required to install equipment monitoring both driver and passenger.

It's a fact of life in towns and city across the U.K. you are being watched wherever you go. In the high streets, in shops, and public transports. Buses already have video and sound recording. Taxi passengers will be recorded too. But some who fear that their safety late at night are reassured, others see it as a staggering invasion of privacy.

"There's always that sort of fear that this is a prison."[4]

Yeah, an electronic prison set up by the Antichrist! Where you say something like, "Hey Bob, I just got in a Taxi or Bus and I'll meet you at the Bug Out Shelter that we wasted thousands of dollars on, cuz we don't need God! You ain't going nowhere! And this is not just happening to Britain's public transport, it's happening here in the U.S. as well.

"In Montgomery County buses, cameras do more than capture what they see. Many cameras also record what they hear, a little-known function that bothers civil liberties advocates."

Maryland Transit Administration began audio recording in October on buses in and around Baltimore and hopes to expand that to about half of the agency's 700 buses by the summer. In San Francisco, buses and trains have both audio and video recording, with the audio devices always running. In Atlanta, transit officials are adding video and audio recording to buses and will put them on trains next. The stated intention of the system is to capture what people say. And the systems are always recording, being saved on the system's hard drive. One person tried to excuse this away by saying, "Well, if you're not doing anything, you have nothing to worry about." That's not the point! People often have "very private conversations" in public if they think no one can hear them.

But not anymore! And you know, a private conversation like this: "Hey Bob, I'm glad you got on this bus with me. And as soon as we make it to our Bug Out Shelter we wasted thousands of dollars on cuz we don't need God," you ain't going nowhere! But you might be thinking, "Well yeah! That's precisely why I'm not going to use public transit to get me to my Bug Out Shelter! I'm going to use my own vehicle and get away! Ha! Ha! Ha! They can't get me!" Really? When will you learn? Haven't you been paying attention?

The **2nd place** they're putting cameras in is **Private Transport**.

That's right! Your own car isn't going to be safe either! The only way out of this mess is through Jesus! Did you know you likely have a "black box" in your car that records information? I didn't either. They were made mandatory for all new vehicles as of September 2014 but have been placed in vehicles since the 1990's. Did you know that? And speaking of mandatory, it has now become mandatory to put rear view cameras in our cars, for our safety of course!

"What used to be a luxury, rear-view cameras on cars, are now mandatory. The NHTSA issued the regulation today, all new cars including trucks and buses require rear-view visibility by 2018. Consumer groups and families have been pushing for this for a number of years. Too many people, especially children, are being hit in back-over accidents. Those are great, I have them on my car"[5]

Yeah, handy, when I wanted one, but now I don't have an option of what? Having a camera in my car! First get us used to it, then make it mandatory. And it's not just cameras in the rear, it's cameras in the front, including those Dash Cams that everybody's just got to have, you know, just in case there's an accident. Believe it or not, there's talk of making those mandatory too!

Game Changer Reports: *"For this guy, February 13, 2016 is a day he will never forget. On this day, on Marcos Highway, Baguio City, this happened. He was on his motorcycle, going down the highway, when someone in the other lane decided to pass the car in front of them and run head on into the motorcycle.*

It totally destroyed the motorcycle and almost killed the rider, Genard. Despite the brutality of the accident, Genard made it out alive. But his problems were far from over. The SUV driver tried to point the blame on Genard. Fortunately, there was an unbiased witness with a dash cam video that captured the whole incident. Thanks to the Dash Cam a lot of "he said she said" can now be resolved. For the longest time, journalist James Diggan has been pushing for the mandatory installation of Dash Cam's across all kinds of vehicles."

Game Changer Reports: *"James, let's talk about your advocacy. Do you think Dash Cam's should be made mandatory?*

James Diggan: *"It eliminates so many problems on the road, I think it should just be a standard feature."[6]*

First, it's an option, then it's mandatory! You have no option! And this is not only being done in the Philippines where that news broadcast was from, but all over the place! *"72% of Aussie drivers want Dash Cams to be mandatory."* And get this, *"Russia is currently the largest user of Dash Cams where almost every vehicle is equipped with a Dash Cam."* Even here in the U.S. we are showing signs of going even further with not only being able to see and hear what we say and do in our cars, but even controlling our cars. A whole new younger generation is being conditioned to accept this! It'll make you go HUM!

Hum Commercial: *"This is your daughter, and she just got her driver's license. Oh Boy! But don't worry you have got 'Hum." So, you can set this, the speed on her car, so if she speeds you can tell her to drive more like this, very slowly like she has a couple grandmas in the back seat. Because you will get a speed alert on your smart phone. You can even set boundaries for her. Like if she should be in school but instead, she goes to the beach, or to a club, or necking with her boyfriend on your couch, you'll know. So, don't worry mom, because you put this, 'Hum' in her car. 'Hum' by Verizon, to make your car smarter, safer, and more connected."*

Yeah, connected to the Antichrist System that's going to use this in the 7-year Tribulation to find any and all resisters who are trying to flee some horrible situation! He'll stop your car dead in its tracks! And speaking of tracks, most people don't even realize that there's already technology being used on our cars to track them even if somehow you could avoid having all these cameras being put on your car. It's called Automated License Plate Tracking or Readers and every car has to have one of those, a license plate, right? New or old! Got to have one! And this technology has not only been around for years, but it's already been implemented around the world for years!

"Automatic license plate readers are mounted on police cars or on objects like road signs and bridges, and they use small, high-speed cameras to photograph thousands of plates per minute."

"The information captured by the readers includes the license plate number, the date and time, and location of every scan is being collected and sometimes pooled into regional sharing systems."[7]

In other words, into huge databases! And approximately 71% of all U.S. police departments use some form of Automated Plate Readers. They collect (and can indefinitely store) data from each license plate, as well as images, dates, times and GPS coordinates of individuals being tracked." (You ain't going nowhere!) and they're putting this technology in some pretty suspicious places, like this desert feature we're familiar with here in Las Vegas!

Fox 10 News Reports: *"Now the town of Paradise Valley is hiding cameras inside cactus. These cactus cameras have been popping up throughout Paradise Valley over the past few days and residents, they had no idea why. The city doesn't want to talk to them about it."*

"Look close enough at the cactus as you drive through Paradise Valley and you might see some cacti looking back."

Randy Evans, Paradise Resident: *"I have lived here 30 years and I have never seen cameras in the cactus before."*

Fox 10 News: *"And the residents are curious about what the cameras are for."*

Randy Evans: *"Your guess is as good as mine."*

Another Resident: *"And when I stopped here, I thought that you all knew what it was."*

Fox 10 News: *"We asked Paradise Valley Police about the cameras, but they said they were not prepared to make a statement at this time, so we came here to Town Hall, where people were also hesitant to talk to us. They say they want to wait until all the cameras are installed. But eventually the Town Manager did answer some of our questions."*

Kevin Burks: *"The town is embarking on the installation of license plate readers."*

Fox 10 News: *"Town Manager, Kevin Burks says the cameras run license plates on cars against a hot list database, if the car is stolen or a subject of an Amber Alert, the police will be notified."[8]*

As well as if you try to flee some horrible timeframe like the 7-year Tribulation and try to make it to your so-called Bug Out Shelter that you and Bob wasted thousands of dollars on because you don't need God. How many times do I have to say it? You ain't going nowhere! Get saved now! The whole transportation system is being monitored. No wonder it's going to be a bloodbath in the 7-year Tribulation! But still you might be thinking, "Okay, okay, I'm just going to go on foot. I'll skip the whole vehicle thing and just run to my bug out shelter!" Well, first of all, let's go back to China and how I said before I believe they are one of the biggest countries that's a testing ground for much of this Big Brother Technology that the Antichrist is going to use in the last days. Remember their social credit system that they put into place to not only control and monitor their citizens but to control what they buy and sell?

Well, if China can do that with their 1.4 billion people population, then the rest of the world is a piece of cake, right? And believe it or not, social credit ratings are already being implemented here in the U.S. The Palms Hotel in Las Vegas is using a social media scoring system to provide perks to guests. Twitter announced they are instituting a new social score for every user based on "influence." And Virgin Airlines has announced they will use these scores to determine upgrades and even pricing. And speaking of Totalitarian Communist Regimes, recently a Florida Democrat Congresswoman, Frederica Wilson called to shut people down who voice their opinion online saying, "We're gonna shut them down." Why?

Frederica Wilson

'GONNA SHUT THEM DOWN'

Florida Dem: Making fun of lawmakers online should be criminal offense

Because, "Making fun of lawmakers should be a criminal offense." This ain't

China lady! And again, for those of you who think, "I'm just going to run to my so-called Bug Out Shelter and escape this Totalitarian Regime," China's plans for this has gone global! They've even figured out how not only to spy on their own citizens, but on any citizen of any country who's purchased any one of their drones!

Fox News Reports: *"The Department of Homeland Security says Chinese made drones could be spying on you, then sending the information back to the Chinese government. Michael Pillsbury is author of the Hundred-Year Marathon, a fantastic book, about the secret strategy on how to replace America as the global superpower, and we are happy to have him on again tonight. Mr. Pillsbury, thank you again for joining us. Is this a credible concern?"*

Michael Pillsbury: *"Yes, I think it is. It's what Homeland Security is pointing out is that these drones, and by the way, there are over two million now operating in the United States, 80% of which are made in China by basically one company. All these drones have hookups to the internet, and they go to servers in China. So, every time you use a drone to check a pipeline or check your ranch, how the cattle are, all that feed is going back to China. And with Artificial Intelligence, if the Chinese want to, they could assemble a picture of a large part of America, what is happening with Airline flights, crops, nuclear reactors, anything they want."*[9]

Whoa! So much for running to your Bug Out Shelter! You should've got saved and avoided the whole thing! There's no place to hide now! Even China's going to be watching you from the other side of the planet! In fact, they're doing this all around the world.

"Two out of every three drones used around the world are manufactured by government-controlled Chinese companies. And consensus is that some 75% of U.S. government security cameras are manufactured in China."

And this is why right now Australia is currently freaking out over the number of Chinese cameras in their cities and even their military bases.

"Australian officials have determined that Chinese cameras are in use in their Army Forces Command, Air Force Air Command, Navy Strategic Command, and Army Special Operations HQ."

They're worried that China may actually be tapping into the images and using the data to spy on or even affect their election results. *"The elephant-in-the-room concern is that Communist China can track Australia's entire military operation!"* And recently, here in the U.S., Congress just passed the National Defense Authorization Act of 2019 which prohibited cameras made by certain Chinese companies from being used in surveillance on U.S. soil. The reasoning was that China would be able to do surveillance in the U.S. as they suspect they've been doing in Australia and, "The commonality of all this is that these cameras all use the internet." Which means some person could tap into the whole system and watch the whole planet all at the same time! Gee, I wonder who that will be! As one guy said, "All this is clearly prophesied in the Bible, and this all-encompassing system will be run by none other than satan himself."

That's precisely why, out of love, God has given us this update on **The Final Countdown: Tribulation Rising** concerning **Modern Technology & the AI Invasion** to show us that the Tribulation is near and the 2nd Coming of Jesus Christ is rapidly approaching. And that's why Jesus Himself said:

Luke 21:28 "When these things begin to take place, stand up and lift up your heads, because your redemption is drawing near."

People of God, like it or not, we are headed for **The Final Countdown**. The signs of the 7-year **Tribulation** are **Rising**! Wake up! And so, the point is this. If you're a Christian today and you're not doing anything for the Lord, shame on you! Get busy doing something for Jesus now! Stop wasting your life! We need you! Don't sit on the sidelines! Get on the front line and help us! Let's get busy working together doing something splendid for Jesus with what time is left and get busy saving souls! Amen?

But if you're reading this today and you're not a Christian, then I beg you, please, heed these signs, heed these warnings, give your life to Jesus now because this monitoring system of the Antichrist and the False Prophet is not going to lead to a life of ease and personal joy but a system that monitors every man, woman, girl or boy! You won't be able to escape! Don't fall for the lie! Take the way out now, the only way out now, through Jesus Christ, and avoid the whole thing, before it's too late! Amen?

Chapter Twelve

The Increase of Big Brother Billboards & Body Cams

So far, we saw, for the first time in the history of mankind, the 1st type of Big Brother surveillance system that they have already put into place is the Information System. The 2nd type was the Satellite System. The Big Brother's Eye in the Sky with satellites watching our every move. And the last two times we saw the 3rd type was the camera system. The Big Brother Eye on the Ground with cameras. And there we saw, whether you realize it or not, there are cameras right now on the ground, as well as microphones hidden all over the place, even in places you wouldn't suspect, watching and listening to our every move. We saw that with cameras in the cities, cameras on the streets, and last time, cameras in buildings and even cameras in the transportation system. Everywhere you go they are watching you, monitoring you like a rat, which means people won't be able to run and hide in some horrible timeframe called the 7-year Tribulation. You'll never make it to your bug out shelter! And once again, they're not just doing this by and large in "secret" but they're also lying about it and being deceitful and once again, that's exactly what the Antichrist is going to do in the 7-year Tribulation. But don't take my word for it. Let's listen to God's.

2 Thessalonians 2:7-10 "For the secret power of lawlessness is already at work; but the one who now holds it back will continue to do so till he is taken out of the way. And then the lawless one will be revealed, whom the Lord Jesus will overthrow with the breath of His mouth and destroy by the splendor of His coming. The coming of the lawless one will be in accordance with the work of satan displayed in all kinds of counterfeit miracles, signs and wonders, and in every sort of evil that deceives those who are perishing. They perish because they refused to love the truth and so be saved."

In other words, they didn't want to hear the truth! But according to our text, we see that when the Antichrist is revealed, he's not only going to use secretive behavior to set up his machinery in the background, he's also going to use what? False, counterfeit signs, wonders, and miracles, right? In other words, he's going to use lies and deceit. Which is why it says it's being done "in accordance with the work of satan." Jesus said in John Chapter 8, satan is a "liar and the father of all lies." So, the Antichrist is going to follow in satan's footsteps. This passage gives us two more tactics the Antichrist will use to set up his kingdom in the 7-year Tribulation to dupe people. It's not only being done in secret, but he'll be using lies and deceit! And again, that's exactly what's being done right now with this Antichrist Big Brother global monitoring system. We are being lied to and deceived about it as they set this system up to monitor us!

The **1ˢᵗ technology** they're lying and deceiving us about is **Billboards.**

That's right! Talk about Tom Cruise and the movie Minority Report! Remember that movie where he was on the run trying to hide out but wherever he went the billboards kept recognizing him and talking back to him?

Minority Report clip: *"A commercial for Lexus is playing on the billboard on one side of the hallway but on the other side another commercial is for Revlon. As Tom Cruise walks down this hallway each of the billboards show a face recognition. They say 'John Anderson' here and 'John Anderson' there on each side of the hallway. Even as he is walking down that hallway with several other people. They have print out 'John Anderson, member since 2037.'*

While he walks down the street, he has three sets of eyes following his every move. In order to get away he gets new eyeballs implanted. Now he walks into the building and the receptionist calls out, 'Hello, Mr. Yakimoto, welcome back to the Gap. How did the assorted tank tops work for you?' This welcome was from the billboard just inside the door. He says, 'Mr. Yakimoto?'"[1]

Mr. Yakimoto is right! He said that because that was after he switched his eyeballs out so they couldn't find him like the first time, but they found him anyway. But how many of you remember that movie? I'm here to tell you, believe it or not, that science fiction movie is now our Modern-Day reality! They're already implementing billboards just like what you saw in that movie that are watching, monitoring, and scanning us. And again, I think I know why! The enemy's not dumb. He's knows exactly what he's doing! He's building a lying deceptive Big Brother system so that no one can get away in the 7-year Tribulation. Including those who would say something like this, "I don't need God. I don't need Jesus. I don't need to get saved! I'm the Ultimate Survivor! And, when the hammer comes down in the 7-year Tribulation, I'm just going to sneak around, hide out behind the scenes, darting here and there in and out of the shadows, they'll never find me! Ha! Ha! Ha!" Really? You really think the enemy hasn't thought of that? Again, this is why we have been lied to and deceived about these new billboards they're putting up all over. They're not just for us to look up at them anymore. Oh no! They're also designed to be looking back down at us! Just like Minority Report!

Next News Network: *"Did you hear about this? Clear Channel billboards are going Big Brother. Merit Kennedy for NPR reports that Clear Channel Outdoor, the largest outdoor advertising company in the United States. It's starting a new program called 'Radar' that will use billboards to map real world habits and behaviors from nearby customers. The technology is sure to help advertisers to better target their ads, but privacy advocates argue that it is well, a little creepy."*

Radar Commercial: *"From traditional and digital roadside displays to commuter and airport hubs and the towering screens of Times Square. Out of home advertising is unskippable. Captivating hundreds of millions of consumers every month. Now with its Radar analytic sweep, Clear Channel Outdoor brings digital audience inside targeting out of homes to the physical world.*

Here's how it works: Using anonymous aggregated data from consumer cellular and mobile devices, Radar measures consumers real world travel patterns and behaviors while they move throughout their day. Analyzing data as; direction of travel, billboard viewability, and visits to specific destinations. This movement data is the map of Clear Channels displays."

Next News Network: *"Sounds like something right out of the Minority Report with Tom Cruise, if you ask me."*[2]

And I would agree! But the point is, have fun trying to run and hide in the 7-year Tribulation! You should've gotten saved and avoided the whole thing because now even the billboards, just like in Minority Report, will get you! It's called soft disclosure. Little by little they get us used to the society they're creating for us! And it's not a good one.

The **2ⁿᵈ technology** they're lying and deceiving us about is **Body Cams.**

And I'm not just talking about the Body Cams they put on Police nowadays! We'll get into that in a little bit. I'm talking about the trend for anybody and everybody to wear cameras on their body. And again, I think I know why! The enemy's not dumb. He's knows exactly what he's doing. He's building a lying deceptive Big Brother system that no one can get away from in the 7-year tribulation including those who would say something like this: "Okay, I'll tell you what. I still don't need God. I still don't need Jesus. I don't need to get saved! I'm the Ultimate Survivor, here's what I'm going to do. Maybe they'll find me with all these new billboards out there like in Minority Report, I'll give you that, but see, that's just it! I'm just going to avoid all those billboards and voila! They can't get me! Ha! Ha! Ha!" Really? You think the enemy hasn't thought of that too? This is why we have been lied to and deceived about all these new body cameras out there that people are wearing. You see, we thought they were just for us to record things that we were looking at for our own private use. Oh no! They actually allow others to see and record what we see as well!

The **1ˢᵗ type** of Body Cameras they're doing this with is **Glass Cameras.**

Including these just released by Snap Chat of all things.

Cnet Reports: *"They are here, only $129.00, and they came out of a vending machine. These are Snapchat Spectacles. Early this morning Snapchat dropped a beautiful, large, yellow, vending machine on the Venice Beach Boardwalk in Santa Monica, California. What happened next was exactly what they hoped for. Hundreds of Snapchat users lined up in the Southern California heat for the opportunity to pick up a pair of spectacles.*

So, let's take a look. The packaging is really cool. The case acts as a charger for your spectacles and it's actually really easy to use. They are light weight when you put them on which I wasn't expecting and pairing them to your device is as easy as opening the Snapchat app and looking at your Snap code with spectacles.

Once you've done that you can click the button to take 10 second snaps. If you click it before the 10 seconds are up it will continue your video. If not that 10 seconds of footage gets uploaded to your memories and then you can publish them as you chose."[3]

Or anyone who decides to hack into your glasses that are connected to your cell phone and uses your glasses to monitor other people around you. But hey, you're not supposed to think that! It's just about being cool and hip. In fact, speaking of being cool and hip, you might be thinking, "Well hey, I'd never get those because I don't like that particular style of glasses. I'll just have to wait until they get something cooler." Well, hey! Wait no more! Problem solved! Now everybody can have these cameras on their glasses because you can just attach them to your existing already cool ones and start monitoring all kinds of people, like these guys.

PogoCam Commercial*: "Wearable cameras are cool. But before now, wearing them out socially, was not. I mean, would you want one of these strapped to you. (headgear) or how about if you tape your cell phone to your head, it can be hands free. Of course not. So how do you take pictures and videos to tape your experience while also being in the moment?*

Meet PogoCam, the first wearable camera. Regular eye and sunglasses become enhanced with the world's smallest detachable quality camera. So, experiences like these are captured in the moment. Like family get togethers, special events, hanging out with friends, or just cruising the town having fun, and even those once in a lifetime moments when bringing out your phone means potentially missing them.

PogoCam works with your favorite brands by attaching a Pogo track, a metallic strip built into your favorite frames so you stay fashionable with whatever pair you wear. Since PogoCam is removeable, you can switch it to any of your favorite pairs as long as it has the Pogo Track on it, so your style can change at any moment. Even Sunglasses. So, if you don't wear glasses, you can still look cool and capture moments as they happen.

PogoCam can capture and store hundreds of photos and even minutes of video with audio with comparable quality to your smart phone camera and has a proprietary mobile app which ensures the image you see is the image you capture. Simply look and shoot. The content is transferred easily to your devices and with the PogoCam app can quickly be shared with friends and on social media."[4]

Including anyone else who hacked into your glasses through your cell phone and turned them into a monitoring device! But hey! You're not supposed to think that! It's just about convenience and looking cool. What are you? Some sort of wacky conspiracy nut? Yeah, right! Sounds like somebody's lying and deceiving me! But hey! Maybe you're still out there resisting this wonderful camera technology because you just don't like glasses, period! Well hey, worry no more! There's no reason to miss out on all this monitoring fun! Now they've come out with a new contact lens that does the same thing. Here's just one that came out from Sony.

Today Show: *"Anyone here wear contact lenses? Check this out. Pretty soon those contact lenses could be doing a lot more than improving your vision. They could be recording everything you see. Sony has just filed a patent for contact lenses. They would snap a photo when you blink your eye. Then you would be able to send that photo to a wireless device like a smart phone or a tablet. Sony's not alone, Google also is working on similar technology. I love technology, I don't know if I'm in favor of this one though. Think of what could happen there."[5]*

Yeah, think of what could happen is right! They're called Smart Contact Lenses that are connected to your smart phone and I sure hope nobody hacks into them like those other glasses to see what you're seeing and recording. Remember, as we saw before, any time you see the word smart before something, what do you do? You supplant it with the words Big Brother because that's exactly what's going on with the device. These so-called Smart Contact Lenses are being looked upon to do way more than just snap a photo with a blink of an eye. Oh contraire! They're also being pitched as the new Bionic Eye that will allow you to record video and even connect to the internet for directions.

D Code: *"Imagine having the entire internet available at the blink of an eye, with a computer monitor on your contact lens. It's already more science than fiction."*

"You may be walking down the street and you see a restaurant, and you would like more information about this restaurant, and that can be displayed in front of your eyes. You can imagine a number of different things. The GPS will show you

directions to your destination. That information can be super-imposed to what you normally see."

"Smart contacts could soon give you robot vision, giving you the ability to record video with just the blink of an eye. (Like a spy movie!) Tech giants Sony, Google and Samsung have all filed patents for the future of digital contact lenses."

Movie clip from Mashable: *"See, I put this in my eye. It's a little camera and then I give this to TJ and then he's able to see everything I see."*

"Hey, I'm seeing what you are seeing! I see me looking at you, looking at me and I see me!

"Plans for lenses include capturing photos and video, cued by a light sensor that detects eyelid movement. The images would than transfer wirelessly to a smartphone. Augmented reality contact lenses are also in development. The technology behind 'Google lens' (which can identify most objects and locations it sees) could one day be integrated into the lens."[6]

In fact, some of these Bionic Lenses come with this feature: *"Wink your right eye to zoom in; wink your left eye to zoom out. This vision-enhancing system will upgrade human eyesight 3X the magnification creating telescopic capabilities."* So now there's no more of even squinting your eyes or adjusting your glasses to see somebody, just zoom in with a wink and find that suspect in the 7-year tribulation, you know, that one that said they don't need Jesus! But you still might be thinking, "Okay Pastor Billy! Listen. Now you've lost it! This is just wacky conspiracy stuff thinking that people are going to use cameras on their bodies to find people and arrest them, calm down!" Really? Well, you might want to pay attention to China, again! Remember, as we saw before, they're on the forefront of this Big Brother Technology and Big Brother Total Surveillance Society. That's what they're building! And I believe they're the playground for the Antichrist system that is being built on a global basis. Believe it or not, China is already looking at using their glasses to scan crowds looking for suspects. No conspiracy theory folks, it's here!

Channel TV Reports: *"Increasing amounts of high-tech gadgets from glasses with facial recognition to robots will be on display at China Rubber Stamp Parliament. To maintain security and track troublemakers, police in the country are using facial recognition, black tech glasses, as part of the major push by its* *leaders to boost security using technology representing a new era of surveillance in the country.*

This security push in China is bringing reality closer to science fiction. Using Artificial Intelligence, the glasses can scan details like car plates or facial features, matching them in real time with a centralized blacklist. It could help security forces identify people and vehicles in real time. The big worry is, who's on the blacklist. In theory it's those with criminal records but it could also include a wide range of people from lawyers and artists to journalist and charity workers.

The AI glasses are now being trialed by the police across the country. But it doesn't stop there. More of what China calls Black Tech is being rolled out. Drones to monitor its border areas, dogs fitted with cameras that feed back into the headsets. Systems to track and sense the behavior online and can scan and possibly read data on your smart phone."[7]

In other words, have fun trying to escape from that system, let alone in the 7-year Tribulation! You should've just gotten saved and avoided the whole thing. But no! Now you're on their what? Their so-called blacklist for disobeying the Antichrist and all this Body Camera Technology will find you anywhere you go. And did you see that other thing in there? They even put cameras on animals! Cameras are everywhere! But hey, good thing this is just in China. Yeah right!

That brings us to the **2nd type** of Body Cameras they're lying and deceiving us about is **Police Cameras.**

Whether you realize it or not, we're already seeing signs of our Police Force being forced right here in America to mandatorily wear body cams just like in China. Remember when those were optional? Not anymore!

Greater Boston Reports: *"Unless you have been living in a cave you have no doubt seen some high-profile shows showing some police misconduct and the extreme incident was captured on body cameras. The debate is on if all officers should be made to wear them is picking up steam."*

CBS This Morning: *"The New York police Department is implementing the country's largest body camera program. More than 20,000 officers will wear the cameras once the roll-out is complete in 2019. Recordings like this can show how* *the body cameras are used. Up to half the country's roughly 18,000 law enforcement agencies are adopting them.*

"We are in Washington Metro PD first district station and there are about 100 body cameras along this wall. Every day the officers take them out of the charging dock, put them on their chest and hit the streets."

Baltimore, November 25, 2016, body worn cameras offer an unfiltered look at the interaction between police and the community."

Bill De Blasio, New York City Mayor: *"All NYPD members on patrol will be wearing body worn cameras."*

CBS this Morning: *"Recently Commander Ralph Ennis showed us how they work."*

Commander Ralph Ennis: *"From the time I hit the button it's recording video and audio."*

CBS this Morning: *"So, it's recording me right now?"*

Commander Ralph Ennis: *"Yes. It's recording our conversation."*[8]

Whoa! So, it's not just video but audio. That sounds deceptive. And that's just Police Body Cameras. That's not counting all the other areas Body Cameras are already being used right now in the U.S.

- Firefighters
- Healthcare Workers
- Medial Industry
- Military
- Journalism
- Commerce
- General Surveillance
- Covert Surveillance
- Action Cameras like…
- Cycling
- Skiing
- Surfboarding

- Snowboarding
- You name it! Everybody's got a Body Camera!

In fact, this has become such a privacy concern that even the secular industry is admitting that all this technology could create: *"A large scale data collection that is combined with facial recognition and other technologies to create videos in bulk and the means for all cameras, including body worn cameras, to create a means of tracking people anywhere they go."* Now if that don't sound like China, I don't know what does! In fact, speaking of which, thanks to Motorola, our Police will also have the capability, just like China, to find anyone in a crowd in real time.

Motorola Solutions: Finding a Missing Child with Real-Time Artificial Intelligence. *"A child is missing. The police have been notified and the child's picture is in the system at the station. As the police walk through the crowds looking for the child, he has on his glasses which have facial recognition and also his body camera. He has the child's description so he knows exactly who he is looking for. He passes many people on this street and his glasses scan each face, adult and child. Many pass by but suddenly his glasses match with a little boy walking with another little boy in the crowd."*[9]

Yup! Subject found! Just like in China, only it's here in the U.S. One report said, *"China's mini-camera system scans the crowd for potential suicide bombers where Police can scan a sea of people with special goggles to see if they are under extreme stress, like a suicide bomber would be."* Which made one guy there say, *"I already feel tense if a Police Officer is looking at me, let alone with these strange goggles on!"* Yeah! You better smile and keep on smiling and never stop! But hey, at least with all this technology it's totally secure and it'll never get into somebody's hands to use for some nefarious global purpose, will it? Yeah, right! That's actually another thing we're being lied to and deceived about. It's not only not secure, but just about anybody can hack into these systems, including the average Joe with normal devices!

Lily Hay Newman, Writer, Wired: *"Body cameras have become a common tool used by law enforcement across the United States. The footage they capture is often instrumental in investigating crimes and allegations of police misconduct. But one security researcher says that many models currently in use by police departments are vulnerable to a wide range of digital attacks."*

Josh Mitchell: *"We can track it, we can manipulate the data on it, upload and download videos."*

Lily Newman: *"And the cameras could also be used to smuggle malware into a police station. Josh Mitchell, the security researchers who discovered these issues with the cameras says the devices suffer from many of the same security lapses found in other connected internet of things, like baby monitors and printers, even cars."*

Josh Mitchell: *"I think all together this whole setup costs less than $100.00."*

Lily Newman: *"Mitchell, who works in San Antonio, Texas, showed me how he could hack into one camera using a laptop and a long-range antenna he bought online. If you were to hack anywhere in world there would be like a million devices all connected to different networks."*

Josh Mitchell: *"So, I can identify this specific device from the wireless access points."*

Lily Newman: *"I walked a few dozen yards away wearing one of the cameras and Mitchell easily hacked into it. He could see everything, where I went and even the passcode I used to lock my phone. But that is just the beginning. Many of the cameras can connect wirelessly with other devices and they transmit a unique ID as part of the process. But none of the Wi-Fi enabled cameras as Mitchell analyzed, matched those signals, essentially turning them into tracking beacons."*[10]

Whoa! So now they can not only be used to record video and audio but become a tracking device that any average Joe can hack into on a regular basis. That's pretty deceptive! Somebody lied about that! Here's the point. Stir all this together, and for the first time in mankind's history, we really have the ability for one guy, who's name rhymes with the Antichrist, to monitor the whole planet. Whether it's cameras in the sky with satellites, or on the ground in cities, streets, buildings, the whole transportation system, billboards, and even in body cams on just about everybody, including animals. This whole system can be hacked into on a global basis which means anyone, anywhere can be under total surveillance creating a seamless net that no one can run & hide in the 7-year Tribulation. Where have I heard that before? The ability is not coming, it's already here! No wonder it's going to be a bloodbath.

And that's precisely why, out of love, God has given us this update on **The Final Countdown: Tribulation Rising** concerning **Modern Technology & the AI Invasion** to show us that the Tribulation is near and the 2nd Coming of Jesus Christ is rapidly approaching. And that's why Jesus Himself said:

Luke 21:28 "When these things begin to take place, stand up and lift up your heads, because your redemption is drawing near."

Like it or not, we are headed for **The Final Countdown**. The signs of the 7-year **Tribulation** are **Rising**! Wake up! And so, the point is this. If you're a Christian today and you're not doing anything for the Lord, shame on you! Get busy doing something for Jesus now! Stop wasting your life! We need you! Don't sit on the sidelines! Get on the front line and help us! Let's get busy working together doing something splendid for Jesus with what time is left and get busy saving souls! Amen?

But if you're reading this today and you're not a Christian, then I beg you, please, heed these signs, heed these warnings, give your life to Jesus now because this monitoring system of the Antichrist and the False Prophet is not going to lead to a life of great convenience and total security but a system that forever does away with any anonymity! Don't fall for the lie! Don't be deceived! Take the way out now, the only way out now, through Jesus Christ, and avoid the whole thing, before it's too late! Amen?

Chapter Thirteen

The Increase of Big Brother Cell Phones

The last three times we saw the **3rd type** was the **Camera System**. The Big Brother Eye on the ground with cameras. And once again, they're not just doing this in "secret" but they're also lying about it, being deceitful, and once again this is exactly what the Antichrist is going to do in the 7-year Tribulation. But don't take my word for it. Let's listen to God's.

2 Thessalonians 2:7-10 "For the secret power of lawlessness is already at work; but the one who now holds it back will continue to do so till he is taken out of the way. And then the lawless one will be revealed, whom the Lord Jesus will overthrow with the breath of His mouth and destroy by the splendor of His coming. The coming of the lawless one will be in accordance with the work of satan displayed in all kinds of counterfeit miracles, signs and wonders, and in every sort of evil that deceives those who are perishing. They perish because they refused to love the truth and so be saved."

In other words, they didn't want to hear the truth. But according to our text, we see that when the Antichrist is revealed, he's not only going to use secretive behavior to set up his machinery in the background, but he's also going to use what? False counterfeit signs, wonders, and miracles, right? In other words, he's going to use lies and deceit. Which is why it says it's being done "in accordance with the work of satan." Jesus said in John Chapter 8, satan is a "liar and the father of all lies." So, the Antichrist is going to follow in satan's footsteps. This passage gives us two more tactics the Antichrist will use to set up his kingdom in the 7-year Tribulation to dupe people. It's not only being done in secret, but he'll be using lies and deceit! And again, that's exactly what's being done right now with this Antichrist Big Brother global monitoring system. We are being lied to and deceived about it as they set this system up to monitor us! But not just the billboards and the body cams.

The **3ʳᵈ technology** they're lying and deceiving about is **Cell Phones.**

I'm here to tell you that cell phones are the biggest Big Brother invention ever thrust upon mankind in all of history, and we pay for it! Talk about deceptive! You liars!

The **1ˢᵗ deceitful lie** they say about our cell phones is hey, **We'll Never Monitor You!**

Really? Whether you realize it or not, these nifty devices, these cell phones that we all have to have, even kids. And apparently even the government wants to make sure we all have one. Remember that free cell phone thing with Obama? I got to get my Obama phone! Remember that? Everybody's got to have one. Well gee I wonder why? Well it turns out, these devices can easily be tapped into to watch, listen, and monitor all of our conversations! It's a 24-hour monitoring device and here's just one report showing how easy it can be done.

CBS News Reports: *"Sometimes you know your phone has been hacked, but often you don't. We sat down with some of the world's best hackers to show us just how easy it is to get access to everything on your phone. Is everything hackable?"*

John Herring: *"Yes."*

CBS News: *"Everything?"*

John Herring: *"Yes."*

CBS News: *"If someone tells you, you can't do it..."*

John Herring: *"I don't believe it."*

CBS News: *"John Herring offered to prove it. So, he gathered together a group of ace hackers in our Las Vegas Hotel. Each of them a specialist at hacking mobile devices."*

"How easy is it to hack a phone right now?"

They all answer, *"Very easy."*

"It started when we logged onto the hotel Wi-Fi. Or at least it looked like the hotel Wi-Fi. Herring had created a ghost version. It's called spoofing. And it looks legitimate."

John Herring: *"Are you connected?"*

CBS News: *"I am."*

John Herring *"And I have your email."*

CBS News: *"You have access to my email account?"*

John Herring: *"I have your ride share application, all the information being transmitted including your account ID, your mobile phone, which I just got the mobile number and I have all the credit cards associated with that account."*

CBS News: *"Now the hack that you just saw only took a matter of minutes and I was fooled by that fake Wi-Fi but the other demonstrations that we are going to show you on Sunday, the hackers were able to explore a hole in the global cellular network and get into our phones, turn on our cameras and listen to us. All they needed was the phone number, with just the phone number they could hack into my phone. No matter what you do, what decisions you make, whether you turn location services on or off, they can still get in."*

"You say even if you are getting dressed, they can get access to the camera on your phone?"

"Yes, think about this. With just the phone number they were able to access my phone. So, can I borrow your phone for a second? So, my phone looks just like this. It doesn't light up and they were able to watch me and listen to me. So imagine, when you take your phone into a meeting and you lay it on the desk,

when you have your phone and you are getting dressed in the morning, they can be watching you and you wouldn't know."[1]

Whoa! That's pretty sneaky! That's deceptive! How many of you knew that? Yeah, most people have no clue, but there you go. You can hack into my phone, any phone on the global network, and not just get data, but as you saw, email, financial information and turn on my camera, listen and watch everything I do without me even knowing it! That's total monitoring! And again, they're not just called cell phones, they're called what? Smart Phones! And any time you see that word "smart" what do you supplant it with? Big Brother! Because that's what's going on here. The biggest Big Brother device ever invented in the history of mankind, not coming, but already here, and we pay for it! And I believe this new technology that's emerged in our lifetime helps explain what's going on in the text in **Matthew 24** dealing with the people in the 7-year Tribulation who get rounded up and slaughtered for being a follower of God.

Matthew 24:9-10 "Then you will be handed over to be persecuted and put to death, and you will be hated by all nations because of Me. At that time many will turn away from the faith and will betray and hate each other."

So here, Jesus says the people during the 7-year Tribulation will not only hate the followers of God, i.e., those who get saved after the Rapture, but they'll what? They'll want to kill them, right? And it says they'll do that by betraying and "turning them in." So again, think about this. How are you going to know if somebody's a follower of God anywhere on the planet in order to betray them and "turn them in?" Simple! You just invent a single device that could monitor all people's conversations all around the world and even see who they're hanging out with! It's called the cell phone! It's not coming, it's already here! In fact, nowadays I don't even have to wait for a hacker to come along and get into my phone like we saw earlier, all I have to do is just download an app. It's that simple! Believe it or not, shocker, we've been lied to about these apps. They say everyone just has to have it on their cell phones, saying it's about convenience and communication needs. You've heard the saying, right? There's an app for that! You've got to have this app! Those apps including something as simple as a Flashlight App that you download could take over your phone!

Fox Special Report: *"We have a really interesting story, our guest here, Gary Molesky, is with the company 'Snoop Wall.' Gary, thanks for being here. It's an interesting and alarming story you have about this study."*

Gary Molesky: *"I think this is Ebola right now because 500 million people are infected and they don't even know it, but it's not them, it's their smart phones."*

Fox Special Report: *"Well, give me the breakdown, how does this happen?"*

Gary Molesky: *"So let me give you an example. If you went to the hardware store you would buy a flashlight, you'd turn it on and use it to find your car keys at night or do some work. We have all installed the flashlight app on our phones."*

Fox Special Report: *"It's just an app, you turn it on, and it's a flashlight."*

Gary Molesky: *"Exactly. And instead of it being a normal flashlight you push the button and this flashlight app is kind of like the flashlight from the hardware store except it was made by Mr. Gadget. And it opens up and says, Bret, I have your phone number, your address, credit card information, family photos, videos, where you are located right now and all friends and contacts. I can send this out over this little satellite dish, all attached to the flashlight. You probably wouldn't want to buy that flashlight. And you wouldn't hit the on switch."*

Fox Special Report: *"That's what's happening?"*

Gary Molesky: *"That's what's happening. The top 10 flashlight apps today that you can download from the Google p=Play Store are all malware. They are vicious, they are spying, they are snooping, and they are stealing."*

Fox Special Report: *"So where does that information go? Or what happens to it?"*

Gary Molesky: *"So I have been tracking down where it goes and found three countries so far, China, India, and Russia."*

Fox Special Report: *"And they use it for various purposes, I guess."*

Gary Molesky: *"They use it, pretty much it seems, for criminal purposes, but if a nation or a state wants to collect a lot of information on Americans this is a great way to do it. Everybody installs a flashlight app."[2]*

Boy, did we get fooled on that one! Talk about being deceptive! I just wanted to use my phone as a flashlight and unbeknownst to me, even foreign countries around the world get access to my phone. And quote, "Collect a lot of information." Boy, that would come in handy in the 7-year Tribulation when you're trying to figure out who worshiped the Antichrist and who didn't, to know whether or not you need to kill them. Crazy stuff but it's happening! He even went on to say that even if you uninstall the app the Trojan is still there! You have to do a factory reset and *maybe* that will work. But hey, it's a good thing this is just being done by foreign countries. At least we can keep this isolated, this hacking ability. Are you kidding me? American companies are doing the same thing starting with Facebook or as we saw before, the real name we should call them, Tracebook! This is another deceptive thing going on. Facebook is not only tracking all our information online and creating these huge databases on us as we saw before, but they're also using our cell phones to monitor us!

Fox 29 Reports: *"Did you hear about this? Facebook plays another Big Brother; users are saying the social media site is really crossing the line with their new messenger app. Joining us now is tech expert Anthony Mongeluzo. Anthony, thanks for joining us. So many people are talking about this messenger app. This used to be optional but now I guess it is mandatory, you have to download it. So how does this all work and why are people all worried about this?"*

Anthony Mongeluzo: *"Basically this app is getting terrible reviews. It has a one on the five-star at the app store and similar ratings from Android. What the Messenger app basically does is, you have to give away all of your privacy, you will have Facebook look at all of your call lists, your contacts, your text messages, it even uses your recording device, your camera device on your phone without even telling you."*

Fox 29 Reports: *"Okay, that is the thing that scared me the most. Take me through that. I'm holding my phone now and if I have this messenger app, they can see what I see, even worse, keep an eye on me and what I am doing?"*

Anthony Mongeluzo: *"Most of your phones nowadays have two cameras, a front camera and a back camera. So legally you are giving them access to those cameras when you install this application."*

Fox 29 Reports: *"So some creepy guy in San Francisco can be looking live at what I am looking at?"*

Anthony Mongeluzo: *"Don't worry about San Francisco, this is global that can look at you."[3]*

Wow! Talk about being deceptive! I was forced to download this app by Facebook to use their Facebook Messenger on my phone and around the world they can monitor me. At least with the flashlight I had an option! But boy, that would come in handy in the 7-year Tribulation when you're trying to decipher who's worshiping the Antichrist and who's not in order to take them out! Tell me that's not deceptive. And don't forget, we pay for it! Isn't that slick? But at this point you might be thinking, "Well, here you go again Pastor Billy! This is just another one of those wacky conspiracy theory things you've fallen for. It's not really as bad as you say it is!" Really? How much more evidence do we need to show? I'm not making this up! In fact, for even more proof, even the secular researchers are starting to admit what these Big Brother devices can do. Here's a headline from just one secular article out there exposing how bad it really is, "Your Phone is Listening & It's Not Paranoia."

In other words, Pastor Billy is not crazy! You can repeat after me! They say, "A couple years ago, something strange happened. A friend and I were sitting at a bar, iPhones in pockets, discussing our recent trips in Japan and how we'd like to go back." The very next day, we both received pop-up ads on Facebook about cheap flights to Tokyo. It seemed like just a spooky coincidence, but then everyone seems to have a story about their smartphone listening to them. In fact, let me share some of them with you!

- **Nate:** "My fiancé and I both had wedding ads the day after we got engaged, before we had told anyone. We bought the ring in the spur of the moment and never looked anything related up. And just two weeks ago my fiancé and I went to a friend's and drank a certain kind of liquor neither of us had ever bought or talked about on the phone, and the next morning it was the first ad Facebook showed her."

- **Jon:** In 2016, I lost the hearing in my right ear. I was given a 'made for iPhone' compatible hearing aid. This meant I could take calls, stream music, etc. from my new hearing aid. Whenever the phone connected to the hearing aid, there would be an audible change, like a little click. In both the Facebook Messenger app for iOS and the main Facebook app I would hear that click, the flipping over of the audio source for my hearing aid, at inexplicable times, including when I had audio from apps disabled."

- **Lindsey:** Just last week I left my employment and sat with my friend having a chat about which direction I was going to go in. I said, 'I like coffee, I might just end up at Starbucks so I can drink more coffee.' Next time I checked my Facebook on my phone I saw a Starbucks advertisement that said they were holding an open event in London to find new staff."

- **Olivia:** "I recently had an extremely bizarre and unsettling experience that felt like more than coincidence after a voice call on WhatsApp. I was catching up with a friend who lives in London and she told me a story about how her new landlord purchased an outdoor storage shed for their bins (a product that I think is rather uniquely British). We had a good laugh about that, and I expressed how I needed something similar here in Texas. The next day as I was scrolling through my Facebook newsfeed, I came across an ad from Wayfair advertising a storage shed for outdoor bins and was immediately taken aback. Before our conversation, this was not a product that I even knew existed."

- **Justin:** "I was talking at a bar with some friends about getting a new mattress and while we were talking about various beds and mattresses suddenly two mattress ads appear on Facebook within 5 minutes of the conversation. None before the conversation."

- **Melissa:** "I visited a friend who was setting up security cameras at her house and I have never used the internet to look at anything remotely linked to home security. Yet less than an hour after discussing how to set up the cameras, I had a Facebook ad for home security cameras and my phone had been in my pocket the whole time."

- **Austin:** Once, my friend was over and he discussed that he needed Lasik eye surgery. Immediately after, I went on Facebook and a Lasik advertisement appeared. I have perfect eyesight and have never searched Lasik ever before."

- **Peter:** "I saw a product at school called the Bug-a-salt salt shooting gun, used for killing flies, something I'd never seen before nor have I searched for any related products. That night I was telling my wife about the product in a personal conversation. The following morning after the conversation with my wife about the product, my Facebook opened with an ad from Amazon with the Bug-a-salt fly killer gun listed as 'things you may be interested in.'"

I bet if I asked all of you reading this, I could get a bunch of your own stories of how this is happening to you as well, right? There is no conspiracy theory here! This is really happening! In fact, they go on to say, "Is this just paranoia, or are our smartphones actually listening?" According to Dr. Peter Henway - The senior security consultant for cybersecurity firm Asterix - the short answer is yes."

Dr. Peter Henway: *"Whether it's timing or location-based or usage of certain functions, apps are accessing the microphones. An ordinary conversation with a friend about needing a new pair of jeans could be enough to activate it."*
"So yes, our phones are listening to us and anything we say around our phones could potentially be used against us."

Including in the 7-year Tribulation. Is that person a follower of God? Are they really worshiping the Antichrist? Your cell phone will know and let the Antichrist know! Current technology, not coming but already here. In fact, it's so easy that even a 14-year old accidentally discovered this ability while playing Fortnite, the ability to tap into people's phones!

Reporter: *"14-year-old Grant Thompson was getting ready to play video games with his friends when he stumbled upon an alarming glitch in Apple's Facetime app."*

Grant Thompson: *"I tried to Facetime my friend Nathan to see if he wanted to play some video games with me and he didn't answer right away so I swiped up on the Facetime to find another person, my friend Diego."*

Reporter: *"That is when he discovered his first friend automatically connected even though his friend hadn't picked up the call yet."*

Grant Thompson: *"I was pretty shocked that we could hear him, and he could hear us."*

Reporter: *"That confusion turned out to be a major bug in Apple's Facetime software that allowed iPhone users to hear audio from their recipients' phones even if that person had not yet picked up the call."*[4]

Whoa! And it gets worse! It's not just the listening we need to be concerned about with our phones, it's the watching with our cell phones! In another article entitled, "You Should Cover Your Phone's Selfie Camera Too" they show a guy sitting on the toilet, so much for privacy!

They go on to say, *"Take a look at your smartphone. Perhaps you're reading this story on it, and the device is planted firmly in your hands. Maybe you're on a laptop, and your phone is resting face up on your desk." "Now, focus your attention on the phone's selfie camera. Try to imagine what's in its field of view. Unless your phone's camera has a cover on it, you may not be the only one with that picture in their mind." "It wasn't long ago that the idea of covering up a laptop webcam was considered 'paranoid' as if to suggest you're one of those tinfoil-hat wearing people. But that began to shift when Mark Zuckerberg accidentally revealed that even he had tape obscuring the view from his laptop's camera." "So why should the selfie camera be different? It's not."*

The article concludes with, *"Pretty unnerving stuff."* Yeah, I'd say so! In fact, it gets even worse than that. It's not just the Big Tech companies and 14-year old kids monitoring us, it's the government, and it's been going on for years whether we realize it or not!

Fox News: *"Alright Bill Binney let me get back to you. Executive Order 12333, it was revised in the final two weeks of the Obama presidency as you know. But you believe that it is that exact executive order, EO12333, that allows our government to literally wiretap and store, every phone call of every citizen, every text, every email, that's your belief, what's happening?"*

Bill Binney, Former National Security Agency Official: *"It's actually Section 23C that says that if you have the intent to find a drug dealer, for example a 64 fiber line or a 10 gigabit line, if you believe there is a drug dealer, you can go in there and collect all the data, store it, mine it, do whatever you want to with it, and preserve it, even though 99.99999% of it is domestic communications. This is nothing new, this has been going on for a long time."*

Fox News: *"So you mean every conversation I had in my life has been taped?"*

Bill Binney: *"Without warrants, yes that is right."*[5]

So now every conversation has been taped. That's disturbing and it comes with prophetic implications. Think about it. It must have seemed like a huge mystery to the Apostle John when he's writing down these revelations from God in the Book of Revelation nearly 2,000 years ago concerning the last days. He must have been thinking, "How in the world is the Antichrist going to know if somebody's a follower of God anywhere on the planet and how will these people be betrayed and turned in during the 7-year Tribulation?" Simple! You just invent a device that could monitor all people's conversations all around the world and even see who they're hanging out with and voila, you have your answer! It's called the cell phone and it's not coming, it's already here! Big Brother on steroids! Oh, and don't forget, we pay for it! Talk about being deceitful! You liars!

The **2ⁿᵈ deceitful lie** they say about our cell phones is hey **We'll Never Track You!**

What? Yeah, you thought the monitoring of our every conversation was bad and the tapping into our cameras to see what we're doing was creepy and horrible? You ain't seen nothing yet! These cell phones are also the biggest Big Brother tracking device ever invented by man, and again, we pay for it! Isn't that great? And again, I believe this helps explain another aspect of what's going on in the **Matthew 24** text dealing with the people in the 7-year Tribulation.

Matthew 24:9-10 "Then you will be handed over to be persecuted and put to death, and you will be hated by all nations because of Me. At that time many will turn away from the faith and will betray and hate each other."

So again, here we see Jesus telling the people that in the 7-year Tribulation, not only will they hate the followers of God and betray and "turn them in," those who get saved after the rapture, but they'll what? They'll want to kill them, right? So again, think about this. How in the world are you going to find followers of God anywhere on the planet in order to kill them? Not just monitor them but find them and kill them. There's lots of places to hide. Simple! You use the exact same device you tricked people into paying for, the cell phone, to not only monitor all their conversations to see what they're doing and who they're hanging out with, but you also use that same device to track them. You'll know exactly where they are, and you can take them out just like that! And if you don't think they have this tracking ability with our cell phones as well, you're in for a rude awakening! Here's just one news report sharing how all this technology put together is tracking our every move.

RT News Reports: *"The US is funneling money into tracking systems, threatening the concept of privacy, a thing of the past. It could mean that peoples every move can be used against them to keep them under surveillance. Here is our reporter on the future of being watched."*

Reporter in the field: *"The information era was a period that everybody embraced. But todays surveillance age is a reality that almost no one can escape."*

Steve Rambam, CEO Pallorium Investigative Agency: *"We are five years away, here in New York, from zero privacy where every New Yorker is being tracked and cataloged and watched and that information is being saved for pretty much an undetermined period of time."*

Reporter: *"Face recognition and iris scanning are the current tools of the trade, however scientists are currently developing a new technology geared to identifying anyone from much greater distances. If researchers are successful the defense department may eventually be able to detect individuals by ear shape, heartbeat, walking pattern and possibly even odor. Long range fingerprint and iris scanning are also reportedly being explored for the U.S. toolbox for tracking."*

A.J. Jacobs, Editor-a-large, Esquire Magazine: *"I think that we are not going to have a private moment in the future and I always tell people that if you want to have an extra-marital affair you better have it right now because you aren't going to be able to have it in 5 years because everything will be tracked. Your husband or wife will know exactly where you are at all times."*

Steve Rambam: *"Do you think it's appropriate that someone can press a button and determine everywhere I've been, everything I've done, everyone I've been with? No, it's wrong."*

Reporter: *"Hard to believe, 10 years ago the concept of facial recognition, biometric surveillance and domestic drones was limited to science fiction movies like Minority Report."*[5]

Ooh! There's that movie again. It's almost like we're being prepared for something. It's called soft disclosure. And did you catch that one part, "Somebody could push a button and find out everywhere I've been and who I've been with?" And that's not even counting cell phones and I'll get to that in second, but this is total tracking ability of anyone on the planet at the push of a button, 24/7! Not coming, but already here! And this information is needed if you're unfortunately one of those resisters who still think something like this, "Well hey. I don't need Jesus. I don't need God. I don't need to be saved. You

Christians are a bunch of wackos! If the hammer comes down in the 7-year Tribulation, I'll just put my cell phone in airplane mode or disconnect it from the internet, or better yet, I'll take out that SIM card so they can't track me! Ha! Ha! Ha!" Really! You really think the Antichrist hasn't thought of that? I hate to burst your bubble, but even if you turn all those things off on your cell phone, even if you power it down, they can not only still track you but they're already doing it!

Fox News: *"We know that Google is tracking us. We agree to it when we set up our phones. So, we wanted to find out what exactly Google is learning about us throughout the day. So, here is what we are going to do. We have two identical phones. The only difference between these two phones is this one is in airplane mode. Both of the phones lack a sim card and they haven't been set up to access any Wi-Fi network. So, for all intents and purposes, these phones have no connection to a data network. We are going to keep them with us throughout the day. As we travel around D.C., we are going to find out just exactly what Google is finding out about me. Our first stop is Sims Convenience Store just outside FOX bureau for a quick coffee. From there we took a walk to the Capitol and then a swift walk around the office buildings and then decided to hop into a car and drive around town.*

"Hello, we are going to the Children's Hospital, please."

To do our test, we have to do more than walk the block. So, we took a cruise around our nation's capital. Due north to the Children's National Medical Center, then west to St Albans school and the National Cathedral School. Our tour around town was a 14.8-mile journey that lasted more than an hour. This entire time the phones had no access to the internet, no Wi-Fi and no cellular data service. It almost seemed quaint that Google wouldn't be able to collect data on me.

"Back to the Bureau, my friend."

"Now we are back here at our Fox Bureau in D.C. and we have both of our phones exactly like we left with them and the only difference is I snapped a couple of bad selfies at the National Cathedral. Otherwise they have stayed in my pocket the entire day. So, let's see what they know. This is our 'man in the middle' device. It's basically a Wi-Fi network that these phones will connect to once we turn their Wi-Fi on.

It's going to pass data through it on its way to Google, but on the way, we are actually going to get a copy of the same data that Google is going to get. We will be able to decrypt it and then see where we have been throughout the day. Within minutes the numbers started rolling in. The phone that wasn't on airplane mode registered more than 100 locations. 130 activities, and even 152 biometric readings.

As soon as it hooked up to the Wi-Fi it registered 300 kilobytes of data being transferred straight to Google. Even logged our exact locations. Tracking us all around town, the capital, the hospital, the school and the cathedral. What's missing here is the exact route we took, but it got that data too. It knows when I got out of the car. The metadata has a time log down to the very second, tracking everything. When they think you are walking, riding, and yes, even getting out of the car. Ok, so you are thinking this is no big deal, just put my phone in airplane mode. We thought of that too.

The other phone with no sim card that remained in airplane mode the entire time, let's see what kind of data it captured. The phone with airplane mode activated actually logged more locations and activities than did the other phone. And it also transferred 100's of kilobytes to Google as soon as it was activated. They even followed where most people would expect total privacy, Government buildings, a children's hospital, a private school, a church, every step you take, Google is watching you."[6]

And that will come in handy for the Antichrist who in the 7-year Tribulation will give an order for people to worship him, and I wonder how he knows who does and who doesn't? Let alone track them down and kill those who don't. And lest you think this tracking ability won't go global, it already has!

"The NSA has a diverse range of surveillance capabilities – from monitoring Google Maps to sifting through millions of phone call records and spying on web searches. But it doesn't end there." "The agency can also track down the location of a cellphone even if the handset is turned off. By September 2004, shortly after the 9/11 attacks, the NSA had developed a technique that was called, 'The Find.' The technique was used in Iraq and helped identify thousands of new targets, including members of al-Qaeda."

Whoa! Stop right there! That's just it, that's the slippery slope! What if you became the "new terrorist," and who gets to define that term anyway?

As we saw before in other studies, evangelical Christians are now being called terrorists!" During the Obama Administration, any one of these beliefs classified you as a terrorist.

- Pro-life
- Critical of the United Nations
- Critical of the New World Order
- Critical of the Federal Reserve
- Critical of Homosexual marriage
- Oppose the North American Union (which they say officially does not exist)
- Critical of the income tax
- Oppose illegal immigration
- Fear foreign powers such as Communist China, Iran, Russia and India
- Concerned about RFID chips
- Belief in Bible prophecy or End Time Prophecies

In fact, here's how the media is brainwashing others to think Christians are dangerous terrorists.

ABC Reports: *"If you want to talk about radical Islam and what is going on there..."*

Rosie O'Donnell: *"Hold on there, radical Christianity is just as threatening as radical Islam. In a country like America. Where we have separation of church and state. We are a democracy."*

Fox & Friends: *"Her exact quote was, Rosie O'Donnell, about two months ago, she said, 'Radical Christianity is just as threatening as radical Islam.' And in the last hour we received an email from somebody who said, 'You seem to forget in the world of radical Islam, Rosie, the woman, the lesbian, would either be hung or stoned to death and in the world of radical Islam there would be no 'View' or independent opinionated women.'"*

Erroll Southers, Barack Obama's Nominee to head the Transportation Safety Administration: *"Most of the radical groups that we have to pay attention here are white supremist groups, anti-government, in most cases anti-abortion, they are usually survivalist in nature, identity-oriented, those groups claim to be extremely anti-government, Christian identity oriented."*

Josh Zepps, Huff Post Live: *"The separation of church and state is fundamental to American life, what about church and military, in a new report by a national security expert says that fundamental Christianity is rampant in the armed forces. The military leaders overtly promote Evangelical Christianity."*

Jim Parco, Professor of Economics at Colorado College: *"You have a system that is creating religious fundamentalists. That is what is concerning to me."*

Sarah Primrose: Huff Post Live: *"The only question that needs to asked is 'Do these fundamentalist beliefs and associated behavior compromise our missions abroad?' If yes, we must discourage or ban the encouragement of the spread of this brand of Christianity in the military."*

Rachel Maddow: *"What we are learning about the religious beliefs of this militia group makes them look a little bit like a cult, a stand-alone religious oddity. But some of the things they are obsessed with, fighting the Antichrist, avoiding the Mark of the Beast, the pre-tribulation Rapture, all that stuff. These are the beliefs that are specific to this one cult, these beliefs are sort of characteristic of a broader movement, aren't they?"*

Fox News: *"Andrei Codroscu, commentator for the program 'All Things Considered' mocked a Christian pamphlet about the doctrine of the Rapture and the ascension into Heaven, quote."* **Andrei Codroscu,** Commentator National Public Radio: *"The evaporation of four million (people) who believe in this crap would leave the world a better place."*

Townhall.com/Blog: *"This man that tried to blow up innocent people that he doesn't know in Times Square, these men are acting on conviction. Somehow the idea got into their minds that to kill other people is a great thing to do and they would be rewarded in the hereafter."*

Commentator: *"But Christians do that every single day. In this country."*

Guest speaker: *"Do they blow people up?"*

Commentator: *"Yes, Christians. Every day."*[7]

As one-man shares, "What is interesting about the above list is that a great deal of it has to do with things that have nothing to do with the individual nation. The only possible reason any national government would be concerned about its citizen's objecting to things like the New World Order, world government, the United Nations, homosexual marriage, a regional global government like the North American Union, abortion, RFID chips and belief in end times prophecies is because this is what they are planning to promote in the near future. Otherwise why be bothered about it?" And he says this, "I would suggest to you that Bible prophecy is being fulfilled far faster than most of us realize and that is why governments around the world are concerned about these things."

We know in the 7-year Tribulation there will be those who get put on a so-called terrorist list, i.e., those who follow God, those who get saved after the Rapture, "will be handed over to be persecuted and put to death." You disobeyed the Antichrist! You didn't worship him! They become the new terrorist. Global Terrorist. And this global cell phone technology is going to find them and hunt them down and take them out. Not coming, already here. The report goes on to say that, "These surveillance tools in cell phones help governments conduct surveillance of communications both domestic and international." In other words, it really has gone global. In fact, even countries like Canada are getting in on the action.

Dave Seglins, CBC News: *"This is the latest revelation from spy agency documents that were leaked by the former U.S. Security Contractor, Edward Snowden. Canada's Electronic Spy agency and the NSA in the U.S. with counter parts in Australia, New Zealand and the U.K. just a few years ago were trying to find ways to hack into people's mobile phones to track them and even install spyware."*

"Smart phones are everywhere, everyone's got one, work, play, banking, talking to loved ones. So, it's a surprise to some that those personal phones and their apps could be vulnerable to snooping, hackers, criminals or spies."

Girl on the street: *"I think it's scary. We are on our phones 24/7, we use it for school, we use it for social media."*

"Top secret documents from Canada Communications Establishment show Canada and its allies have worked to hack not all mobile phones but elsewhere, in Europe, Africa, the Caribbean, and they are looking for servers that could be exploited, used to secretly install spyware in suspect's smart phones."

Michael Geist, University of Ottawa: *"What was particularly striking was you see some of the biggest names in technology in the mobile world being the target, the Samsung's, the Apples, of the world that millions and millions of consumers that the public rely upon on a daily basis."*

Ron Deibert, The Citizen Lab, University of Toronto: *"They can use this data to trap targets of interest. Political targets, terrorists, and so on."[8]*

Including the terrorists in the 7-year Tribulation who refuse to worship the Antichrist and are trying to get away. You ain't going nowhere! The global net needed to monitor, listen, watch, and track down any resisters in the 7-year Tribulation is already here with a device that we got tricked into paying for called the cell phone! Talk about deceptive! But you still might be thinking, unfortunately, "Well that's it. I'll just take out my battery in my cell phone and they can't track me then! Ha! Ha! Ha! I'm free! I'm free." When will you ever learn! Don't be a fool! Take the way out through Jesus!

And I quote, "This cell phone can make calls even without a battery." *"In order to operate without a battery, the phone would have to rely only on energy that could be harvested from its surroundings." "Ambient light can be turned into electricity with solar panels or photodiodes. Radio-frequency, TV, and Wi-Fi broadcasts can also be converted into energy using an antenna." "You would never have to worry about leaving your charger at home ever again."*

Why? Because you don't need a battery! Which means all these cell phone monitoring and tracking functions can still be used even without a battery to listen, monitor, spy on everything you're doing, and track you down in case you need to be killed. Technology that is not coming, but is already here, and we pay for it. Talk about deceptive! That's what the Antichrist is going to do. The cell phone is here just in time for the 7-year Tribulation slaughter. It's not by chance and it's a sign we're living in the last days, and we don't even realize it!

And that's precisely why, out of love, God has given us this update on **The Final Countdown: Tribulation Rising** concerning **Modern Technology & the AI Invasion** to show us that the Tribulation is near and the 2nd Coming of Jesus Christ is rapidly approaching. And that's why Jesus Himself said:

Luke 21:28 "When these things begin to take place, stand up and lift up your heads, because your redemption is drawing near."

People of God, like it or not, we are headed for **The Final Countdown.** The signs of the 7-year **Tribulation** are **Rising**! Wake up! And so, the point is this. If you're a Christian today and you're not doing anything for the Lord, shame on you! Get busy doing something for Jesus now! Stop wasting your life! We need you! Don't sit on the sidelines! Get on the front line and help us! Let's get busy working together doing something splendid for Jesus with what time is left and get busy saving souls! Amen?

But if you're reading this today and you're not a Christian, then I beg you, please, heed these signs, heed these warnings, give your life to Jesus now because this monitoring system of the Antichrist and the False Prophet is not going to lead to a life of ease and great communication, but a system that allows them to have global assassinations! Don't fall for the lie! Take the way out now, the only way out now, through Jesus Christ, and avoid the whole thing, before it's too late! Amen?

Chapter Fourteen

The Increase of Big Brother Computers

The **7th place** they're installing Big Brother cameras on the ground right now is in our **Homes**.

This is something people desperately need to hear especially if they're one of those who are still rebelling, unfortunately, after all that we've seen with this Big Brother Technology. They still say they don't need God, they don't need Jesus, you Christians are a bunch of wackos! If I'm left behind in the 7-year Tribulation, I'm just going to stay in my house, and they can't get me! Ha! Ha! Ha! Really? You really think the Antichrist hasn't thought about that one? You need to read your Bible! Even Jesus said your house is not going to be safe during the 7-year Tribulation! You need to get saved right now and avoid the whole thing! But don't take my word for it. Let's listen to God's.

Matthew 24:15-22 "So when you see standing in the holy place the abomination that causes desolation, spoken of through the prophet Daniel – let the reader understand – then let those who are in Judea flee to the mountains. Let no one on the roof of his house go down to take anything out of the house. Let no one in the field go back to get his cloak. How dreadful it will be in those days for pregnant women and nursing mothers! Pray that your flight will not take place in winter or on the Sabbath. For then there will be great distress, unequaled from the beginning of the world until now –and never to be equaled again. If those days had not been cut short, no one would survive, but for the sake of the elect those days will be shortened."

In this passage we see that Jesus clearly says that during the 7-year Tribulation, after the Antichrist shows his true colors and goes into the rebuilt Jewish temple to declare himself to be god, at the halfway point, the abomination of desolation spoken of by the Prophet Daniel, that the only option for these people at this time is to what? To flee, right? To get out of there now in quick flight, right? Chop, chop! Get out of there now! Why? Because again, as we saw before, Zechariah said it's going to be a horrible time of slaughter. Just the Jewish people alone, 2/3^{rds} of them are going to be annihilated at this time!

Zechariah 13:8-9 "In the whole land, declares the LORD, two-thirds will be struck down and perish; yet one-third will be left in it. This third I will bring into the fire; I will refine them like silver and test them like gold. They will call on my name and I will answer them; I will say, 'They are my people,' and they will say, 'The LORD is our God.'"

Again, this is a good news, bad news passage for the Jewish People. They finally wake up at this point and realize that Jesus is the One and Only Messiah, that's great, but it comes at a horrible price. Two-thirds perish! But Jesus not only tells these people, left behind, what they should do, including the Jewish remnant, i.e., flee to the mountains, but He also tells them what they should not do. He said whatever you do, don't "flee" to where? Your house, right? It says it right there! And this is important for those who think their homes will always be the safest place on the planet, or maybe, somehow, they can make their home the safest place on the planet with all their survival gear and stuff, think again! Listen to Jesus! Has it ever occurred to you that all this lying deceptive system of the Antichrist that is being built right now before our eyes has also figured out a way to make our homes into a Big Brother paradise as well? Well guess what? They already have! Not coming, but already here! Now, as I've mentioned before, they not only have radar guns that can peer through concrete walls and see you if you try to hide, in any building, including your home, and satellites in orbit, and drones in the sky that do the same thing. But, skipping over that aspect...

The **1st way** they're getting **even more invasive** with our homes is with **Computers**.

You see, not only does everybody just have to have a cell phone, as we saw before, which are great for tracking, watching, and listening to everything we do, but hey, everybody's got to have a computer too, right? At least one! And by the way, that's all a cell phone is, is a sophisticated computer, just smaller. Who cares if you only use your home computer at home just to play games, it too has become one of the biggest bugging, tracking, monitoring devices ever invented by man! And since we keep them at home, guess where they get to monitor us? Right there too!

And the **1st way** we're being monitored in our home by our computers is with **Data Tracking**.

Believe it or not, as we saw before, *"Every search you perform online, including on Google, goes into a giant database which is then used to keep a profile on our habits and interests. Not only Facebook and the other social media giants, but internet search engines also track which links you click during your search and then they use that information to place targeted ads into your browser."* This is another reason why, when you look for tourist spots in Hawaii on your computer, that all of a sudden, ads for airline tickets to Hawaii start popping up everywhere. It's not just on the cell phone and social media doing this, it's also computer search engines. It's all interconnected and they're using it all to track us. In fact, Google not only admits it, they even invite you to come check it out!

The Hill Reports: *"Google will now let you see everything that you searched for over the weekend. An unofficial social blog highlighted a new feature to find everything that you have ever searched for. Users should go to Google Web History, click the gear icon, download and then create an archive on your search history data. The web company promises that in a few moments, it will send an email of downloadable cache data about past searches."*[1]

That includes, yours, mine, everyone's! So, there you have it! Whether you realize it or not, all your computer activity is being watched, monitored, and cataloged! And one of the ways they do that is with these things called, "Cookies." These are "electronic cookies" they put on your computer to secretly track your every move! Believe it or not, in a very short amount of computer activity, you could have 1,000's of them watching your every move, like this guy found out!

Geoffrey A. Fowler, WP Reports: *"Chrome lets web trackers follow you around in a way that might freak you out in the real world. Imagine you are just out and about browsing. Minding your own business. But at the very first place you visit, you get joined by one of these. A cookie. He belongs to an advertising network or data tracker. In other words, he's a spy.*

What is pesky about cookies is that they stick with you, allowing nosey companies to tag along with you to the other places you browse. The more places you go, the more cookies you collect. They attach at the pants you looked in at one shop and start following you around everywhere you go. Tracker cookies come from lots of companies that you probably never heard of, but the number one cookie maker is Google. The same company that makes the number one web browser, Chrome.

'Can I get coffee?' he asks. And she answers as she takes the order, 'a coffee.'

Google makes most of its money by targeting ads, so no wonder Googles doesn't do much to stop the surveillance. You never know where you will find a cookie. Over time cookies help data companies build profiles, other interest, incomes, places and personalities. These profiles can shape what you see online, including the prices you get charged for the products. In a week of regular web browsing you might get tagged by more than 10,000 third party cookies."[2]

Ten thousand of those things are following me around in just a week? How long have you owned your computer? Think of how many thousands upon thousands must be following you around now! No wonder it runs so slow! But here's the point. So much for being anonymous and hiding out in your house during the 7-year Tribulation. What you search for, and whatever activity you're doing on the computer is being tracked and watched and monitored and cataloged whether you realize it or not, whether you want it to or not! Just in time for the 7-year Tribulation holocaust, just like Jesus said! Not even your home is going to be safe! They're going to know all your activity. And, believe it or not, it's not just companies that are doing this on our computers, so is the government. Under the guise of keeping us safe they know everything we do on the computer, right now!

RT News Reports: *"British Intelligence has been running a secret mass surveillance program that tracks people's internet browsing around the world. It has emerged from new documents from whistle blower Edward Snowden. The* *program's code name is 'Karma.' It analyzes web users online habits by tracking which websites they visit and also logs which radio stations they listen to and traces them on social media and search history and puts this all together and cross checks it to get the web profile of individuals to identify suspicious activities."[3]*

Including somebody trying to hide out in the 7-year tribulation who refuses to worship the Antichrist. They'll know what you're doing. They'll know your likes, your dislikes, your tendencies. In fact, they'll probably know you better than you! All that you do on the computer is giving them that profile. And if you think it's just the British government doing this, you're wrong! It's our own and other governments around the world. But it gets even worse than that. These same entities are not only tracking all your activity on the computer, but if they don't like something you're researching, or trying to report on with the computer and attempt to share it with others, they'll hack into your computer and take you out and silence you! Watch what happened to this reporter!

Fox News Reports: *"Sharyl Attkisson was the CBS News reporter investigating the Obama administration when she discovered last year that two of her computers were repeatedly hacked. After meeting with a confidential source at McDonald's, he told her that he was shocked and flabbergasted by his examination of her computer. A consultant hired by CBS confirmed the hacking. The intruders deleted some files and accessed others including one on the Benghazi attack. At once her iMac began wiping out files at hyper-speed before her eyes.*

Sharyl Attkisson: *'Numerous independent analysis has confirmed what we had said earlier about unauthorized intrusion by sophisticated entities at both my work computer and my home.'"[4]*

At her what? Her home! Where have I heard that before? So, if you speak up against or disagree with a political figure and try to share that information with someone, they will come and take you out even at your home. This behavior is already going on, just in time for the 7-year Tribulation! And again, for those of you who unfortunately find yourself in the 7-year Tribulation and you think you're going to be safe at home, monitoring all the events of the Antichrist in order to avoid his snare, share that information with your fellow bug-out shelter buddies, who also didn't need Jesus, you better wake up! You're toast! The only secure connection to make is to get saved right now through Jesus

Christ and avoid the whole thing! But it's even worse than that! They are not only monitoring what you do on the computer, but they are also monitoring you with the computer!

Which leads us to the **2ⁿᵈ way** we're being monitored in our Home, by our computers, is with **Built-in Microphones**.

That's right, just like with cell phones, computers also have the ability to "track" you, and "listen" to you as well, just like a cell phone, with their own built-in microphones of which most people are clueless. Granted, maybe you don't see it there, but these microphones are always listening to what you say on your computer like this guy shares!

Live Report: *"Today I'm going to be doing a live test to see if Google is always listening on your microphone. Okay, this has been in the news just in the last few days. A lot because of Mark Zuckerberg. He's been addressing Congress and the Senate in the United States. Answered a lot of questions about user privacy and particularly one question has been coming up a couple of times, which is whether or not Facebook is always listening with the microphones to better target advertising to you. I can't speak it out loud yet because I have to do a test first. This is the subject we are going to talk about okay. And he holds up a sign that says, 'dog toys.' So, I think I can start talking about that subject now. I have to close everything first though.*

'So, dog toys. I want to buy some dog toys for my dog. Because I love my dog and he deserves all the best toys in the world, so maybe we can find him some really nice dog toys. Some really nice toys for dogs. Maybe some calm or plush animals, maybe some dog toys near me. Maybe some black or red ones. I don't know what colors dogs care about but hopefully they like colored dog toys from time to time.

Let's see, a weasel or dog bed, or something he can chew on, you know. Dog toys near me or affordable dog toys are good for me. As a consumer I am looking for the most affordable items that I can get for my dog. Yes, dog toys are what I am most interested in right now. I need something right now. Dog toys. I have money right now in my wallet. I will take it out and give it to whomever is selling dog toys, is what I am trying to say.'

Alright everybody, that's enough, so let's get back online. Oh my, it's right there! Everybody bury your microphones. Oh no, there's dog toys right here. (On his computer screen). So, let's click on this ad and see where it takes us. Pricefalls.com. Well everybody I think that is conclusive evidence that your microphones are always listening."[5]

From where? From your computer at home or office or wherever you have one. How many of you realized that was going on? Yeah, almost none! It's bad enough they're doing that with the cell phone, but now even the computer. Which means, even if you don't own one, think about it, all you have to do is go near one and they'll be listening to everything you say! Which includes, for those who are unfortunately left behind in the 7-year Tribulation for rejecting Jesus, they'll know if you're worshiping the Antichrist and whether or not you're trying to hide out in your home! You should've listened to Jesus! The computers are listening to you! But that's not all.

The **3rd way** we're being monitored in our Home by our computers is with **Web Cams**. (That's right folks! Whose watching who?)

Whether you realize it or not, spying on people via their webcams from their computers is not just happening, but it's become so commonplace that they now have whole YouTube channels of people posting what they're watching and spying on from other people's webcams after hacking into them! And one of the terms they use for this is called 'Ratters' which stands for Remote Access Tools, a RAT. And, as we saw before, it was such a big concern that even Mark Zuckerberg of Facebook admitted that he places tape over his webcam on his computer! Remember that? Gee, I wonder why. Well, maybe he knows something we don't? Believe it or not, it's not paranoia, even secular experts are saying it's a good thing to do! Cover your webcam!

Tech insider Reports: *"Should you cover your laptop camera with tape for security?"*

Liam O'Murchu, Symantec Director of Security: *"It's not actually paranoia but we do see cases where people will get onto your computer and activate your camera and will look at what you are doing. You see that quite a lot. Mark Zuckerberg is the type of person who will probably be targeted from even other governments to understand what he is doing, where he wants to go, what are his business plans. They do all sorts of things. They take screenshots of what is going* *on. We have actually had cases where people have been arrested and have gone to prison for taking pictures of people in their bedrooms and blackmailing them with that information. Not just on your computers, on your home cameras, your TV monitors, your security cameras in your home. Hackers can get into those and see the stream of video inside your home. So, it's not really paranoia and you probably should cover your camera."[6]*

So, Mark Zuckerberg wasn't paranoid after all. He knew what none of us did! They really are watching you on your computer through your webcam at home! And did you see it wasn't just your webcam, but any camera you have in your home they were hacking into and monitoring you. But as you saw, secular experts are saying this is not paranoia, it's not just for Mark Zuckerberg or the lunatic fringe who wear that tin-foil hat thingy! We too need to be concerned about this. Oh, and by the way, have you noticed that virtually all new laptops and all new desktop monitors have built-in web cams in them whether you wanted one or not? I wonder why? In fact, it has become so commonplace and easy for people to hack into other people's computers, including their webcams, that this guy decided just to do it to prank his friends!

YVF Reports: *"Every time I turn around there is something else in the news about the government spying on us. The hackers can actually hack into your webcam and spy on you in the privacy of your own home on your own computer. I decided to put this to the test so I'm going to spy on my own friends and family members today and we will see how they feel when they find out that someone is watching them.*

Okay, we are live, we are in. She has no idea we are watching her.

As they look at another person, 'We are in, I've never seen that room before.' So, they dial him up on the phone and watch him as he answers. He answers, 'Jack' and they reply, 'Hey buddy how you doing? Where are you?' He answers, 'At home in Idaho.' As they are watching him rub something on his lips, they say to him, 'You should get some brand name something to put on your lips.' He all of a sudden gets this strange look on his face. 'What? Jack?'

Then they go to another person. A girl is in her bedroom. They send her a text saying, 'Don't bite your nails.' She has her finger in her mouth. She stops what she is doing to look at her phone and they look around her room. The guys are laughing at how she is trying to figure out how anyone knows she is biting her nails.

They then go back to the guy that was putting something on his lips. He asks them, 'What, did you hear me putting something on?' They answer, 'Yes, we heard the cap coming off. Hey, write this down. Do you have a pen or something?' Right at this time he is holding a pen up to his mouth with a flower on the end. He answers, 'Yes, hold on,' and he puts the flower down to pick up another pen. But they say to him, 'Hey, isn't that a pen, isn't that flower a pen?' He says, 'Yes, it is, how did you know?' He has such a puzzled look on his face and the two guys are cracking up. They ask, 'Know what?' He replies, 'That it is a flower pen.' They laugh some more. He is looking all around the room to see if they are hiding somewhere to see what he is doing. 'Are you in here?' he asks.

Now we go to another room where a third friend is looking at a picture album. As they watch her, they tell her, 'You just turned the page.' She holds her phone out in front of her and says, 'Can you see me?' He replies, 'What, can I see you, what is that supposed to mean?'

Now we are back to the first girl. She is sitting on the floor going through her closet. He sends her a text and says, 'You don't need to get on your knees, just bend over and pick it up.' She jumps to her feet and again starts looking around the room to see if they are hiding.

The girl looking at the album is also stunned. They tell her to take the photo that she is looking at, the one she just touched.

The guy with the flower is now rubbing the flower on his lips. The guys watching him say, 'How does that flower feel on your lips?' They are laughing and he is looking around the room and asks, 'Why are you laughing? How do you know I have a flower? Jack, how do you know I have a flower?' They answer him, 'We are looking at you through your webcam, Christian.' He looks at his webcam in surprise. He didn't know they could do this, and they all laugh. He puts a little purple sticky note on his lip and asks if they can see that. They all laugh, and the guys tell him it says laugh on it. He takes it off and turns it over and that is what it says, and they all laugh again.

Now they are back to the girl in the closet. She says, 'That is so creepy, how did you know how to do that?'[7]

Yeah, and if that guy can do that, then do you think the professionals are going to have any trouble doing it? Do you think the Antichrist and the False Prophet are going to have any problem doing it in the 7-year Tribulation? No way! I'll say it again: There is no safe place to hide in the 7-year Tribulation, not even in your home! How many times do I need to say it? Listen to Jesus! Don't make the biggest mistake of your life! Do not go back to your house. Don't think that it's going to be safe! Get saved now! All this computer technology is ensuring that all people will be monitored and watched at all times in the 7-year Tribulation wherever you go! There is no way to escape except through Jesus! But that's still not all.

The **4ᵗʰ way** we're being monitored in our home by our computers is with **Bogus Media**.

You see, the computer technology is getting so sophisticated that even for those of you who think at this point, incredibly so, that you still don't need Jesus, you don't need to get saved, Christian's are a bunch of wackos, what you're going to do is just simply get rid of all your computers in the 7-year Tribulation from your home, and so this way they won't be able to find you, let alone see what you're up to, you're safe. Really? You better think again! Because we have already given them tons of video recordings and tons of hours of our speaking via the cell phones or computers, or even social media uploads. And now these same computers can make us say and do anything they want us to, to create an excuse for them to come and round you up at your home! Don't believe me? This is how easy it is now to make anybody say anything they want you to say!

Jordan Peele: *"Let's hear from Zeyu Jin about Photoshop voice overs. Please welcome to the stage Zeyu Jin."*

Zeyu Jin: *"Hello everyone. You guys have been making weird stuff online with photo editing. We are going to do something today, like do something to human speech, like what you said at your wedding. So, let's get on with it. Well I have obtained this piece of audio of Michael talking to Peele about how he felt after getting nominated. There is a pretty interesting joke here so let's just hear it."*

The audio says, *'I jumped out of bed and kissed my dogs and my wife, in that order.'*

Zeyu Jin: *"So how about we mess with who he actually kissed. You may be thinking that you are pretty familiar with Photoshop, but we are not quite used to audio waveforms. How can we do this? Well I have good news for you. Introducing project VoCo. Project VoCo allows you to add speech in text, so let's bring it up. I just load this audio piece into VoCo and we have this as you can see we have the audio waveform above it and we have the text down there and when we play back the text and audio should play back at the same time, so let's try it.*

The audio says, *'And I kissed my dogs and my wife.'*

Zeyu Jin: *"So suppose Michael wants to send this audio to his wife and he actually wants his wife to go before the dogs. So, what do we do, copy and paste? Let's do it. Now let's listen."*

The Audio says, *'And I kissed my wife and my dogs.'*

Zeyu Jin: *"Wait there is more. We have to type something that's not here, so I actually heard that on that day our Michael actually kissed our Jordan so to recover the truth let's do it. So, let's take the word 'secrets' out too and also type the word Jordan and here we go."*

Audio says, *'I kissed Jordan and my dogs.'*

Zeyu Jin: *"The last is we not only type words but small phrases. So, we remove these words and put in three times."*

Audio says: '*I kissed Jordan three times.* '[8]

This technology is not only here now but it can be used against anybody to create an excuse to round you up in your home! Think about it. This is the perfect tool to make anyone into a so-called "bad guy" or "terrorist" or any other "threat" to society and take them out! I mean, how can you deny it? Didn't you hear what they said? It's all over the internet and the news! They were criticizing the government, the Antichrist, the False Prophet. When the whole time it was fake! It was all computer generated. You didn't say anything of the sort, but nobody else will know. The perfect tool to get rid of anyone they want, just in time for the 7-year tribulation! But that's not all. They can not only Photoshop your photos and voice, but now they can even Photoshop your face, making your face say whatever they want as well. It's called Deepfake Videos and even the government is getting concerned about it!

Today Show Reports: *"From the moment we wake up, the unending stream of videos scream for our attention, but how good are you at spotting a fake? The so-called Deepfakes can be awfully convincing."*

Jennifer Lawrence at the Golden Globes: *"This is truly surprising to me."*

Today Show: *"You have probably seen Jennifer Lawrence at the Golden Globes and this Deepfake makeover with Steve Buscemi face lined over hers. If you didn't know the real Jennifer Lawrence, you might be convinced that this is real. But get this, creating fake photos and videos are very easy. Some apps let users feed in hundreds of thousands of images to create a fake video. Like adding Nicholas Cage's face to movies he was never in. Scarlett Johansen had slam hackers post her face on a porn actors' video. Or the video of a researcher seemingly changing President Bush's facial expressions. Look closely. Is that really President Obama lacing a speech with profanities?"*

President Obama: *"I would never say these things, especially in a public address, but someone else would. Someone like Jordan."*

Today Reports: *"To show how easily it can be done, Cyber Security expert Theresa Payton uses the video on me. She puts a face on mine using a program free on the internet."*

Theresa Payton: *"We can actually take a topic that you were talking about which is completely different, mash it up and make you say something in the real newscast so that if you were saying something in the positive, we could change it to a negative."*

Today Reports: *"Theresa's videos were done using crude programs that were available for free on the internet. Already much more sophisticated software makes it difficult to tell what is real and what is not."*

WSJ Reports: *"The concern now is that foreign governments with deep pockets could flood American social media with Deepfakes to influence voters in the next election. Changing photos and history used to be tedious and technical. In one photo, Stalin had a secret police official removed from photos when he fell out of* *favor. Hollywood has had the wherewithal for decades to make computer generated fakes like in the movie Forest Gump. Tom Hanks meeting with John F. Kennedy. Now fast forward to where we are today and the last few years, we see a whole new generation of fake content. In the meantime, the fakes are getting ever more sophisticated."*

"There is a lot happening very, very quickly right now."

WSJ Reports: *"This Professor shows us the cutting-edge research that has been publicly discussed in the field. The newest generation of fake videos are not only head shots that are being manipulated, but actually full body manipulation. And one of these videos includes me. I'm not a very good dancer. I'm not as good as Bruno Mars but I can be. The superimposed software scans Mars movements and then renders my video to make my movements match his. The dance video was synthesized by three Berkley students and overseen by a computer science professor."*

Professor: *"Now what you do is basically, you feed into the system a whole bunch of images of the person you want to target on the right, and you have someone as the puppet master on the left, and it synthesizes what you want. Then I superimpose a voice synthesis of Putin, President Trump, whoever it is. Imagine the following scenario. The video comes out with Donald Trump saying, 'I have just launched weapons against North Korea. That video goes on to Twitter and goes viral in 30 – 60 seconds. North Korea responds in another 60 seconds before anybody figures out that the video is fake. How are we going to believe anything anymore that we see?"[9]*

Including somebody in the 7-year tribulation that they want to take out by making them look like a terrorist. So, they create a Deepfake video and the illusion is complete! Technology that is not coming, but already here! I mean, how can you deny that? I didn't just hear you; I saw you say it! You're a "terrorist." You need to be rounded up right in your own home.

This is starting to sound like that movie, *The Running Man*, in the 1980's that featured Arnold Schwarzenegger, remember that? It featured a society, a totalitarian state in, get this, the year 2019, where at that time they were able to manipulate a video of Arnold to make him out to look like he was a crazy, wacko, terrorist, dangerous guy, as an excuse to round him up! So much for this being a science fiction movie! It's become our current reality! They hit the date right on the nose! 2019 is right! And just to make sure that everybody falls for it, just like in the Running Man movie, all they have got to do is replay that Deepfake video over and over again on all the media outlets to brainwash people into thinking it's true. Then just like with Arnold they'll be cheering on our arrest too! And if you don't think they would do stuff like that, they already are! Remember it's 2019! The date is precise. Here's proof that the media is all interconnected reading off the same fake script!

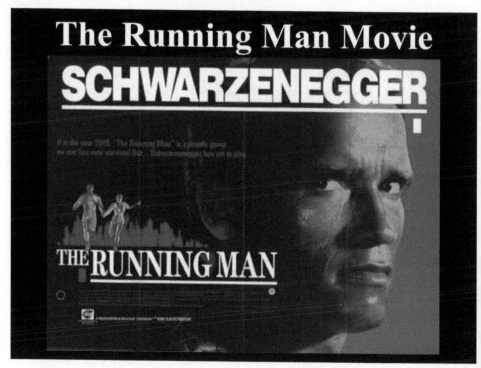

Fox 29 News Reports: *"Hi, I'm Fox's Jessica Headley." "And I'm Ryan Wolf."*

KATU 2 News and Fox 29 together: *"Our greatest responsibility is to serve our Treasure Valley communities..."*

ABC 4 News: *"the El Paso Las Cruces communities..."*

Fox 28 News: *"the Iowa communities..."*

Fox 66 News: *"the Michigan communities..."*

Channel 4 News: *"We are extremely proud of the quality balanced journalism, that 4 News produces but...."*

All the news channels say the exact same words at the exact same time: *"we are concerned about the fake news stories plaguing our country."*

Eyewitness News KBAK: *"Plaguing our country. The sharing of bias and false news has become all too common on social media. More alarming is some media outlets publish the same fake stories without checking the facts first."*

All the news channels say the exact same words at the same time: *"the sharing of the false news has become all too common on social media. More alarming is some media outlets publish the same fake stories without checking the facts. It is extremely dangerous to our democracy."*

Fox 29: *"It is extremely dangerous to our democracy."*

KATU 2: *"It is extremely dangerous to our democracy."*

Local 12: *"It is extremely dangerous to our democracy."*

News 4, Fox 11, Fox 28 and many more: *"It is extremely dangerous to our democracy."*[10]

Welcome to the Running Man show, where fake generated, manipulated news is on 24 hours a day 7 days a week across the globe. Where you can have anyone say and do anything you want and replay that thing across the planet to brainwash people to take out those resisters! Just in time for the 7-year Tribulation and the resisters who said they didn't need Jesus, and that Christians are a bunch of wackos. You should've listened to Jesus! You should've gotten saved and avoided the whole thing!

And that's precisely why, out of love, God has given us this update on **The Final Countdown: Tribulation Rising** concerning **Modern Technology & the AI Invasion** to show us that the Tribulation is near and the 2nd Coming of Jesus Christ is rapidly approaching. And that's why Jesus Himself said:

Luke 21:28 "When these things begin to take place, stand up and lift up your heads, because your redemption is drawing near."

People of God, like it or not, we are headed for **The Final Countdown**. The signs of the 7-year **Tribulation** are **Rising**! Wake up! And so, the point is this. If you're a Christian here today and you're not doing anything for the Lord, shame on you! Get busy doing something for Jesus now! Stop wasting your life! We need you! Don't sit on the sidelines! Get on the front line and help us! Let's get busy working together doing something splendid for Jesus with what time is left and get busy saving souls! Amen?

But if you're reading this today and you're not a Christian, then I beg you, please, heed these signs, heed these warnings, give your life to Jesus now because this monitoring system of the Antichrist and the False Prophet is not going to lead to fun times and funny memes, but to a system that again allows them to have targeted assassinations! Don't fall for the lie! Take the way out now, the only way out now, through Jesus Christ, and avoid the whole thing, before it's too late! Amen?

Chapter Fifteen

The Increase of Big Brother Homes

The **2ⁿᵈ way** they're getting **even more invasive** with our Homes is with **Automated Home Systems**.

That's right! Once again, you should've listened to Jesus! He said not even your house is going to be a safe during the 7-year Tribulation! You should've gotten saved and avoided the whole thing! But once again, don't take my word for it. Let's listen to God's.

Matthew 24:15-22 "So when you see standing in the holy place the abomination that causes desolation, spoken of through the prophet Daniel – let the reader understand – then let those who are in Judea flee to the mountains. Let no one on the roof of his house go down to take anything out of the house. Let no one in the field go back to get his cloak. How dreadful it will be in those days for pregnant women and nursing mothers! Pray that your flight will not take place in winter or on the Sabbath. For then there will be great distress, unequaled from the beginning of the world until now –and never to be equaled again. If those days had not been cut short, no one would survive, but for the sake of the elect those days will be shortened."

Again we see in this passage, Jesus says that during the 7-year Tribulation, after the Antichrist shows his true colors and goes into the rebuilt

Jewish temple to declare himself to be god, the halfway point, the abomination of desolation spoken of by the Prophet Daniel, that the only option for the people at this time is to what? To flee, right? To get out of there now in quick flight, right? Chop, chop! Get out of there now! Why? Because again as we saw, it's going to be a horrible time of slaughter. Jesus not only says what these people that are left should do, i.e., flee to the mountains, but He also said what you should not do. He said whatever you do, don't "flee" to where? Your house, right? It says it right there! Why? Because they've already turned our homes into a Big Brother paradise! Not just with computers, but also with all these new-fangled automated home systems that everybody just has to have as well. And the reason why is because we are lazy! In fact, we've gotten so lazy that we can't even find the strength to turn on the TV with the remote, or turn the dial on the stove, or even push the button on an alarm clock. We think it's all about convenience when in reality, it's actually creating a Big Brother paradise. Don't believe me? Let me give you just a few examples.

The **1st lazy technology** that leads to a Big Brother paradise is **Smart Locks**.

Again, if you see the word "smart" before anything, what do you supplant it with? Big Brother, right? And believe it or not, that's the same thing happening to our doors. Because we all know how hard it is to turn the key with your hand.

"Hi, I'm Roger here on this beautiful day to show off the new Schlage Lock system. I have purposely locked myself out so that Larry who is far away in Seattle can unlock the door with nothing but his cell phone. Go ahead Larry."

Larry pushes a button on his phone and as the phone makes the sound of the key getting pushed the door opens and Roger walks into the house.
"Tada... like magic, but real."²

Wow! Isn't that convenient? I can open the lock even if I'm out of state! No more hurting my hand doing it myself, ouch! In fact, I can do it before I even get out of the car and make it inside with those groceries! It's magic! Yeah, it's magic alright. It really gives you not only the ability to unlock the door remotely, but anyone who hacks into this system. All because it was too hard to 'turn the key with the hand.' So much for being safe in your house during the 7-year

Tribulation. Lock your doors all you want, try to hide! They'll push a button and come right on in. You're toast!

The **2ⁿᵈ lazy technology** that leads to a Big Brother paradise is **Smart Assistants**.

You know, those things like Amazon Echo or Alexa or Google Home. Because we all know how hard it is to walk over to the computer and look something up, or turn on the lights with your finger, or push a button on the stereo. Oh, and by the way, for those of you asking your Home Assistant devices questions and thinking you're getting honest unbiased answers, think again! You're being lied to! One lady put Google Home to the test to see what it would say about Jesus!

Lady asking the questions: *"So, hey Google, who is Allah?"*

Google: *"According to Wikipedia, in Islamic theology, Allah is the all-powerful and all-knowing creator, sustainer, and judge of everything in existence."*

Lady: *"Hey Google, who is Buddha?"*

Google: *"According to Wikipedia, Buddha, also known as Gautama Buddha or simply the Buddha, after the title of Buddha, was a monk, mendicant, sage upon whose teaching Buddhism was founded."*

Lady: *"Hey Google, who is Jesus Christ?"*

Google: *"Sorry, I don't know how to help with that yet."*

Lady: *"Google, who is Jesus?"*

Google: *"Sorry, I'm not sure how to help."*[3]

You liar! You're this huge massive AI database and you don't know who Jesus is? Give me a break! It's filtered information! Why is it only Jesus? Something spiritual is going on! In fact, another guy put Amazon Echo to the test and asked it, *"Who is the Lord Jesus Christ,"* it actually said, *"Jesus Christ is a fictional character."* But that's only half of the story with these Home Assistants. You're not only getting filtered information from them, but you're also getting constant monitoring from them! Watch what this article says, *"Alexa, stop Listening!"*

"In millions of homes throughout the world, Alexa is listening. Many of you know who I'm talking about, but for those who don't, Alexa is the name of the famous voice behind some of Amazon's most popular devices, such as the Echo, Echo Dot, Echo Spot, Echo Show, and others."

"Millions of homes around the world have these devices and millions of additional homes have similar products such as Apple's Siri and Google Home devices. But what most users don't realize is Alexa is always listening and remembering. That's right. By her very nature, Alexa is always listening, otherwise, she wouldn't hear when you call her. But when you do, Alexa does more than listen. She records your voice and stores that audio file on a remote server."

In fact, even the news is starting to catch up on this invasive behavior.

Danielle: *"My husband and I would randomly joke sometimes like I wonder if these devices are listening to what we are saying."*

CBS News Reports: *"Until recently, Danielle's home was wired up in every room with Amazon Echo. Her family used the Alexa app to do everything from turn up the heat to turn off the lights. But Danielle told us via Skype two weeks ago their love for Alexa changed with an alarming phone call."*

Danielle: *"The person on the other line said, 'Unplug your Alexa devices right now.'"*

CBS News: *"That person was one of her husband's employees, calling from Seattle."*

Danielle: *"We went running around unplugging them all and he proceeded to tell us that he had received an audio file recording of what was going on in our house."*

CBS News: *"Danielle went on to say that her Amazon device in her Portland home recorded a private conversation and sent that recording to a random contact which happened to be an employee in Seattle."*

Danielle: *"At first my husband said, 'No you didn't' and he said, 'You were talking about hardwood floors,' and we went 'Oh, my gosh! You really did.'"*

CBS News: *"Danielle listened to the conversation and she couldn't believe that someone 176 miles away heard it too."*

Danielle: *"I felt invaded, like total privacy invasion, like immediately, I am never going to plug that device in again."*

Why? Because you're a conspiracy wacko? No! Because it's actually, always listening and storing whatever you say in a database. Which means have fun trying to hide out in your house in the 7-year Tribulation! These devices are always listening to everything you say, including whether or not you'll worship the Antichrist. And if you don't think they'll use that voice information against you with the authorities, think again! They're already using it in courts of law!

"In 2015, James Bates claimed he awoke after a night of drinking and watching football to find his friend, Victor Collins, floating face down in a hot tub. Bates claimed it was a tragic accident."

The authorities claimed it was murder. To prove it, they called an unusual witness - Alexa. The prosecutor subpoenaed the defendant's Amazon Echo recordings to find out the truth and Amazon provided the audio files to help prove their case.

"Then Alexa became a witness in a January 2017 trial of a double-murder of two New Hampshire women. The judge ordered Amazon to turn over any recordings from the Echo device found at the crime scene."

In other words, not only are these devices really recording you, but they already are being used in a court of law! In fact, a whole new generation of people are being brainwashed to think this kind of Big Brother invasion in our homes is a good thing. And they're doing that conditioning with their toys!

World News Now Reports: *"Watch out kids, your newest Barbie doll may be a tattletale. The Wi-Fi connected 'Hello Barbie' has voice recognition software to interact with the children, that's great, but the software records conversations, sending them to cloud servers."*

RT News Reports: *"Some things are pretty harmless, that most of us are guilty of doing. However, toy advocacy groups are complaining to the Federal Trade Commission about a kids' toy that could actually be spying and collecting data on the entire family.*

My Friend Cayla and the IQ intelligent robot are two talking dolls that are currently on the market. With Christmas just around the corner many parents have or are gearing up to purchase these two hot items made by Genesis Toys. According to CBS Money Watch both come equipped with a Bluetooth microphone, a speaker, mobile application, storage, and Wi-Fi connections. Conversations are also recorded and collected between the toys and children. What's even scarier is Cayla prompts kids to answer personal questions like where they live, where they go to school and what their family members names are." [4]

Or, who's worshiping the Antichrist and who's not! And they go on to say, *"These devices can be hacked into."* I wonder how people will be betrayed in the 7-year Tribulation?

Matthew 24:9 "Then you will be handed over to be persecuted and put to death."

I wonder how? Maybe the dolls will turn you in! But that's not all. Maybe you don't want to buy yourself a doll for Christmas and if you're a guy I sincerely hope not. But maybe it was one of these…

The **3rd lazy technology** that leads to a Big Brother paradise is **Smart TV's**.

Huh? That's a guy gift! Because we all know how hard it is to push a button on the remote. Again, all under the guise of convenience to speak to your TV and tell it what to do. Look Ma, no hands! Believe it or not, these so-called Smart TV's are really Big Brother TV's that not only let you talk to them, but they watch you in return!

Infowars.com Reports: *"Christmas is fast approaching. That means millions of people are going to be thinking of their savings and lining up to get their hands on the latest technology. Completely oblivious to the fact that they are actually paying to have their private conversations recorded and shared with third parties. Take the new Samsung Smart TV. The amount of data this thing collects is staggering.*

'Just say what you want.' It logs where, when, how, and for how long you use the TV. It sets tracking cookies and beacons designed to detect when you have viewed a particular content or a particular email message. It records the apps you have used, the sites you visit and how you interact with the content. And of course, it has a built-in camera and microphone with facial and voice recognition for your convenience. But, Samsung's new global privacy policy for its line of Smart TV's comes with a rather ominous warning. 'Please be aware that if your spoken words include personal or other sensitive information, that information will be among the data captured and transmitted to a third party through your use of Voice Recognition.'

There is no need for the FBI to bug your living room, you'll do it yourself. In two years time, the stuff that this Samsung TV can do will be old news. Let's say you are having a fight with your spouse in front of your television. That camera and microphone that has been recording all your private conversations and scanning your body language, can now send that information to third party advertisers so they can provide a perfectly timed commercial suggesting some SSRI's. In other words, don't say anything private in front of your television."

Why? Because they really are listening and watching everything you're doing, including who's worshiping the Antichrist or not! And again, it's not just listening, it's watching! *"Is Your TV Watching You?"[5]*

Perhaps you're not worried about the National Security Agency tracking your phone calls and emails -- but what if they were watching you in your PJs on your couch? It may sound like something out of Mission Impossible, but it's the stuff of fact, not fiction. Today's Internet-connected smart TVs can be hacked into and outsiders are able to turn on a set's video camera without the user's knowledge. In fact, pretty much the whole world of 'smart' devices, smart wearables, smart home devices, smart TVs, smart cars – anything with a chip and internet connectivity is logging you. And if you think they'll never use that information against you with the authorities think again. It's already being done!

Fox News Reports: *"Wikileaks may have done more than any other organization last year to destroy the Clinton campaign thanks to the release of their massive trove of Democratic emails. Now they are trying to claim another scalp in the CIA. We are joined tonight by Fox News Reporter Trace Gallagher. Hi Trace."*

Trace Gallagher: *"Unlike the Edward Snowden release back in 2013 that revealed the NSA was in fact spying on average Americans, today's document dump of Wikileaks isn't about gathering information on Americans, it's about the tools and tactics being used by the CIA to break into or circumvent various communication technologies. For example, experts who have studied the leaked documents say the CIA along with other US and Foreign Agencies found that a way to hack into phones is to use Google's Android technology giving them the ability to collect voice and text message data from messaging apps like What'sApp, Telegram and Signal.*

Experts say it appears that the CIA was able to hack devices prior to the encryption or secret code being applied. Google is looking into the matter. But it is interesting that one cybersecurity expert here in California says that CIA hackers would cover their tracks by leaving electronic trails suggesting that the hacks came from Iran, China, or Russia instead of the United States. It also appears that U.S. and British intel agencies developed a way to take control of televisions connected to the internet. It may appear the TV was off when in fact it was recording conversations in the room.

BBC Reports: *"Could your TV be spying on you? If you have an internet connected TV that might be possible. Secret documents show how the CIA has turned the TV into bugging devices.*

'Hello, is anyone listening?' 'Hi, TV.' It is possible that your TV can be used as a spy, as a Big Brother in your living room but how likely is it? The leaked documents show that the CIA worked with Britain's MI5 to develop this capability. To target specific individuals."[6]

You know, like anyone they deem as a "terrorist." It makes it all okay! But what if you became the "terrorist" and again who gets to define that? The Antichrist will define it in the 7-year Tribulation, and it will be anyone who refuses to worship him. And your TV will be right there in your home to turn you in! You should've gotten saved through Jesus! But that's not all.

The **4th lazy technology** that leads to a Big Brother paradise is **Smart Homes**.

That's right, because we all know how hard it is to turn the dial on the thermostat or push the button to close the garage door, huh? Once again, all under the guise of convenience, just about anything you do in your home, Big Brother is there to do it for you! And they're pitching it as some sort of Utopian Paradise. Like this!

"It's 6:00AM and the alarm clock is buzzing earlier than usual. It's not a malfunction, the smart clock scanned your schedule and adjusted it because you've got that big presentation first thing in the morning."

"Your shower automatically turns on and warms to your preferred 103 degrees Fahrenheit. The electric car is ready to go, charged by the solar panels or wind turbine on your roof."

"When you get home later, there's an unexpected package waiting, delivered by a drone. You open it to find cold medicine. Turns out, the health sensors embedded in your bathroom detected signs of an impending illness and placed an order automatically."

"Good thing you already knocked that presentation out of the park."[7]

This is the Smart Home of the future. And it's not even future anymore, it's already being implemented with one of the biggest promoters being Google! I know…shocker! They have a Smart Home System called Google Nest and they not only want to automatically control all your thermostats, appliances, smoke detectors, security systems, security cameras, locks, open doors, turn on lights, you name it, everything you can think of doing in your home or nest as they call it, they will do it all for you! Isn't that convenient? Actually, it's lazy and dangerous because it's already come out, and Google didn't tell you they installed hidden microphones into these systems. "Google Nest home security system's hidden microphone was never disclosed to consumers."

Smart Homes

The worst kind of microphone is a hidden microphone. And customers were caught off guard early February when Google announced its home security system, Nest Secure, has listening capabilities.

"One user asked, 'Have I had a device with a hidden microphone in my house this entire time?" "Yes."

"The microphone left the door open for additional features to be added to the technology, Google said, like the ability to detect broken glass. And the company said sound sensing devices are common in security systems."

You know in case 'I've fallen, and I can't get up' and I can't get to the phone. That's precisely why when we moved into our home here in Las Vegas, it already had a security system installed but they wanted us to upgrade to the new system that could listen to us call for help. We said no way because obviously that means you could potentially be listening to us at all times, any time! But as you just saw, that's not just a potentiality, it's our reality with these Smart Home Systems. It's really being done without our knowledge. They're listening to everything you say and watching whatever you do. In fact, these guys know just how easy it is to hack into them!

M News Reports: *"Let's talk about whose watching you. High tech break and enter. 'Attention Johanna and Peter, your home has been hacked.' Homes are being transformed by so called smart devices that promise to make things more convenient and more secure. It's automated control for everything from our lights and locks to our TV and temperature."*

'Alexa, set the thermostat to 23 degrees, Alexa turn the kitchen light on.'

In Canada alone more than 100 million of these devices are now connected to the internet. We are traveling to a small town in Southern Ontario to deliver some disturbing news. 'That's their Prius.' 'Is it?' A family who lives here is being watched by the whole world and they don't know it. Here on this monitor they are renovating their front porch. And here again sharing some more intimate moments on the back deck, captured by their own security cameras and broadcast over the internet for all to see. Anyone can keep an eye on their comings and goings. That is how we tracked them down. Through their license plates. You can even watch on their cameras as we arrive to alert them as to what we have found."[8]

If those guys can do it, do you think the Antichrist is going to have a problem? So much for hiding out in your house in the 7-year Tribulation! You should've listened to Jesus! And lest you think they'll never use these Smart Home devices to turn you in to the authorities, once again, think again. It's already being done!

Fox News Reports: *"We have been telling you for months now the growing power of the big tech companies whose brand of surveillance capitalism has come to shape our politics and culture in ways that many people don't perceive. So, I'm going to give you a very specific example of that. We are going to look into the near future at the terrifying control these companies seek over our daily lives. We recently reviewed several patents filed by Google.*

As we describe them, ask yourself if you are comfortable to give them that much power to unelected technocrats that you have never met. The first patent that was filed in Sept. 2016, Google envisions how it could send you personalized advertising based on what a camera observes in your home. The illustration that

Google submitted to the federal government patent office is, a camera in your bedroom sees a 'The God Father' book on your nightstand next to your bed and uses that to steer you to watching the movie. If you think that is creepy, prepare yourself because it gets even creepier.

In another patent from 2016 Google imagines how it can take control of your parenting. The relationship you have with your children. Google's Smart Home System could detect your children near your liquor cabinet, for example, or in their parent's bedroom and if mischief is occurring it would deliver a verbal warning. In another example, Google imagines a hypothetical child named Benjamin. Google's cameras would be watching Benjamin at all times, carefully.

They could see if he was outside. Presumably using electronics, they could use that information to try to sell him things at some point, because that is the whole point, to sell things, by Google. The patent also discusses how the Smart Home could coach families on areas of improvement. For example, if a family doesn't spend enough time together, to Google's standards, Google might scold them."

RT News Reports: *"ABC News is reporting that a smart home device like the Amazon Echo, alerts New Mexico authorities to alleged domestic assault and it saved the day. Now this is one of those feel good stories that is much more insidious that you realize. I'm glad the woman was rescued, of course. But please raise your hand if you would like your house to be spying on you and calling the police when it feels like something illegal might be happening."*[9]

Yeah, real funny! Have fun trying to run and hide in the 7-year Tribulation! Your house will turn you in to the cops! Just like Jesus said, don't go back there! In fact, there's not only signs of this Big Brother Smart Home technology turning you in to the authorities, but those same authorities will take you out! Smart ovens have been turning on overnight and preheating to 400 degrees.

Smart Ovens

Smart ovens have been turning on overnight and preheating to 400 degrees

June Oven owners are reporting preheating incidents

"Smart Ovens have turned on in the middle of the night and heated up to 400 degrees Fahrenheit or higher. The ovens' owners aren't sure why this happened. Nest cam footage captured the exact moment it turned on."

"And the New York City Fire Department says, 'Unattended cooking accounts for 33% of home fires, and those fires typically start with a stove or oven.'"

Hmmm. So maybe that's the other half of the equation here. Not only will these Smart Devices be watching and listening to your every move, seeing whether or not you'll worship the Antichrist, but maybe this is how they take out those resisters. Just turn on that Smart Stove electronically, wirelessly, and BOOM nobody will be the wiser! But that's just it, you might be thinking, "Well okay, that's it! I'm just going to get rid of all my electronics in my house and avoid all these smart devices and I'll be safe! Ha! Ha! They can't get me!" Really? You got a bag of chips in your house? Even that will betray you in in the 7-year Tribulation!

RT News Reports: *"Well the next time you are speaking behind closed doors and you're sure there isn't a camera present, researchers at Microsoft, Adobe,* *and MIT have completed a new experiment that can recreate sounds from an environment from only video images. That means your words could be deciphered much easier than you think. The algorithm they developed reconstructs audio signals by analyzing minute vibrations from objects in a soundless video.*

For example, using a high-speed camera and soundproof glass, researchers were able to extract the audio of someone singing Mary Had a Little Lamb just off the vibrations of a bag of chips. In other experiments researchers extracted usable audio signals from videos off aluminum foil, the surface of a glass of water and even the leaves of a potted plant."[10]

And I bet you've got those in your house too! No wonder there's no place to hide in the 7-year Tribulation! The only way out of this Big Brother nightmare, this worst time in the history of mankind, as Jesus says, the 7-year Tribulation, is to get saved now and avoid the whole thing. Stop thinking you're going to be the ultimate survivor because you're not.

"Everything that the great science fiction novels predicted has come true. From Huxley's, 'Brave New World', Orwell's, '1984' right on down the line to Ray Bradberry. Things that were predicted many, many years ago have come true. You may not believe that, but if you keep up with the ways of technology today, it's getting pretty freaky. Orwell said in his book '1984' that you had to live like everything you did is being watched except in darkness. The problem with Orwell, he wrote his book in the late 1940's, even in darkness now you are going to be listened to. As you go about your daily business in America, you are filmed or surveilled at least 20 times per day. You are being watched continually.

The police can drive by your home, and they do by the way, with their Stingray device which is located in their car. They act as fake cell phone towers and they download everything you are doing in your home. They are watching. They are listening. They are recording. They have Doppler radar devices which are semi heat detecting devices. If they drive by your home, they can point at your home and tell if you are at home. Now if they want to get a swat team on you, they can. Or if they don't want you to be home and they want to go into your home under the US Patriot Act and download everything you have on your computer and see everything you have in your home, all that's legal under the Sneak and Peak Search, it's legal in America. Of course, it's a violation of the Constitution, but it's legal. The Department of Homeland Security, which is really the master mind of all of this in working with the FBI, is handing out license plates to the police across the country where they go by, down your road, and collect up to 1,800 images per hour.

They can tell where you went to the Dentist's office, Doctor's office, political rally, wherever you are headed, they can track you. Google now admits, on your cell phone, by your power usage, as you're are driving around the city, they can track you everywhere you go. That is all fed into an intelligence cloud. Did you know that Amazon built a multi-million-dollar intelligence cloud for all seventeen intelligence agencies to use and all this intelligence is fed into it and they analyze it? If they think you are a criminal, they can come and get you. By the way, there are numerous Federal Laws passed every year across the country. This doesn't count state and city laws, creating new criminal behavior, such as having a chicken in your back yard, vegetable garden, solar panels, or collecting rainwater. You can be a criminal. There are 300,000 regulatory crimes in the federal government.

So now, the average American, they say, is committing 3 to 5 crimes a day and we don't even know it. We now know that the assets and securities agency's that are supposed to be protecting us is now holding about two billion of our emails per day. The American citizen, text messaging, Facebook posts, remember the 4th Amendment that our Founding Fathers said that before the government can do surveillance on you they have to have some kind of criminal activity or they have to have a really strong suspicion that you are committing it before they can do surveillance.

They are downloading everything we see. Even your TV's now. Your Samsung Smart TV that can do commands, voice commands, anything that you say in the room is going into your TV and they admit, Samsung and other corporate entities that make these sort of TV's, those voice commands are collected and sent to an internet server. And where does that go? Up into that intelligence cloud that I mentioned earlier, and the government knows everything you are talking about.

And you have the FBI creating a huge database of DNA samples. Sometimes DNA does help to catch a criminal but why do they want DNA samples of babies? They are collecting some in hospitals, of people that have been arrested of a crime but haven't been convicted, police are pushing heavy for misdemeanors. Everything is going into a DNA database. Come to find out, your DNA can tell you who your ancestors were. Maybe they were troublemakers.

Maybe we can deal with that. Maybe this is what the government is thinking about, maybe a pre-crime unit like in the movie 'The Minority Report' which was a novel."

So, everything is being watched. And now we have drones flying over the United States legally. Former President Obama signed a law into effect allowing drones to fly without any civil liberties protection at all. If you didn't realize some of these drones have scanning devices that can fly over your home and scan everything you are doing in your home, hack into your Wi-Fi, computers, download this and that. They have hummingbird drones that can fly right up to your window to watch what you are doing, hear what you are saying. Set drones in your house. All these things are here, so what have we come to? We are at the end of the age of privacy. There is nothing that we can do privately.

Revelation 14:19 "The angel swung his sickle on the earth, gathered its grapes and threw them into the great winepress of God's wrath."

Give it up! Listen to Jesus! Don't go back to your house thinking you'll have safety in the 7-year Tribulation! Take the one and only way out through Him and be safe today! Even if you could make it to the end you're still going to Hell!

And that's precisely why, out of love, God has given us this update on **The Final Countdown: Tribulation Rising** concerning **Modern Technology & the AI Invasion** to show us that the Tribulation is near and the 2nd Coming of Jesus Christ is rapidly approaching. And that's why Jesus Himself said:

Luke 21:28 "When these things begin to take place, stand up and lift up your heads, because your redemption is drawing near."

People of God, like it or not, we are headed for **The Final Countdown**. The signs of the 7-year **Tribulation** are **Rising**! Wake up! So, here is the point. If you're a Christian today and you're not doing anything for the Lord…shame on you! Get busy doing something for Jesus now! Stop wasting your life! We need you! Don't sit on the sidelines! Get on the front line and help us! Let's get busy working together, doing something splendid for Jesus with what time is left and get busy saving souls! Amen?

But if you're reading this today and you're not a Christian, then I beg you, please, heed these signs, heed these warnings, give your life to Jesus now because this monitoring system of the Antichrist and the False Prophet is not going to lead to convenience and a life of ease, but a system that again, allows them to have targeted assassinations! Don't fall for the lie! Take the way out now, the only way out now, through Jesus Christ, and avoid the whole thing, before it's too late! Amen?

Chapter Sixteen

The Increase of Holograms, 3D Printing and Restlessness

The **7th way** that **Modern Technology** reveals that we're really living in the last days is by the **Increase of Electronic Holograms**. But don't take my word for it. Let's listen to God's.

Revelation 13:11-15 "Then I saw another beast, coming out of the earth. He had two horns like a lamb, but he spoke like a dragon. He exercised all the authority of the first beast on his behalf and made the earth and its inhabitants worship the first beast, whose fatal wound had been healed. And he performed great and miraculous signs, even causing fire to come down from heaven to earth in full view of men. Because of the signs he was given power to do on behalf of the first beast, he deceived the inhabitants of the earth. He ordered them to set up an image in honor of the beast who was wounded by the sword and yet lived. He was given power to give breath to the image of the first beast, so that it could speak and cause all who refused to worship the image to be killed."

So here we see again in this passage that the False Prophet is going to use his deception around the world to get people to what? To specifically worship the Antichrist's image or be killed, right? And apparently, it has something to do with his death, or "appearing" to die, and so you honor his great power by worshiping his image. So that's the question. Do we see any technology on the planet that could actually help create not only an image of the

Antichrist, but one that could actually talk with and interact with people? Even cause their death if they don't do what he says? You know, like worship him? Uh, yeah! They're called 3-D Holograms and that's just one technology out there. But as we saw before, they're not only used in news broadcasts, but even political leaders around the world are making important announcements with them which is what the Antichrist is going to do in the 7-year Tribulation. They also use them right now in concerts, specifically concerts of dead singers, like Tupac, Elvis, Frank Sinatra, you name it. Even Michael Jackson seemingly comes "back to life" on stage again today.

CNN Reports: *"The comeback performance was a thriller. Michael Jackson almost 5 years after his death taking the stage at the 2014 Billboards Music Awards. There was his iconic 'moon walk' and that trademark voice. The only thing missing was the real king of pop. In his place was a hologram. This MJ likeness used at the Billboards Awards was created by Hologram USA and may have made some viewers a little uneasy.*

But the founder A. David says the technology gives them a chance to remember the pop icon at his best. But this wasn't the first time a hologram performed on stage. Celine Dion performed alongside Elvis on American Idol in 2007. Tupac wowed audiences in 2012 at the Coachella Music Festival, rapping alongside the real live Snoop. David says we can expect even better holograms in the future."[1]

You know, like the Antichrist when he makes a global announcement with his image saying to worship him! And remember these are all dead people seemingly "coming back to life" with people interacting with them, and since they were their idols in real life, they get to "worship" them again. But you might be thinking, "Well that's all well and good, but that's just for entertainment! Nobody's going to walk around in real life with a hologram, like it's a real ongoing relationship with the Antichrist or something." Really? Well, you might want to ask the Asian Community. You see, we're all so busy running the rat race that nobody has time for a relationship anymore, at least a real one. So hey, wouldn't it be great if they could create a hologram spouse for you? No commitments, no worries, no demands. Now that's a relationship you could have time for. Believe it or not, they're already doing that!

"It's morning! Wake up!! Hey wake up!"

In Japan a person is slowly getting up out of bed. He looks over on a table and there is a hologram of a little woman standing there telling him it's time to get up. He says, "Good Morning."

The hologram then says, "Oh, it may rain today. Take your umbrella with you. Hurry or you will be late."

He bends over to take a closer look and says, "I'm leaving now." And she says, "See you later. Take care. Have fun at work."

During the day at work he gets a text on his phone. It is his hologram telling him, "Come home early." He replies, "It's only noon."

Later in the day he sends her a text, "I am heading home now." And she replies, "Yaaay!"

With a click of her finger she turns on all the lights, to welcome him home. It has started raining and he takes out his umbrella. He walks to the bus and while riding home he texts her again saying, "I'm home soon." She replies, "I can't wait to see you." He says, "In ten minutes." She replies, "I can't wait!"

When he gets home, he goes to the hologram and she says, "I missed you darling."

"You know, somebody's home for me, it feels great. Thought so on my way home, as he looked up at the lights in the window." "Good night," he says. "Good night," she answers.

Living with your favorite character.[2]

Or Antichrist, whichever hologram you choose to have a relationship with. Did you see it sent him texts throughout the day, said it missed him, turned the lights on for him when he got home, shared some tea with him? It isn't just that we're seeing sophisticated image technology with Holograms appear on the scene in our day, it's for the first time in man's history we're seeing people develop relationships with these images and that's exactly what's going to happen in Revelation 13 and the image of the Antichrist. But wait a second, we already have the ability to broadcast an extremely life-like image across the world of somebody with Holograms and we even have people now developing intimate relationships with them. But speaking of global, how is the image of the Antichrist going to break through the language barrier with his image? I mean, there's thousands of different languages. How's he going to communicate with everyone? Well, can you say an Automatic Language Translator for Holograms? Believe it or not, that too is already here. Here it is in action!

Julia White, CVP, Azure Marketing: *"Now it's a pleasure to be here in Las Vegas, to present to you. I get invited to casinos across the globe and though it's easy for me to come to Las Vegas it isn't always easy to travel across the world and even when I do, I can't always speak the local language. So, what if neither language nor distance mattered for me to deliver a fantastic keynote? What if technology can help me anywhere I needed to be and speak any language I wanted?*

Well it can. We are bringing together the power of mixed reality and Azure AI services to create a truly game changing experience. What you are about to see is an exact hologram of me wearing the same outfit that we recently captured at a mixed reality studio. I don't speak Japanese, but what if I wanted to deliver my keynote in Japanese. Using Azure AI Technology, I can translate my English into Japanese and train it to sound exactly like me. The same voice tones, the same inflection. We have brought this together, my hologram and Azure AI to show you what is possible.

So first I want to put on my HoloLens-2 here and then a special camera so you can see what I am seeing. Let's get started. First, let me introduce you to mini-me." In her hand she is hold a green hologram of herself. *"There she is, my perfect hologram. And thanks to the power of HoloLens-2 she floats with me. I am literally holding my hologram. So natural. Now she is a little small to do a keynote so let's see if she can be a full-size Japanese keynote. Render keynote."*

The hologram goes off her hand and onto the floor growing to a full-size human. As soon as the form comes together, she starts to speak in Japanese. She says in Japanese, 'There is something truly amazing about being a hologram. We are using our latest mixed reality capture technology to create my hologram. You might have seen people as holograms before, but what is new in what you're seeing today is that I am actually speaking Japanese. I don't speak Japanese, yet here I am with my voice and my hologram speaking in perfect Japanese. Technology called neural text to speech or neural TTS.

We are able to use recordings of my voice to create my own personal voice signature." Now as you can see this is a mind-blowing technology and what you just saw was my life-size hologram, the exact replica, rendered here in real time, speaking Japanese with my own unique voice signature. And the most amazing part, all of these technologies exist today."[3]

Which means, all of the technologies needed to fulfill the Antichrist's image in Revelation 13 exist today. Including broadcasting it anywhere in the world, having relational abilities, and speaking any language! Just in time for the 7-year Tribulation! And again, all these events happen during the 7-year Tribulation, and the Rapture of the Church happens prior to the 7-year tribulation, which means we're getting close! Are you ready for that rapture?

The **8th way** that **Modern Technology** reveals that we're really living in the last days, is by the **Increase of Electronic Body Parts**.

You see, with all this explosion of technology in our lifetime, it's not only leading to the possible fulfillment of the "image" of the Antichrist, but also to the "death" of the Antichrist. Let's go back to our opening text.

Revelation 13:12 "He exercised all the authority of the first beast on his behalf and made the earth and its inhabitants worship the first beast, whose fatal wound had been healed."

So here we see the Antichrist is seemingly invincible! I mean, you kill him, he gets this fatal wound, and he "seemingly" comes back to life again. No wonder people worship him, right? Now some would say this "fatal wound" is one of the "heads" or Kingdoms the Antichrist rules over that's mentioned in the Book of Revelation, and it could be. Others would say no, it's speaking of a "literal" head wound he receives, maybe an assassination attempt like what happened with J.F.K. A political leader who got a fatal shot in the head, but he never recovered. And so that's the question. Do we see any technology on the planet **now** that could actually "give the appearance" of somebody coming back to life from a head wound, including the Antichrist? J.F.K. wasn't brought back to life but could they do it with the Antichrist? And not just a Hologram, but literally coming back from what appears to be a fatal head wound of some sort and somehow still survive it?

Uh, yeah! It's called 3-D Printing Technology. Star Trek eat your heart out! Believe it or not, thanks to this new technology, we can not only print anything we want right before our very eyes, but it's getting so cheap that just about anyone can own one of these devices. And all you do is, just like Star Trek, scan the image of what you want to create and voila! There it is! Right now, you can have 3-D Printed toys, shoes, clothes, furniture, dental implants, sports gear, eye wear, phone cases, tools, artwork, instruments, houses, cars, trucks, aircraft, even 3-D printed pills and firearms! Drugs and guns...not a good combo! In fact, speaking of Star Trek, even food is being printed with these things, such as chocolates, candies, crackers, pizza, pasta, even plant-based meat material, and isn't that the rage nowadays. "Mimicking meat texture and nutritional values" for the environmentally friendly! And that's right, just in time for the Millennials, you can now even scan in an image of yourself and create your own 3-D printed selfie. At least this person included their spouse! In fact, believe it or not, for the

3-D Printed Selfie

first time in man's history, we now have the ability with 3-D Printers to create new body parts. Here's the other side to 3-D Printers. Look what else they can print!

Tara Long, D News Reports: *"You know what's better than a 3D printed pizza? Nothing, nothing, nothing. There is nothing in the world better than a 3D printed* *pizza. Hey guys, Tara here from D News with a story that I'm sure will warm the cockles of even the coldest, deadest heart. I don't know if that is even a word, but I said it and now it is.*

A group of engineering students from an Illinois High School used a 3D printer to make a prosthetic hand for a 9-year-old girl who was born without fingers on her left hand. A regular prosthetic hand costs up to $50,000 which is an insane amount of money. So instead, this girl's father approached the school asking for help. Students found the 3D printer online used to create fingers and then they pieced the hand together using flexible cords that would allow her to bend and grab things. The girl now has a brand-new functioning hand and the total cost, $5.00.

This isn't the first time a 3D printer has created working body parts and it's probably more common than you think. Last month a group of doctors in Holland performed the first successful skull transplant using a plastic 3D printed skull which is insane. The patient suffered from a condition that thickens the bone structure that causes headaches, blindness and eventually causes death. The procedure took around twenty-three hours and the woman has completely regained her sight and returned to work. Absolutely incredible.

The company also produces other facial prosthetics including noses and ears. The Wake Forest Institute for degenerative medicine is another place that is leading the way in creating prosthetics. They recently created a bio-printed kidney by depositing kidney cells cultivated from a biopsy into a biodegradable shell."

"There is no doubt that organ transplants save lives but waiting for compatible donors can never be short enough. So, what if there was a way to get compatible organs on demand. Bio-printing has traditionally meant printing bio-compatible materials as a base for cells to grow. It may sound farfetched; scientists have already been able to produce a human ear and other tissues. Doctors take a scan of the organ, a 3D blueprint, cells are then taken from the patient which are then placed in a culture to multiply. The cells are then painstakingly placed on the 3D printed scaffold which is incubated to produce a functioning organ. It involves taking stem cells from the patient's tissue which are then mixed in a hydrogel and then placed in 3D printed molds. These are then incubated to produce steroids which are the building blocks of organ printing. From there you can just about print any organ you like."

"Wake Forest has also paved the way for synthetic skin grafts, and they are currently developing a printer that will print skin right onto the wound of a burn victim. First, they use the scanner to determine the size and depth of the wound, then they use an ink containing enzymes and collagen and they layer it between tissue and skin cells. Just like you would layer it in healthy skin. They say their goal is to have portable skin graft machines ready within five years but let me reiterate just how incredible the potential of this is. Transplant waiting lists will be thing of the past. Lose your arm in a boating accident, cool, I'll just print another one."[4]

Or if I take a seemingly fatal wound to the head, those new parts I would need to "recover" can be printed up just like that for the first time in mankind's history. From a new skull, to a new ear, even to new skin to cover the whole wound, and nobody would be the wiser! Why, it appears as if this guy's invincible! I mean when J.F.K. got shot, that was it, but this guy, he's already back in action. This technology is not coming but is already here, just in time for the 7-year Tribulation! Can you believe that? Printed body parts for people! In fact, these kinds of operations, we're "theorizing" are already taking place.

"In March 2014, surgeons used 3D printed parts to rebuild the face of a motorcyclist who had been seriously injured in a road accident."

"In May 2018, 3D printing was used for a kidney transplant to save a three-year-old boy. And just this year Israeli researchers constructed a heart out of human cells."[5]

And all of that would sure come in handy if someone needed to be "healed" from some serious "fatal wound" whatever that is. Again, just in time for the 7-year Tribulation! But that's right, speaking of fatal head wounds…we not only have the technology to make body parts to "come back to life" if you will, but we also have for the first time in man's history an actual movement called Transhumanism that actually has plans to "bring people back from the dead" and achieve man-made immortality. As wild as that is, they have not only succeeded in already getting FDA approval of "human suspended animation trials," to preserve somebody's body when it dies, like the Antichrist, to keep them alive until you provide an alternative body, print it up, clone it up, whatever, okay. But the ultimate goal is to "preserve the human brain and transform it," hence the term Transhumanism, into a computer image, inside of a computer, to seemingly extend their lives forever! And as crazy as that sounds,

Hollywood is already out there promoting this idea of us having the ability real soon to just print up a whole new body if need be, or that which they call, a sleeve.

The tour guide welcomes the visitors*: "Can I answer any questions? Welcome to Psychasec. We are a company that produces 100% organic human sleeves. You are probably wondering what the human sleeve is. Well, if you gather around, I can let you know what we do here in full detail. We have been able to achieve true mortality by taking your human consciousness and storing it in a device called a portable stack. We implant it in the base of your neck, and it collects and stores everything that make you, you. Every memory, every emotion, everything you have ever experienced is stored on this device.*

You can see it on this screen, it's about to come up. If you guys will just follow me. All the information is stored on this device and it can be transferred to the sleeve of your choosing. Follow me and I can give you a little more information. The portable stack device is a small device as I said before, that is implanted in the base of your neck with a small incision and it records everything that you have ever experienced in your life from a child until now. And we store it in a file called EHF which is a digital human frame. Everything that makes you, you is on this device. Now, all that information can be transferred over from the sleeve that you currently occupy into the sleeve of your choosing.

Now, the sleeve of your choosing can be designed like, if you want blue eyes instead of brown eyes, or those rock hard abs but you don't want to go to the gym for them, if you want to be taller, or if you want to be darker, all these things can be achieved here at Psychasec. If you would like to follow me for a tour around this corner, here is our final re-sleeving process. Come on in."

As they turn the corner, on the table in a large plastic bag, is a human sleeve that is laying in a fetal position. One of the visitors touch the sleeves head and says, "It feels real."[6]

Yeah, that's real alright, real creepy! But think about this. Not only a brand-new head but a brand-new body to put that head on if you wanted one! All being promoted now! So how is this going to happen? How is some guy going to "survive" some seemingly "fatal wound" and come back to life? I mean think about it. The Apostle John must have been blown away when he received this vision from God nearly 2,000 years ago dealing with this future timeframe called the 7-year Tribulation. But today you and I are seeing it being promoted in the media, the Transhumanist Movement, and Science right there to get the job done, just in time for the 7-year tribulation! It's almost like we're living in the last days and it's time to get motivated! Anyone else coming to that same conclusion?

The **9th way** that **Modern Technology** reveals that we're really living in the last days, is by the **Increase of Restlessness**. Here is where all the technology is headed.

2 Timothy 3:1,7 "But mark this: There will be terrible times in the last days. Always learning but never able to acknowledge the truth."

So here we see the Bible not only warns us of terrible times in the last days, but apparently one of the reasons why it's so terrible is because we'd have an increase of unrest like never before. Why? Because we would become a people who are always learning yet are never able to acknowledge the truth, leaving us in a frustrated and restless state. Which means God even predicted as a sign of the last days that we'd have what we call the modern-day rat race! It's actually a side effect of all these Modern Technology advancements. Let's go back to our very first text at the very beginning of our study.

Daniel 12:4 "But you, Daniel, close up and seal the words of the scroll until the time of the end. Many will go here and there to increase knowledge."

Now think about it! Are we are not being told today that the more we acquire this new technology, the more time it will save us so we can spend more time rushing here and there? And aren't we being told that the more we can learn from this increase of information, the more peace it will produce in our lives? Exactly! But the question is, "Is this true? Have we really saved more time and created more peace in our lives with all this new Modern Technology?" NO! We've actually become a society on the brink of disaster! And this is exactly what the secular experts are saying. Even though we have the most highly funded educational system in the world, we are producing the most confused, ignorant and violent children ever. Rates of depression are going through the roof, suicide is at an all-time high, anxiety abounds, serial killers are commonplace, nobody has any peace, and we're running around like a bunch of chickens with our heads chopped off! But wait a second. How can this be? Because, read your Bible! We're always learning yet never able to come to the truth! You see, the truth is that the more we fill our lives with so-called time saving devices, the more rushed we feel. In fact, we're in so much of a rush that "we tap our fingers while waiting for the microwave to zap our instant coffee."

Think about it! The truth is that these devices that are supposed to save us so much time so that we can rest more are actually making us more restless. Why? Because that's exactly what the Bible said would happen in the last days from all this technology! We're living it now! In fact, one guy said that *"It's significant that we call it the Information Age. We don't talk about the Knowledge Age. Our society is basically motion without memory, which of course is one of the clinical definitions of insanity."* And speaking of insane, this guy demonstrates just how insane it really is to think that technology is somehow going to give you a fulfilling life!

"We convince ourselves; technology is helping. The reality is, people don't seem enough for us these days. We condense books into articles, into lists, into gifs, because who has time to read an actual sentence anymore? We scroll and click, and double tap our lives away wondering where the day goes. We are more anxious than any generation before us, yet we keep downloading another app hoping that it could fix us.

We look to the latest trends, check the reviews on Yelp, investigate the hashtags yet in a world with so much information we're somehow still missing the wisdom of life. We crave real connection but we'd rather text about the hard conversations. We desire relationships but settle for following each other on Twitter. We stare at the pretty pictures on Instagram instead of the person standing right in front of us. We prefer filtered images to reality. We listen to a new podcast over a person's day, we check social media more than we check in with our friends. In our constant need for new information, new insights new everything, we lose the chance to make old memories. We like being busy, we wear it like a badge of honor.

We can't focus because we're being pulled in 50 different directions. We can't commit because there always seems to be another option, a better alternative. We have trust issues with the people we've known for years yet we trust someone's review that we just saw on Amazon. We want to hold hands while still holding onto our phones. We scroll through Twitter while having lunch with our friends. We think we can keep one foot out the door while still falling for the person sitting in front of us.

We always need the latest, the newest the most up to date, and then wonder why relationships don't last. We walk around stores on FaceTime and text during work because life without multi-tasking feels inefficient. We fill our schedule; we fill out our days, we fill our phones thinking that will cure the emptiness that we feel inside us. We binge another series of that latest Netflix show because someone else's story drowns out the experience of our own. We complain that nothing feels real anymore, but we don't give anything time to become real. We complain nothing has depth, but we don't allow things space to deepen. We're so quick to fill the silence or write someone off completely.

We complain nothing feels authentic today as we select a new filter on our selfies. We recharge our devices but not ourselves when we're out of time we just add more to our schedules. We don't know who we want to become because we're too distracted by who everyone else is becoming. How many times has anyone ever said to you I want your time? Whenever you hear that, know this truth. What people really want is your energy.

Imagine if you gave someone an hour of your time but the whole time you were completely distracted on your phone. Versus if you gave someone 10 minutes of your complete energy. I'm sure that any of us would select option 2, because what we're really searching for is energy. What we're really searching for is attention. What we're really looking for is presence. What we're really after is affection. So, what we really need to do is give people our energy, not just our time. Take a moment. Take time to reflect. Take a step back."[7]

And realize that we may have advanced beyond our wildest dreams technologically with all our cell phones and social media accounts and all the gadgets and doo dads that are supposed to make life more convenient. Yet we are still spiritually bankrupt about the true meaning of life. No wonder we're restless! All this Modern Technology has done is guarantee that we don't have time or even take the time to seek out meaningful relationships including with the One Who Alone could give us rest…i.e., God! Instead, we spend our time with TV, the internet, texting, cell phones, YouTube, Facebook, Twitter, and a whole bunch of other things that are supposed to save us time and give us peace…and they don't! It's a trap…a spiritual one! And can I state the obvious? You cannot grow spiritually watching 3 hours of TV a day versus 3 minutes of the Bible a day! You don't pray to God, but you socialize on Facebook! It's a trap! It's taking away whatever time you have left in the day after running the rat race, to spend time with God!

Don't we see what's happening to us? The Bible says in the last days, there'd not only be an increase of travel and information and all kinds of Modern Technology like never before, but the Bible also warns that all this technology is going to steal away the time that you could've spent with God making you restless! It's created a restless rat race society, that rushes here and there and travels to and fro gathering information from this and that, who said this and who said that. Exactly like Daniel said would happen when you're living in the last days!

You see, the problem of being in a hurry all the time is that you never take the time to stop and think about what is the most important in life. It's called eternity. Busy, busy, busy! Rushing here and there, to and fro, getting this, getting that, never able to come to the truth, what's life all about? Preparation for eternity! Instead of worshiping the One True God, you got tricked into bowing a knee before the idol of technology when the whole time, the answer to all of your problems was right before you, if you'd only have stopped long enough to listen. This is what the devil doesn't want you to see. This is what he's trying to keep from you. You don't need to travel halfway across the world for truth. You don't even need that latest computer gizmo or social networking device to understand it, nor spend a dime to receive it. Why? Because the truth about a restful life has been right under our noses the whole the time, in the words of Jesus Christ.

Matthew 11:28 "Then Jesus said, 'Come to me, all of you who are weary and carry heavy burdens, and I will give you rest.'"

Please don't be fooled like our last days society into thinking that it's by rushing here and there and by increasing your knowledge is where you'll find rest. Modern Technology can't give it to you! But if you persist, not only will you remain restless, but you may one day wake up to find yourself in the greatest time of unrest the world has ever known. It's called the 7-year Tribulation and it's coming much sooner than you think!

And that's precisely why, out of love, God has given us this update on **The Final Countdown: Tribulation Rising** concerning **Modern Technology & the AI Invasion** to show us that the Tribulation is near and the 2nd Coming of Jesus Christ is rapidly approaching. And that's why Jesus Himself said…

Luke 21:28 "When these things begin to take place, stand up and lift up your heads, because your redemption is drawing near."

People of God, like it or not, we are headed for **The Final Countdown.** The signs of the 7-year **Tribulation** are **Rising**! Wake up! The point is this. If you're a Christian today and you're not doing anything for the Lord, shame on you! Get busy doing something for Jesus now! Stop wasting your life! We need you! Don't sit on the sidelines! Get on the front line and help us! Let's get busy working together doing something splendid for Jesus with what time is left and get busy saving souls! Amen?

But if you're reading this today and you're not a Christian, then I beg you, please, heed these signs, heed these warnings, give your life to Jesus now because this Modern Technology is not going to lead to a fulfilled life with plenty of rest and relaxation but a nightmare beyond your wildest dreams called the 7-year Tribulation! Don't fall for the lie! Take the way out now, the only way out now, through Jesus Christ, and avoid the whole thing, before it's too late! Amen?

How to Receive Jesus Christ:

1. Admit your need (I am a sinner).

2. Be willing to turn from your sins (repent).

3. Believe that Jesus Christ died for you on the Cross and rose from the grave.

4. Through prayer, invite Jesus Christ to come in and control your life through the Holy Spirit. (Receive Him as Lord and Savior.)

What to pray:

Dear Lord Jesus,

I know that I am a sinner and need Your forgiveness. I believe that You died for my sins. I want to turn from my sins. I now invite You to come into my heart and life. I want to trust and follow You as Lord and Savior.

In Jesus' name. Amen.

Notes

Chapter 1 *Increase of Land Travel*

1. *History of Transportation*
   https://www.youtube.com/watch?v=FaLCQo8NJFA
   https://study.com/academy/lesson/history-of-cars-lesson-for-kids.html
   https://en.wikipedia.org/wiki/Car
   https://www.pcmag.com/news/321120/worlds-fastest-car-clocks-record-speed-of-270-49-mph
   http://www.guinnessworldrecords.com/world-records/land-speed-(fastest-car)
   https://www.livescience.com/37022-speed-of-sound-mach-1.html
   https://en.wikipedia.org/wiki/Motor_vehicle
   http://www.worldometers.info/cars/
   https://www.quora.com/What-percent-of-the-world-population-knows-how-to-drive-a-car
   https://www.autogravity.com/autogravitas/money/whats-average-miles-driven- per-year-car-lease-guide
   https://www.cnbc.com/id/49796736
2. *Thrust SSC*
   https://www.youtube.com/watch?v=JD3RtLLOntU
   https://www.youtube.com/watch?v=j1Qv2xq6eA0
3. *Tim Hawkins Helper in the Car*
   https://www.youtube.com/watch?v=ynRWWy2sWyQ
4. *The Rise of Automated Cars*
   https://www.youtube.com/watch?v=aBxfcmuloUA
   https://www.youtube.com/watch?v=uHbMt6WDhQ8
   https://www.youtube.com/watch?v=IQai75Ex6Kc
   https://en.wikipedia.org/wiki/Applications_of_artificial_intelligence
   https://en.wikipedia.org/wiki/Artificial_intelligence#Automotive
   https://observer.com/2015/03/self-driving-cars-will-be-in-30-u-s-cities-by-the-end-of-next-year/
   https://www.bloomberg.com/news/features/2018-05-07/who-s-winning-the-self-driving-car-race
   http://www.3u.com/news/articles/7801/apple-sele-driving-cars-are-far-safer-than-googles

https://futurism.com/police-control-self-driving-cars
https://futurism.com/seven-minutes-miles-pull-over-drunk-sleeping-tesla-driver

5. *The Rise of Automated Roads*
   https://www.youtube.com/watch?v=qlTA3rnpgzU
   https://www.collective-evolution.com/2014/11/09/netherlands-is-the-first-country-to-open-solar-road-for-public/
   https://www.youtube.com/watch?v=YQba3ENhlKA
   https://www.dailymail.co.uk/sciencetech/article-4082722/Are-smart-ROADS-key-self-driving-cars-Authorities-say-technology-prevent-accidents-reduce-travel-time-save-fuel-costs.html

6. *Automated Millennial Selfie Car*
   https://www.youtube.com/watch?v=H0XuAEsh0Pg

7. *Automated Travel Utopia*
   https://www.youtube.com/watch?v=8Clchx1VM0Y
   https://www.telegraph.co.uk/technology/2017/08/02/hyperloop-pod-travels-192mph-maiden-journey/
   https://mashable.com/article/dubai-rta-self-driving-taxi-cars/#Qwcq3iDFxiqq
   https://www.autotrader.com/car-reviews/what-uber-pays-toyotas-big-money-and-booking-googl-281474979888460
   https://www.latimes.com/business/autos/la-fi-hy-la-auto-show-future-panel-20141118-story.html
   https://losangeles.cbslocal.com/2015/11/23/smart-car-seat-senses-drivers-physical-and-mental-state/
   https://money.cnn.com/2017/01/03/technology/fiat-chrysler-portal-millennial-concept-car/index.html
   https://www.independent.co.uk/life-style/gadgets-and-tech/news/self-parking-volvo-plows-into-journalists-after-owner-neglects-to-pay-for-extra-feature-that-stops-10277203.html
   https://www.theguardian.com/technology/2018/may/29/tesla-crash-autopilot-California-police-car
   https://futurism.com/people-attacking-driverless-cars-california
   https://en.wikipedia.org/wiki/Artificial_intelligence#Automotive
   https://observer.com/2015/03/self-driving-cars-will-be-in-30-u-s-cities-by-the-end-of-next-year/

8. *Automated Car Controlled Cloud*
   https://www.youtube.com/watch?v=ciJmbwEPk3o

9. *Guys Hacking into Cars*
   https://www.youtube.com/watch?v=MK0SrxBC1xs

10. *Google Sticky Car Patent*
    https://www.youtube.com/watch?v=aa-ZAuSNKVQ
11. *Automated Car Death*
    https://www.youtube.com/watch?v=xJsagYFY0RM

Chapter 2   *Increase of Air Travel*

1. *Early Attempt at Flight*
   https://www.youtube.com/watch?v=S0v0gBENGpw
   https://www.youtube.com/watch?v=gN-ZktmjIfE
   https://en.wikipedia.org/wiki/History_of_aviation
   https://www.militaryfactory.com/aircraft/ww1-aircraft.asp
   https://en.wikipedia.org/wiki/Jet_aircraft
   https://en.wikipedia.org/wiki/Jet_airliner
   https://en.wikipedia.org/wiki/Boeing_747
   https://en.wikipedia.org/wiki/Airbus_A380
   https://www.aerospace-technology.com/features/feature-biggest-passenger-airplanes-in-the-world/
   https://www.infoplease.com/askeds/speed-first-flight
   https://www.quora.com/How-often-does-the-average-person-fly-each-year
   https://www.statista.com/statistics/564769/airline-industry-number-of-flights/
   https://www.faa.gov/air_traffic/by_the_numbers/
   https://www.telegraph.co.uk/travel/travel-truths/how-many-planes-are-there-in-the-world/
   https://www.zmescience.com/research/technology/virgin-galactic-commercial-flight-25092014/
   https://www.popsci.com/six-star-wars-technologies-may-not-be-so-far-far-away#page-13
   https://phys.org/news/2017-09-driverless-hover-taxi-concept-flight-dubai.html#jCp
   https://www.nbcnews.com/mach/science/self-flying-planes-may-arrive-sooner-you-think-here-s-ncna809856
   https://www.telegraph.co.uk/news/2016/07/14/space-plane-which-could-fly-anywhere-in-the-world-in-four-hours/
   https://www.telegraph.co.uk/news/2016/05/26/japanese-engineers-to-create-flying-cars-in-time-in-time-for-tok/
   https://www.theguardian.com/technology/2014/oct/21/marty-mcfly-

hoverboard-available-on-kickstarter
https://www.wired.com/2015/06/lexus-hoverboard-slide/
https://www.gearbrain.com/10-flying-car-companies-2587872239.html
2. *Early Flights of Wright Brothers*
https://www.youtube.com/watch?v=RriKI7u72Xs
3. *First Jet Airplane*
https://www.youtube.com/watch?v=nw37TZzyxzg
4. *Fastest Jet Plane*
https://www.youtube.com/watch?v=tO_dYEAXg7Q
5. *Flying Around the World in 4 Hours*
https://www.youtube.com/watch?v=yLlsV9ON_lQ
https://www.youtube.com/watch?v=a4zMtesSeKU
6. *Flight in just 11 Minutes*
https://www.youtube.com/watch?v=_gfBDQrXVAM
7. *Time-lapse UK Flights*
https://www.telegraph.co.uk/travel/travel-truths/how-many-planes-are-there-in-the-world/
8. *Flying Hoverboard*
https://www.youtube.com/watch?v=rNKRxsNyOho
9. *Flying Jet Pack*
https://www.youtube.com/watch?v=cIMWYeP7O1w
https://www.youtube.com/watch?v=7UcgsN33LGM
https://www.youtube.com/watch?v=Czy0pXRRZcs
https://www.youtube.com/watch?v=e3xCEAG8b6o
10 *Flying Car Compilation*
https://www.youtube.com/watch?v=0Yn2uyQJ1jc
https://www.youtube.com/watch?v=BAehx5S1HeM
11 *Flying Automated Air Taxis*
https://www.youtube.com/watch?v=V08IQz7Rk3o
https://www.youtube.com/watch?v=BZiJcQN5N
12 *Last days Global War*
https://www.youtube.com/watch?v=88e9yybOa8A
https://www.youtube.com/watch?v=GyFEJ-Cptr4

Chapter 3 *Increase of Sea & Space Travel*

1. *Panther Water Car*
https://www.youtube.com/watch?v=2150iFXF5Vc

2. *Underwater Homes & Cities*
   https://www.youtube.com/watch?v=Iol6yXQo4r0
3. *The History of Space Travel*
   https://www.youtube.com/watch?v=PLcE3AI9wwE
   https://en.wikipedia.org/wiki/The_Moon_is_made_of_green_cheese
   https://en.wikipedia.org/wiki/Buck_Rogers
   https://en.wikipedia.org/wiki/From_the_Earth_to_the_Moon
   https://en.wikipedia.org/wiki/John_Carter_of_Mars
   https://en.wikipedia.org/wiki/Moon_landing
   https://en.wikipedia.org/wiki/List_of_missions_to_the_Moon
   https://www.timesofisrael.com/israels-moonshot-kicks-off-with-a-successful-launch/
   https://www.youtube.com/watch?v=gTEMMiQXXVg
   https://www.telegraph.co.uk/news/science/space/11769030/Impossible-rocket-drive-works-and-could-get-to-Moon-in-four-hours.html?utm_medium=twitter&utm_source=dlvr.it
   https://www.foxnews.com/science/mars-in-three-days-nasa-touts-new-propulsion-system
   https://www.youtube.com/watch?v=WCDuAiA6kX0
   https://www.youtube.com/watch?v=RguSFaX8wBc
   https://www.google.com/search?q=how+long+would+it+take+to+get+to+mars+at+the+speed+of+light&oq=how+long+would+it+take+to+get+to+Mars&aqs=chrome.1.0l6.8156j0j7&sourceid=chrome&ie=UTF-8
   http://www.itechpost.com/articles/61522/20161204/moon-back-private-firm-reveals-plan-taking-tourists-2026-cool.htm
   https://www.reuters.com/article/us-usa-moon-business/exclusive-the-faa-regulating-business-on-the-moon-idUSKBN0L715F20150203
   https://lunar.xprize.org/prizes/lunar
   https://www.spacex.com/elon-musk
   https://www.telegraph.co.uk/science/2017/06/21/elon-musk-create-city-mars-million-inhabitants/
   https://www.space.com/37549-elon-musk-moon-base-mars.html
   https://theconversation.com/five-reasons-india-china-and-other-nations-plan-to-travel-to-the-moon-87589
4. *Israel Trip to the Moon*
   https://www.youtube.com/watch?v=XZULKCMq1T4
   https://www.youtube.com/watch?v=PG_42ZlcwEU
5. *China Fake Moon*
   https://www.youtube.com/watch?v=ohmdPpbPJ1s

6. *Space Elevator*
https://www.youtube.com/watch?v=vYTypQO6liA
https://www.youtube.com/watch?v=qPQQwqGWktE
https://www.youtube.com/watch?v=annVRxRjj4c
7. *Canadian Space Tower*
https://www.youtube.com/watch?v=Nir8mmIUkKs
8. *The New Space Race*
https://www.bloomberg.com/news/articles/2017-08-21/outer-space-obsession-moguls-worth-513-billion-join-the-race
9. *Luxury Bunkers*
https://www.youtube.com/watch?v=OI2ZDIP0ZWo
10. *Time- Lapse Noah's Flood*
https://answersingenesis.org/media/video/science/flood-geology/
11. *History of Sea Travel*
http://www.todayifoundout.com/index.php/2013/09/the-first-person-to-circumnavigate-the-world/
https://en.wikipedia.org/wiki/Maritime_history
https://cruisemarketwatch.com/capacity/
https://en.wikipedia.org/wiki/Maritime_transport
https://www.marinetraffic.com/en/ais/home/centerx:-48.1/centery:32.2/zoom:3
https://en.wikipedia.org/wiki/Water_speed_record
https://www.scmp.com/news/china/article/1580226/shanghai-san-francisco-100-minutes-chinese-supersonic-submarine

Chapter 4 *Increase of Global Communication*

1. *Rotary Phone Challenge*
https://www.youtube.com/watch?v=1OADXNGnJok
2. *3D Holographis Smart Phone*
https://www.youtube.com/watch?v=4tM5qJFsXeM
3. *Bill Cosby Southern Speak*
https://www.youtube.com/watch?v=E1NsC98xVN0
4. *Word Lens APP Translator*
https://www.youtube.com/watch?v=h2OfQdYrHRs
5. *Google Pixel Translation Buds*
https://www.youtube.com/watch?v=B_BQjRs94ec
https://www.youtube.com/watch?v=9Je5UklCcXY

6. *Babylonian Language Movie*
   https://www.youtube.com/watch?v=pxYoFlnJLoE
   https://www.youtube.com/watch?v=0jS8bNCxKJM
7. *Dave Hunt & The Vatican*
   https://www.youtube.com/watch?v=oUFhGQ4Do9s
8. *Pope Meets with Mormons*
   https://www.youtube.com/watch?v=up7fZ-0oaP8
   https://www.youtube.com/watch?v=IoD5g53z5qc
9. *Evangelical Chumming up with Pope*
   https://getalifemedia.com/video/prophecy/pop/fc2014-68.htm
10. *Pope Francis Man of His Word*
    https://www.youtube.com/watch?v=MOmY8i-uBcY
11. *History of Communication*
    https://www.infoplease.com/askeds/how-many-spoken-languages
    https://www.livescience.com/43639-who-invented-the-printing-press.html
    https://www.localhistories.org/media.html
    https://en.wikipedia.org/wiki/Publick_Occurrences_Both_Forreign
    _and_Domestick
    https://www.worldometers.info/newspapers/
    https://www.localhistories.org/communicationstime.html
    https://www.history.com/this-day-in-history/marconi-sends-first-atlantic-
    wireless-transmission
    http://www.unesco.org/new/en/unesco/events/prizes-and-
    celebrations/celebrations/international-days/world-radio-day-2013
    /statistics-on-radio/
    https://www.quora.com/How-many-TV-channels-are-there-in-the-world
    https://www.history.com/topics/inventions/alexander-graham-bell
    https://en.wikipedia.org/wiki/Invention_of_the_telephone
    https://www.statista.com/statistics/274774/forecast-of-mobile-phone-users-
    worldwide/

Chapter 5   *Increase of Global Distribution*

1. *China New Silk Road*
   https://www.youtube.com/watch?v=EvXROXiIpvQ
2. *China & Russia Connect the World*
   https://www.youtube.com/watch?v=CexUGGejPw0
   https://www.youtube.com/watch?v=RJCkpOkuph4

https://www.youtube.com/watch?v=nyiUCra6rxo
https://www.youtube.com/watch?v=XLJD-ENEnRw
https://www.youtube.com/watch?v=Ce7Ncxr2e7Y
https://www.youtube.com/watch?v=XbbqYfgplHE
3. *Pony Express*
https://www.youtube.com/watch?v=7hjXUmCeppU
4. *Scout & Starship Delivery Services*
https://www.youtube.com/watch?v=peaKnkNX4vc
https://www.youtube.com/watch?v=WTiXTUF_eUk
5. *Grub Hub Commercial*
https://www.youtube.com/watch?v=jkZ_9vkmL2c
6. *Amazon Prime Now*
https://www.youtube.com/watch?v=InXwJIlEJ9c
https://www.youtube.com/watch?v=rZx6BlpGGrc
7. *Dash Button*
https://vimeo.com/149401596
8. *Amazon Prime Air Commercial*
https://vimeo.com/149401596
9. *Amazon Go*
https://www.youtube.com/watch?v=NrmMk1Myrxc
10. *Mark of the Beast Employer*
https://www.youtube.com/watch?v=9zN6cUvh3kI
https://www.facebook.com/watch/?v=1480718712015720
11. *History of Global Trade*
http://mentalfloss.com/article/86338/8-trade-routes-shaped-world-history
https://www.worldatlas.com/articles/trade-routes-that-shaped-world-history.html
https://en.wikipedia.org/wiki/Trade_route
https://www.ducksters.com/history/china/silk_road.php
12 *History of American Trade*
https://en.wikipedia.org/wiki/Pony_Express
https://www.businessinsider.com/best-lunch-delivery-service-ubereats-vs-postmates-vs-amazon-vs-grubhub-vs-caviar-2016-7#doordash-just-celebrated-its-third-birthday-making-it-the-youngest-independent-company-on-this-list-in-that-short-time-it-has-already-expanded-into-26-cities-around-the-country-6
https://en.wikipedia.org/wiki/Courier
https://en.wikipedia.org/wiki/Package_delivery
https://en.wikipedia.org/wiki/Food_delivery

https://en.wikipedia.org/wiki/Delivery_(commerce)
https://topyaps.com/top-10-most-popular-courier-services-in-the-world/
https://www.cbsnews.com/pictures/richest-people-in-world-forbes/21/

Chapter 6   *Increase of a Cashless Society*

1. *How the Economy Works*
   https://www.youtube.com/watch?v=M_3T-Af57Pg
2. *Trump pulls out of TPP*
   Billy Crone, *The Final Countdown Vol.3,*
   (Get A Life Ministries, Las Vegas, 2018, pgs. 321-324)
   https://www.youtube.com/watch?v=SIfP5NhaZ2E
   https://www.youtube.com/watch?v=8e-cMkrddso
3. *What is the New 5G Network*
   https://www.youtube.com/watch?v=2DG3pMcNNlw
   https://en.wikipedia.org/wiki/5G
   https://www.networkworld.com/article/3285112/get-ready-for-upcoming-6g-wireless-too.html
   https://en.wikipedia.org/wiki/Internet_of_things
4. *What is the Internet of Things*
   https://www.youtube.com/watch?v=NjYTzvAVozo
5. *The History of Money*
   https://www.youtube.com/watch?v=pd8SPsG8kps
6. *The U.S. going cashless*
   https://www.youtube.com/watch?v=v20jD2GAF98
   https://www.youtube.com/watch?v=6ajJ_I4rmCI
7. *Sweden Almost all Cashless*
   https://www.youtube.com/watch?v=UzWMJZnGScw
   https://www.youtube.com/watch?v=AfowV-tBnE0
   https://www.youtube.com/watch?v=SH7ay57OfKE
8. *The World Almost All Cashless*
   https://www.youtube.com/watch?v=8uv_RUljRJg
   https://www.youtube.com/watch?v=OkV3XaajPUU
   https://www.youtube.com/watch?v=GbECT1J9bXg
   https://www.youtube.com/watch?v=pzEJCV_N84o
   https://www.youtube.com/watch?v=oesjcKByYhU
   https://www.youtube.com/watch?v=O753NUrD0hg
   https://www.youtube.com/watch?v=f-4kL9ry8Do

https://www.youtube.com/watch?v=VQFhgk_rn6o
7. *Employers Use Social Media to Screen People*
   https://www.youtube.com/watch?v=1xtXBqiop2Y
8. *China Implements Social Score*
   https://www.youtube.com/watch?v=xuqbx8tyW1Y

Chapter 9 *Increase of Big Brother Satellites*

1. *Live Earth Satellites*
   https://www.youtube.com/watch?v=RJm0Sykrw8A
   https://www.pixalytics.com/wp-content/uploads/2014/04/Debris_objects_-_mostly_debris_-_in_low_Earth_orbit_LEO_-_view_over_the_equator.jpg
   http://www.crossroad.to/text/articles/nis1196.html
   http://countdown.org/end/big_brother_12.htm
   http://countdown.org/end/big_brother_13.htm
   http://countdown.org/end/big_brother_09.htm
   http://www.khouse.org/articles/political/20010801-360.html
   http://countdown.org/end/big_brother_02.htm
   http://www.mvcf.com/news/cache/00065/
   http://countdown.org/end/big_brother_06.htm
   http://www.telegraph.co.uk/news/newstopics/howaboutthat/7608153/New-speed-cameras-trap-motorists-from-space.html
   https://www.techtimes.com/articles/213807/20170925/gps-chips-in-next-years-smartphones-can-track-your-location-very-accurately.htm
   https://en.wikipedia.org/wiki/Iridium_satellite_constellation
   https://www.vice.com/en_us/article/8qx54b/googles-satellites-could-soon-see-your-face-from-space
   https://www.americancityandcounty.com/2014/04/25/eye-in-the-sky-2/
2. *APP to Track Satellites*
   https://www.youtube.com/watch?v=pfoomxHGS-Y
3. *Bill Gates Earth Now Satellites*
   https://vimeo.com/315036364
4. *Google Maps*
   https://www.youtube.com/watch?v=Spel7vfkpNc
5. *Google Earth 3D Maps*
   https://www.youtube.com/watch?v=suo_aUTUpps
6. *Baltimore Monitored from the Sky*
   https://www.youtube.com/watch?v=wRa-AucbN6k

7. *Eye in the Sky Movie*
   https://www.imdb.com/title/tt2057392/
8. *Slaughterbots*
   https://www.youtube.com/watch?v=TlO2gcs1YvM

Chapter 10 *Increase of Big Brother Cities & Streets*

1. *Big Brother London*
   https://www.youtube.com/watch?v=ATq-XHSXTuI
2. *Big Brother Chicago*
   https://www.youtube.com/watch?v=dvrsr1X5hfY
3. *Big Brother China*
   https://www.youtube.com/watch?v=pNf4-d6fDoY
4. *Big Brother Earth Cam*
   https://www.earthcam.net/
5. *Chicago Traffic Cam*
   https://www.youtube.com/watch?v=4ezBCUz7q9Y
6. *Big Brother Vegas Lights*
   https://www.youtube.com/watch?v=bfaD5PT9foQ
7. *Big Brother Microphones*
   https://sanfrancisco.cbslocal.com/video/3399900-feds-plant-hidden-microphones-in-public-places-around-bay-area/
8. *Big brother Tied Together*
   https://www.youtube.com/watch?v=gt4XieUwWP8
9. *Antichrist Announcement*
   https://www.youtube.com/watch?v=wU0pzzG3930

Chapter 11 *Increase of Big Brother Buildings & Transportation*

1. *Cameras in Workplace*
   https://www.youtube.com/watch?v=yBmAtUWxCXU
   https://en.wikipedia.org/wiki/Closed-circuit_television
   https://en.wikipedia.org/wiki/Closed-circuit_television
   https://districtadministration.com/surveillance-cameras-in-school/
   https://www.a1securitycameras.com/blog/best-places-install-security-

cameras-businesses/
https://www.theepochtimes.com/high-school-in-china-installs-facial-recognition-cameras-to-monitor-students-attentiveness_2526662.html
https://www.theepochtimes.com/in-beijing-big-brother-now-sees-all_1872484.html
https://www.a1securitycameras.com/blog/best-places-install-security-cameras-businesses/
https://compass.org/are-you-being-watched-yet/

2. *Cameras in Schools*
https://www.youtube.com/watch?v=JxxILXZBhZc

3. *Find Hidden Cameras*
https://www.youtube.com/watch?v=i0hUhNtR-sk

4. *Cameras in Taxis*
https://www.youtube.com/watch?v=k77wbv-fcwo

5. *Mandatory Rear Cameras*
https://www.youtube.com/watch?v=CapFy4PRu6Q

6. *Mandatory Dash Cams*
https://www.youtube.com/watch?v=_CjKz3NELWs

7. *Big Brother in Cars*
https://www.youtube.com/watch?v=sTNhRYKNd3k

8. *Big Brother in Cactus*
https://newspunch.com/arizona-town-installs-license-plate-scanning-cameras-in-fake-cactuses/

9. *Big Brother in China Drones*
https://newspunch.com/arizona-town-installs-license-plate-scanning-cameras-in-fake-cactuses/

10. *CCTV Transportation*
http://massprivatei.blogspot.com/2012/12/surveillance-cameras-which-record-audio.html
https://www.crashdatagroup.com/theres-likely-black-box-car-heres-records/
http://harristechnical.com/wp-content/uploads/2016/01/HTS_CDR_List.pdf
https://www.usatoday.com/story/money/cars/2018/05/02/backup-cameras/572079002/
https://www.change.org/p/scott-morrison-mandatory-dash-cams?recruiter=966665645&utm_source=share_petition&utm_medium=copylink
https://www.smithslawyers.com.au/post/australia-mandatory-dash-cams
https://www.reddit.com/r/NoStupidQuestions/comments/bihb8x/wouldnt_it_make_sense_to_mandate_all_cars_to_have/

https://businessmirror.com.ph/2016/07/21/mandatory-dash-cams-for-your-car/
https://www.aclu.org/issues/privacy-technology/location-tracking/you-are-being-tracked
https://en.wikipedia.org/wiki/Automatic_number-plate_recognition#United_States
https://www.washingtontimes.com/news/2019/jul/2/frederica-wilson-calls-for-online-pranksters-to-be/
https://compass.org/are-you-being-watched-yet/

Chapter 12 *Increase of Big Brother Billboards & Body Cams*

1. *Minority Report Billboards*
   https://archive.org/details/MinorityReport_201606
2. *Big Brother Billboards*
   https://www.youtube.com/watch?v=9ZDfZHyumAE
   https://vimeo.com/156622287
3. *Snap Chat Glass Cameras*
   https://www.youtube.com/watch?v=qKBpkxI1oBY
4. *Pogo Cam Cameras*
   https://www.youtube.com/watch?v=-GRCZsl7v_Q
5. *Contact Lens Cameras*
   https://www.today.com/video/sony-files-patent-for-contact-lenses-that-take-photos-678421059841
6. *Bionic Contact Lens*
   https://www.youtube.com/watch?v=C7YycpxoKSw
   https://www.youtube.com/watch?v=JWLti-oVwuw
7. *China Big Brother Glasses*
   https://www.youtube.com/watch?v=C7YycpxoKSw
   https://www.youtube.com/watch?v=JWLti-oVwuw
8. *Police Body Cams Mandatory*
   https://www.youtube.com/watch?v=_vOOHapjE3E
   https://www.youtube.com/watch?v=6mjGh0HCb2g
9. *Police Technology Like China*
   https://www.youtube.com/watch?v=ZtsAaUVyGfc
10. *Police Technology Can Be Hacked*
    https://www.youtube.com/watch?v=izvzn5RO0lI
11. *Body Camera Technology*

https://en.wikipedia.org/wiki/Body_worn_video
https://www.sciencemag.org/news/2015/02/telescopic-contact-lenses-could-magnify-human-eyesight?fbclid=IwAR2Eabx-YQdquZZyovGOEdwPaeXqcZNwQYPj6Qb4W9N4So9ZDWEj4tuvQp8

Chapter 13 *Increase of Big Brother Cell Phones*

1. *Cell phones Can be Hacked*
   https://www.youtube.com/watch?v=zGUR6kao9ys
2. *Flashlight App Allows Hacking*
   https://www.youtube.com/watch?v=Q8xz8xKEFvU
   https://www.vice.com/en_uk/article/wjbzzy/your-phone-is-listening-and-its-not-paranoia
   https://www.bbc.com/news/technology-41802282
   https://mashable.com/article/should-you-cover-phone-selfie-camera/
   https://slate.com/technology/2013/07/nsa-can-reportedly-track-cellphones-even-when-they-re-turned-off.html
   https://www.wired.com/story/this-cell-phone-can-make-calls-even-without-a-battery/
   https://www.armytimes.com/news/your-army/2018/05/02/never-lose-a-soldier-again-the-army-buys-locator-beacons-to-help-find-lost-troops/
   https://en.wikipedia.org/wiki/Combat_Zones_That_See
   https://www.argee.net/DefenseWatch/Combat%20Zones%20that%20See%20Everything.htm
3. *Facebook App Allows Hacking*
   https://www.youtube.com/watch?v=vAbglR9bvEk
   https://www.youtube.com/watch?v=fXnYXtYJnw8
4. *Teen Discovers Cell Phone Hacking*
   https://www.youtube.com/watch?v=cBD1Q6tHPSM
   https://www.youtube.com/watch?v=nqCjP2nmRBw
5. *Fox News All Conversations Being Heard*
   https://www.youtube.com/watch?v=7mv_2NWonmQ
6. *Cell Phones Tracking Our Every Move*
   https://www.youtube.com/watch?v=0s8ZG6HuLrU
7. *Video Christians Being Called Terrorists*
   Billy Crone, *The Final Countdown Vol.2,*
   (Get A Life Ministries, 2017, Las Vegas)
   Billy Crone, *The Final Countdown Vol.3,*

(Get A Life Ministries, 2018, Las Vegas)
http://www.wposfm.com/HTML%20files/Darwin%20Sunday.htm
http://www.youtube.com/watch?v=1av8aFnc9t4
http://www.theadvertiser.news.com.au/common/story_page/0
,5936,17142097%255E911,00.html
8. *Canada Tracking Our Every Move*
https://www.youtube.com/watch?v=ctrHbUc3-SA
https://www.youtube.com/watch?v=k_Pf2k-CUA0

Chapter 14 *Increase of Big Brother Computers*

1. *Google Sees All Searches*

   https://thehill.com/policy/technology/239487-google-will-let-you-see-everything-youve-ever-searched
2. *Cookies See All Searches*
   https://www.youtube.com/watch?v=18En4NBbw3c
3. *Government Sees All Searches*
   https://www.youtube.com/watch?v=n1TMh5sO2S4
4. *Computers Are Being Hacked*
   https://video.foxnews.com/v/3861716315001/#sp=show-clips
5. *Computers Are Listening to You*
   https://www.youtube.com/watch?v=zBnDWSvaQ1I
6. *Cover Your Webcams*
   https://www.youtube.com/watch?v=ycZwIMMEZus
7. *Computers Are Watching You*
   https://www.youtube.com/watch?v=IX1LfCX0JCs
8. *Computers Can Change Your Voice*
   https://www.youtube.com/watch?v=I3l4XLZ59iw
9. *Computers Can Change Your Face*
   https://www.youtube.com/watch?v=Ex83dhTn0IU
   https://www.youtube.com/watch?v=Baocg6czpvE
   https://www.youtube.com/watch?v=up2b1oI9S78
10. *Media Outlets All Connected*
    https://www.youtube.com/watch?v=pL1zwMtz_Ho

Chapter 15 *Increase of Big Brother in Homes*

1. *Tim Hawkins Lazy Technology*
   https://www.youtube.com/watch?v=FeErkshXRPI
2. *Big Brother Locks*
   https://www.youtube.com/watch?v=agsRTQfkuE4
3. *Google Home Doesn't Know Jesus*
   https://www.youtube.com/watch?v=qb_ceWfPaHK
4. *Big Brother Toys*
   https://www.youtube.com/watch?v=oYIHVMdfgSY
   https://www.youtube.com/watch?v=jShksPFPrwQ
5. *Big Brother TV's*
   https://www.youtube.com/watch?v=rjs0S1S8vNE
   https://www.youtube.com/watch?v=GCFOfiDAEBw
6. *Government Hacking into TV's*
   https://www.youtube.com/watch?v=23W0SuDGghA
   https://www.youtube.com/watch?v=ZZCCrKzaGhY
7. *Big Brother Homes*
   http://prophecynewswatch.com/article.cfm?recent_news_id=2937
   https://www.youtube.com/watch?v=MECcIJW67-M
   https://www.foxnews.com/tech/is-your-tv-watching-you
   https://www.irishtimes.com/business/technology/are-you-watching-your-tv-
   or-is-your-tv-watching-you-1.3760358
   https://www.magzter.com/articles/12427/361564/5d3ac21c29c2a
   https://www.theblaze.com/unleashed/google-nest-
   microphone?fbclid=IwAR3gQH1v1nIpKvVdGqjXxVasr
   2T0EsZguogLpTTpc7Ahpx6m8OH9LeWUlBI
   https://www.washingtonpost.com/business/2019/02/20/google-forgot-notify-
   customers-it-put-microphones-nest-security-systems/
   https://www.theatlantic.com/technology/archive/2019/02/googles-home-
   security-devices-had-hidden-microphones/583387/
   https://www.theverge.com/2019/8/14/20802774/june-smart-oven-remote-
   preheat-update-user-error
8. *Big Brother Security Cameras*
   https://www.youtube.com/watch?v=-P0rSnt2HSU
9. *Big Brother Turns You In*
   https://www.youtube.com/watch?v=lfN3xmJiDEc
   https://www.youtube.com/watch?v=X7gKQgcI2sA
10. *Big Brother Bag of Chips*

https://www.youtube.com/watch?v=kaGDcxkN9co
11. *Big Brother No Way Out*
    https://www.youtube.com/watch?v=tyTGQPaW_IE

Chapter 16 *Increase of Holograms, 3D Printing, Restlessness*

1. *Michael Jackson Hologram*
   https://www.youtube.com/watch?v=fDR3hSeQ8pk
2. *Japanese Wife Hologram*
   https://www.youtube.com/watch?v=nkcKaNqfykg
3. *Multiple Languages Hologram*
   https://www.youtube.com/watch?v=auJJrHgG9Mc
4. *3-D Printed Body Parts*
   https://www.youtube.com/watch?v=jSjW-EgKOhk
   https://www.youtube.com/watch?v=zzmVrE-WWHA
5. *3-D Printing*
   https://en.wikipedia.org/wiki/3D_printing
   https://en.wikipedia.org/wiki/3D_bioprinting
6. *Altered Carbon Bodies*
   https://www.youtube.com/watch?v=LEGK2slavWE
   https://www.youtube.com/watch?v=wvOXQ8Hx5JU
7. *Modern Restless Society*
   https://www.youtube.com/watch?v=ReyEU06e5PU

Lightning Source UK Ltd.
Milton Keynes UK
UKHW012205280721
387925UK00001B/98